The Writing Game

The Writing Game

□

A BIOGRAPHY OF
WILL IRWIN

ROBERT V. HUDSON

The Iowa State University Press

AMES

To Dorothy Davis Hudson

ROBERT V. HUDSON is Professor of Journalism, Michigan State University.

© 1982 The Iowa State University Press
All rights reserved

Composed by Compositors, Cedar Rapids, Iowa 52405
Printed by The Iowa State University Press, Ames, Iowa 50010

First edition, 1982

Library of Congress Cataloging in Publication Data

Hudson, Robert V. (Robert Vernon), 1932–
     The writing game.

     Bibliography: p.
     Includes index.
     1. Irwin, Will, 1873–1948. 2. Journalists—
United States—Biography. I. Title.
PN4874.I7H8   070'.92'4   [B]   82–150
ISBN 0–8138–1931–8   AACR2

CONTENTS

PREFACE

WILL IRWIN was an American "journalist and writer" who lived from 1873 to 1948. He was a "frequent contributor of fiction and articles to magazines," an "excellent journalist, and a writer who [knew] the uses of suspense and mystery," and a "crusading journalist and official biographer of Herbert Hoover." The most succinct and appropriate definition of Irwin appeared in *Time* at his death: "Jack-of-all-letters."[1] Besides contributing to magazines, he wrote newspaper pieces, plays, poems, and fact and fiction books on many subjects. He also edited newspapers and magazines and served as a propagandist for the Committee on Public Information. In his obituary the *New York Times* described him this way: "Wide ranging, versatile, personally genial, a story-teller who delighted his cronies, he searched and wrote in just about every field available to an extraordinary curiosity."[2] But it is as a reporter that he is best remembered. And it is the reporter who reflected the culture of his changing times with whom this biography is primarily concerned.

I am indebted to the following individuals, repositories, and libraries for permission to use and quote from the source materials on Will Irwin, his family, his friends, and his associates: Donald Gallup, curator of the Collection of American Literature, Beinecke Rare Book and Manuscript Library, Yale University, and Rutherford D. Rogers, university librarian, for authorization to quote from the Will Irwin Collection; Patricia King, director of The Schlesinger Library, Radcliffe College, for permission to quote from the Inez Haynes Irwin Collection; James D. Hart, director of The Bancroft Library, University of California, Berkeley, from the Will Irwin holdings; Charles Schlessiger, Brandt and Brandt, from the literary agency's files; and Margaret Cookman and Inez Sturges, from unpublished documents written by Inez Haynes Irwin and Edith Haynes Thompson. Also, I am indebted to Rodney G. Dennis, curator of manuscripts, Harvard College Library, for permission to quote from the Corinne Roosevelt Robinson collection; to Nicholas B. Wainwright, director, The Historical Society of Pennsylvania, from Irwin manuscript material; to Jacqueline

Kolle Haring, college curator, from the Knox College Archives; and to Flora Elizabeth Reynolds, librarian, and Mary Manning Cook, reference librarian, Mills College, from letters in the Albert M. Bender Collection of Rare Books and Manuscripts. I am especially grateful to William Hyde Irwin for granting permission to quote from his father's, mother's, and grandmother's writings, for showing me memorabilia concerning his father, and for answering my frequent questions.

Also, Bill and Susan Irwin, Donald Irwin, Wallace Irwin Jr., Eban and Phyllis Given, Roscoe and Inez Sturges, Edith Haynes Thompson, and Constance Smith Whitman (all relatives of Will and Inez Irwin) shared their memories of Will Irwin with me. I am thankful not only for their assistance but also for their hospitality.

Many other institutions and people assisted me. In addition to the archives and libraries mentioned previously, several other depositories provided a variety of material. Those include the California State Library; the Library of Congress; the Herbert Hoover Presidential Library; the Huntington Library; the National Archives; the Sutro Library; the California and Colorado state historical societies; the Indiana, Columbia, and Stanford universities libraries; and the Boston, Denver, New York, and San Francisco public libraries. Through the courtesy of Stanford University archivists, I had access to many of Irwin's early published works, and through the courtesy of the university registrar, to Irwin's academic record. At Michigan State University, interlibrary loan librarian Walter Burinksi was of special assistance.

Three other people deserve special thanks. Michael Myerberg shared his recollections of Irwin during their work on *Lute Song* and opened to me his scrapbooks about the play. Dan Gilson took me on a tour of the Bohemian Club and alerted me to valuable background on Irwin's era in *The Annals of the Bohemian Club: From the Year Eighteen Hundred and Ninety-Five to Nineteen Hundred and Six Inclusive,* vol. 4 (San Francisco: Published by the Club, 1930), compiled and edited by Clay M. Green. Don Griswold copied by hand and annotated for me an important interview story in the files of the old *Weekly Carbonate Chronicle.* Questions about other important slices of Irwin's career were answered by the staffs of the Authors League of America and PEN.

For insight into Irwin's CPI job, I am much indebted to Jackson A. Giddens. Dr. Giddens not only pointed out essential sources, but also shared some of his own extensive research (including an early draft of a book) into American foreign propaganda in World War I.

Two organizations were particularly helpful in the completion of this biography. The Graduate School, University of Minnesota, provided partial financial support for the preliminary stages of my research, and Michigan

State University provided subsequent funds that helped me to continue that work.

Last but foremost, I thank five people for their very special support. Drew and Marsha Hudson helped me in countless ways, nonetheless by welcoming Will Irwin into our household like a member of the family. Two gentlemen and scholars, Professors Edwin Emery and J. Edward Gerald, set by example high standards of accuracy and thoroughness, which I have sought to attain. It was Professor Emery who in 1966 suggested to me a biography of Will Irwin and who guided my initial immersion into the subject. For help in the final stages, I am especially indebted to Professor Linda W. Wagner.

Robert V. Hudson

East Lansing

CHRONOLOGY

1873
    Born in Oneida, New York, on Sept. 14

1879
    Moves to Colorado

1892
    Graduated from West High School, Denver

1894
    Enters Stanford University

1898
    Expelled from Stanford
    Secretly marries Harriet Sophia Hyde

1899
    Receives A.B. degree from Stanford
    Joins San Francisco *Wave*

1900
    Stanford Stories published
    Joins San Francisco *Chronicle*

1901
    Publicly marries Harriet Sophia Hyde

1903
    Son William Hyde Irwin born
    The Reign of Queen Isyl published

1904
    The Picaroons published
    Joins New York *Sun*
    The Hamadryads produced (later published)

1906
    Writes "The City That Was" for *Sun* (also published as book)
    Joins *McClure's Magazine*

1907

Resigns from *McClure's* to free-lance for *Collier's*, other magazines

1908

Divorced from Hallie Hyde Irwin
Pictures of Old Chinatown published

1909

The Confessions of a Con Man published
Warrior, the Untamed published

1910

The House of Mystery published
The Readjustment published

1911

"The American Newspaper" series published in *Collier's*

1912

Where the Heart Is published
The Red Button published

1914

Beating Back published
Becomes war correspondent in Europe

1915

Breaks English censorship with beat on "Splendid Story of Ypres"
Reports on German gas attack
Men, Women and War published

1916

Marries Inez Haynes Gillmore
The Thirteenth Chair opens

1917

The Latin at War published
Right ear damaged by shell explosion near Caporetto

1918

Becomes Chairman of the Division of Foreign Service, Committee on Public
  Information
A Reporter at Armageddon published
Returns to Europe to cover war for *Saturday Evening Post*

1921

The Next War published
Columbine Time published
Lectures on Lyceum and Chautauqua circuit

1923
    Writes about League of Nations in Europe for *Collier's*
    Christ or Mars? published

1925
    Youth Rides West published

1927
    How Red Is America? published
    Highlights of Manhattan published

1928
    The House that Shadows Built published
    Herbert Hoover published
    Cecilie and the Oil King published

1930
    Pi-Pa-Ki produced

1936
    Propaganda and the News published
    Scituate, 1636-1936 published

1940
    Receives Doctor of Humane Letters degree from Knox College
    Spy and Counterspy published

1942
    The Making of a Reporter published

1943
    What You Should Know About Spies and Saboteurs published
    Thirty-Eighth Anniversary of the Dutch Treat Club published

1946
    Lute Song opens on Broadway
    Letters to Kermit from Theodore Roosevelt, 1902-1908 published

1948
    Dies of cerebral occlusion on Feb. 24

1952
    A History of the Union League Club of New York City, completed by others,
    published

He knew the writing game from alpha to omega, and for more than forty years, most intimately, the editors, publishers and fellow authors in our New York life.

—INEZ HAYNES IRWIN

CHAPTER ONE

Fledgling

WILLIAM HENRY IRWIN was derived from colonial American stock. Through his veins coursed the blood of Scottish Highlanders crossed with that of New England Puritans, with a few drops of German blood from his vague, distant past. It was probably from the maternal Puritan side of the family that he acquired his artistic tastes and from the paternal Scottish side that he acquired his roving bent.

His paternal grandfather, Admah Irwin, was descended from a large clutch of Irvins, immigrants from Irvine's Bay, Ayrshire, Scotland, in the formative years of the United States. Admah was a tyrant who strived to live down the sinful reputation of his biblical namesake. A militant teetotaler and a Bible-thumping fundamentalist of strict principles, he switched from the Presbyterian to the Baptist church when the Calvinists became too liberal for him. By applying rigid determination and burly strength to the fertile soil near Erie, Pennyslvania, he made himself a prosperous farmer. Two of his wives, unable to withstand the rigors of frontier life, died young; his third and last, Mary Elizabeth, would outlive him. She was the mother of David Smith Irwin.

David was born in northwestern Pennsylvania on Feburary 8, 1844, youngest of the three sons and one daughter of Admah.[1] Convivial and easygoing, young David showed less drive or ambition than his father. Browbeaten by Admah, he fled to New York state as soon as he could make his own way. At twenty-one he completed a course in double entry bookkeeping from Bryant and Stratton's Mercantile College in Buffalo, his only formal education beyond elementary school.[2] He found employment with a railroad, moved to Oneida, and met Edith Greene.

Born in Canandaigua on February 23, 1848, Edith was the eldest of the three daughters of Charles Chauncey and Emily Danks Greene, both descendants of early settlers of Rhode Island.[3] Her ancestors included a Quaker convert, a colonial lieutenant governor with a reputation for scandalous conduct, an importer who lost his wealth when his Tory partner skipped to England with their money, a lieutenant colonel decorated for Revolutionary War service, and a young actor who later became a respectable farmer. The last, Thomas Greene, begot Edith's father, a painter and eccentric.

Charles Chauncey Greene was a colorful, virile artist and friend of Edgar Allan Poe and Nathaniel Hawthorne. A radical, he was an early feminist, a participant in the Brook Farm experiment, and an abolitionist. Around 1870 he went to Lowell, Massachusetts, to paint murals and vanished, never to be heard from.

His eldest daughter acquired his humanism without his eccentricities. A sensitive, spirited young woman with delicate features, she appreciated the artistic aspects of life and sympathized with the feminist movement. She was twenty-six when on Christmas Day, 1872, the Reverend S. H. Thompson married her to David S. Irwin at her home in Canandaigua.[4] The newlyweds settled in Oneida.

David was an agent for the American Express Company and a lumber salesman when their first son was born on September 14, 1873, a few days before the financial panic. He was named in memory of President William Henry Harrison. Except for a missing joint in his thumbs, Willy was a normal, healthy baby. A year and a half later, as the economic depression deepened, Wallace Admah was born.

As the brothers grew older, they drew closer in interests and appearance. Willy was taller than his chubby brother, but both had high foreheads and long yellow curls. The family moved to Clayville, a farming and milling center south of Utica, and the boys played together in the woods along Sauquoit Creek. At Grandmother Greene's colonial house near Canandaigua Lake, they played among the old books, broken easels, twisted tubes, gummed palettes, and unfinished canvases that grandfather had left behind. From their mother they acquired an appreciation of the arts, and from their father they picked up a waggish sense of humor.

David Irwin was in his middle thirties when he heard of the quick wealth discovered along the Continential Divide. By the summer of 1878 a new town had arisen around the corner of Carbonate Hill from California Gulch two miles high in the Rocky Mountains, and word of its fantastic lodes of ores bearing lead and silver had spread around the world. Silver seekers were streaming into the carbonate camp. Building was booming, and lumber sold as fast as it could be chopped and cut. Banking on his knowledge of bookkeeping and the lumber business to see him through until he struck it rich, he gathered his meager savings and joined the silver rush to Colorado. After he had established himself in the lumber business, his family followed.

*****

Leadville was a lusty, violent town of more than thirty thousand adventurers, most of them prosperous, many suddenly wealthy, others just as suddenly broke, and all easy with their silver dollars. At first the Irwins lived in a pine-board shack adjacent to a sidewalk raised on stilts above the slush, mud, and dirt. The rooms were papered with old pages of the Chicago *Tribune*, upside down, and on bright summer mornings Willy would stand up in bed with his head tilted downward and earnestly read the eastern news of 1872. Eventually, the Irwins were able to move out of the tin-can and wood-shack district into a better home with real wallpaper. Around the spring house in back Willy could hear the plaintive cry of coyotes and the screams of mountain lions.

Wally skipped school when he could get away with it, but Willy liked it. He was an intellectually curious lad and developed an early interest in literature. "When I was little, and already interested in literature," he later wrote,

> a school-ma'am of mine used to read us extracts from "Hiawatha" and "The Vision of Sir Launfal," close the book and say: "Anyone who cannot see the wide difference between real literature like this and cheap work like Mark Twain's will never develop taste!" I was trying to develop taste, God knows, and she used to worry me a lot. I liked Mark Twain. I preferred him to the vision of Sir Launfal, in spite of my better nature.

The publication of the *Adventures of Huckleberry Finn* in 1885 gave Willy the courage to speak up for Twain over Lowell.[5] His preference for popular literature would eventually be reflected in his own writing.

Edith thought her sons were learning very little in the frontier schools, and she personally supplemented their classroom education. Both boys learned Shakespeare from her, and when Willy was around ten he read most of the bard's works. Both boys imitated the sonnets.[6] Their mother's devotion to the artistic aspects of life crystallized in them a desire to write.

Although Willy loved to read and write, he was no bookworm or recluse. Outside of school he spent most of his time like the other boys in the neighborhood, doing odd jobs, scrapping, playing. With Willy and their setter dog, he wandered all over the bustling mining district.

One day he saw a growling mob, its leader carrying a noose, escort a shuffling pair of stolid, yellow-faced figures, their pigtails tied tightly together, to a smoking-car on a siding. The mob kicked the Chinese aboard and relaxing, lapsed into laughter as its leader flourished the noose and described what would happen to those "monkeys" if they ever came back. They had disregarded the camp motto, "no Chinks wanted," by trying to start a laundry. He would remember the incident for many years.[7]

One of his favorite places was the Tabor Opera House. Only New York exceeded Leadville in variety and quality of theaters. Silver king H. A. W. Tabor had given the city a handsome brick, 880-seat theater, some said the finest west of Chicago, with Victorian plush opera chairs, carpeted and mirrored boxes, a frescoed ceiling, and a spacious orchestra pit. On the boards of the Opera House performed Edwin Booth, Rose Coghlan, Maggie Mitchell, Helena Modjeska, Frederick Warde, Oscar Wilde, and other stage celebrities of the 1880s. Willy and Wally became stagestruck when they saw Joseph Jefferson in *Rip Van Winkle*. Willy made friends with the property man, who got him a matinee job as a super in *The Private Secretary*, and he made his debut before the footlights at age eight in the arms of William Gillette.[8] It was a heady experience for the boy.

Although men were striking it rich every day, the Irwins did not prosper. David optimistically continued to pour into a mine the money he made in the lumber business, but the gold did not assay high enough to make the operation profitable. With the end of the metal mining boom, the speculative frenzy died and there was a panic then settling down. Those were especially hard times for the Irwins.

Edith struggled to keep together her household, expanded by the birth of Herman in 1882. She would murmur, "All going in and nothing coming out," but she had an indomitable spirit and seldom complained despite her frail health.[9] When she lost a fourth son soon after giving birth, her physician prescribed relief from the two-mile altitude in the mineral waters of Glenwood Springs, a hot-water resort about a hundred miles west of Leadville where the mountains sloped down into the intermountain plains. Edith basked in the steam rising from the hot pools that flowed out of the caves, and her health improved.

In the spring of 1886 David Irwin moved his family from Leadville to nearby Twin Lakes to try the hotel business. Although his only experience in hotels had been as a transient guest, he sold his interest in the unprofitable mine and purchased a dilapidated, barnlike hostelry eighteen miles from Leadville between two sparkling turquoise lakes plied by sailboats and an excursion steamer in the lovely wilderness summer. It seemed like a natural summer resort for Leadville's smart set.

"The Hotel," as the unnamed place was known during Irwin's proprietorship, required a great deal of remodeling. Broken windows needed replacing and the upside-down Chicago *Tribune*s needed covering with wallpaper. The bleak, empty rooms were ventilated by breezy cracks and infested with hardy mountain rats. During a rainfall there was running water. But by the end of the short mountain summer, when lacy crystal formed along the shorelines, the Irwins had made few improvements.

Their only guest was a wandering German geologist with a knapsack. Although business was slow, the Irwins never went cold or hungry in the bountiful wilderness. There was plenty of fuel wood, and they slept under buffalo robes and woolen blankets. The lakes were full of trout. Game birds, grouse, and prairie chicken abounded. Hunters brought in cuts of meat from brown and grizzly bears and venison from deer and elk.

The fringe of wild forest with its spectral white pines, dark spruces, and Alpine firs and the deep water that reflected the sapphire sky at noon provided a fantastic playground for the Irwin brothers. Willy and Wally ran wild. They learned to smoke cigars and to fish. Willy ranged the meadows between the forests and shot running jack rabbits with a .22 rifle. When the cold west wind brought a snowstorm down from the surrounding peaks and the Arkansas Valley lay sheeted in blinding white, he tracked coyote, deer, elk, mink, mountain lion, ptarmigan, skunk, snowshoe rabbit, timber wolf, weasel, and along the water courses, beaver. There were wonderful places to slide and skate. Twin Lakes was a playground paradise for the Irwin boys.

For their parents it was a disaster. To their frail mother, bringing up three boys and helping maintain the hotel meant hardship and deprivation. To David the hotel meant another financial failure. In a few months he traded it and the Irwins moved back to Leadville and went into the dairy business.

David had the same luck managing a dairy as he had in mining and hotel keeping. The cattle died of malnutrition and other causes, and Willy and Wally looked for other employment to help support the family. As a result, Willy got his first taste of journalism.

The leading editor in Leadville was Charlyle Channing Davis, who published the evening *Chronicle* and the morning *Herald Democrat*. Wally sold the *Chronicle* on the street, doing a lucrative business among the brothels and gambling houses, and Willy rose by four o'clock in the morning to deliver the *Herald Democrat* pony back through blizzards and subzero temperatures into California Gulch and over Carbonate Hill. Riding over the hill one morning, he saw a woman suffering from the effects of poison she had taken by mistake. Showing a news sense at fourteen, he reported it to the editor, who told him to write the story and instructed him how to do it. His first published writing appeared in twelve lines on the back page.

Later Davis employed him as a printer's devil. The publisher was crusading with blazing adjectives and the slogan "The gamblers must go!" to clean up the wild west town, and a reporter was assigned to write what happened in the "gambling hells." Davis believed that the news carried more weight than editorials, and he said so in Willy's presence; it was a lesson that would stick.[10] Willy's on-the-job lessons in journalism—and his crush on vivacious Nellie Davis, the publisher's daughter—came to an abrupt end after three weeks in the shop when he lost the post office key. Davis fired him.

Edith was still dissatisfied with the frontier schools but could teach her boys less and less as they grew older. They could spout pages of Shakespeare, but they were weak in arithmetic. To go to college, her dream for them, they would need a sound educational foundation. She wanted them to have the advantages of better public schools, such as Denver had.

For that and other reasons, including Edith's frail health and David's continued financial failures, the Irwins decided to move "back East." The lower altitude would be better for her and he might find steady employment. In 1889, before Bill was sixteen, they left their bungalow at 125 West Twelfth Street and descended five-thousand feet to Denver.

It was like returning to civilization. In Leadville there had been only two or three carbon arc lamps, and the electric lights in the houses of Denver fascinated the boys. So did the trolley cars. The Irwins' square, brick cottage at 218 South Water Street was modest, but it seemed splendid; it even had a bathroom. Edith, homesick for the familiar flowers of Canandaigua, promptly planted pansies, petunias, and zinnias. David settled down to bookkeeping for Tabor, Pierce, and Company, but it was difficult to clothe a wife and three growing sons on his modest salary, and Bill and Wallace sometimes lacked enough warm clothes for the blustery winters.

Despite their poverty, Bill and Mick, as Wallace was now known, enjoyed school. A teacher at West High School recognized their writing talent and fiercely criticized their first essays and encouraged them to do better. Sara M. Graham, respectfully referred to as "Feroccissima," brought from Boston New England's worship of the classics, both English and Latin, and could bring to life even the pomposities of Virgil. She believed that "getting at the mind is the main thing," and with Edith and Shakespeare, strongly influenced the boys' writing styles.[11]

These three influences were reflected in what may have been Bill's first published poem, "First Sight of the Mount of the Holy Cross" (a fourteen-thousand-foot peak northwest of Leadville). His ode began:

> That afternoon a mountain torrent's roar
>   Banished the silence; springing from our way
>   The gray deer, whistling, ceased his wanton play,
> And far above we marked an eagle soar.
> As the red day-god drowsy sank him lower
>   The shadows slowly lengthened; . . .
>   Where rose the lofty western mountains, there
> The Holy Cross lay, carved in purest snow.

The poem was accepted by a popular Colorado magazine, Harry S. Tammen's *Great Divide*.[12]

Bill struggled through elementary algebra and plane geometry and excelled in American, Grecian, and Roman history and English, French, and Latin language and literature. The classic and poetic influences emerged with a flourish in such essays as "Hanging Up the Sword," completed in his senior year: "How long, O Lord, how long? God of the helpless, till what day in the future wilt thou withhold the might of thy sword?" He prayed for a time "when sounds of peace shall be heard on fields lately groaning with the rumble of war; when men shall lay down the sword and take up the spade and the plow, and with these the human race shall travel forward toward the glories of the millenium." It was a plea deep from his heart, a plea he would renew with increased fervor almost thirty years later. At commencement on June 10, 1892, it won the Allen medal for the best essay.[13]

The author was not present to receive his award. Will H. Irwin was home ill, his health impaired by inadequate nourishment and the intense study required to complete his high school education in less than four years. The salutatory he was supposed to deliver was read by one of his ten classmates.

Three months after his graduation his mother suddenly suffered an embolism in his presence and within a few minutes was dead. Her unexpected and agonizing death was especially hard on her older boys, who had been profoundly influenced by her enthusiasm for the arts. Bill, who acquired her gentleness and kindness, would remember her as a delightful, articulate, and intelligent woman. He missed her terribly.

Sara Graham helped fill the void. A generous woman, she was always helping someone, especially budding writers, and she watched over Bill and Mick. With the sharp wit that would break through her New England reserve, she encouraged Bill to write and to go to college. "Her influence on what I have done is marked," he acknowledged many years later; "she gave me as much encouragement as a loving, understanding mother."[14]

Despite the help of Aunt Susan, who came from Canandaigua to take care of the family, poor health continued to trouble him. Working at odd jobs in Denver, a dry-climate haven for migratory consumptives, he caught what he thought was a severe cold, and at work alone one night he hemorrhaged. Dr. Charles Denison diagnosed the illness as incipient pulmonary tuberculosis and recommended the standard TB prescription of the early 1890s, several months of roughing it.

Bill packed up his dunnage, hired out to a livestock company in the Leadville district, and helped drive herds over the mountains from Colorado down into New Mexico and Texas. He could shoot, ride, and rope, and he thrived on the hardy masculine outdoor life. In a year he was pronounced well.

Leaving the range, he resumed his theatrical career, begun in Leadville. He barnstormed through the west, playing bit parts in such melodramas as "In the Ranks" and "The Great North West." When the theater company went bankrupt in Leavenworth, Kansas, he returned home.

Around Denver he was employed for a while as a coachman, watchman, and then elevator operator. In the summer he ran a pickle wagon, and in the autumn he worked in the hay fields. The older he grew, the fainter became his hopes of ever going to college.

In 1893 the possibility seemed to vanish. When the value of silver crashed, banks, railroads, and other businesses collapsed by the hundreds throughout the nation. The panic hit once silver-rich Colorado hardest, and David Irwin lost his job, his home, and what other few assets he had. Now he could not possibly send any of his sons to college.

But Sara Graham could. She offered to loan Bill the money to supplement whatever he could earn, and he began making plans to attend Harvard University. Because his physician strongly condemned the New England climate as bad for his arrested case of tuberculosis, he looked westward. In California the Leland Stanford Junior University had opened three years before with the largest endowment of any American university of that day, and its reputation for excellence had already spread throughout the West. Its president was a brilliant young zoologist from Indiana University, David Starr Jordan. And it was tuition free. With some outside help, an ambitious young man could work his way to a degree.

In September 1894 Bill arrived by train in Palo Alto. At twenty-one, he resembled "a shaggy and sprawling, frolicsome and friendly Newfoundland puppy in spectacles." He gave no more thought to the future than such a puppy and had no idea what he would do with a university education. He later recalled: "I was infinitely careless—especially in dress—impatient of conventionalities, talkative, indiscreet, sensitive under a protective mechanism of social boldness, an odd mixture of reserve and exhibitionism, of naïveté and premature sophistication, and even more perverse than most boys."[15] He was raw meat for the Victorian faculty, who took seriously their charge of creating useful, productive men from such talented but unrefined material.

Soon after his arrival, he heard that the football team had lost several valuable players; fancying himself an athlete, he tried out. It was a foolish thing for a young man with a recently arrested case of pulmonary tuberculosis to do but a characteristic thing for Bill Irwin, who never would take very good care of his health. He made center on the freshman team and played the varsity in a rough and tumble scrimmage almost daily, rain or shine. The flying wedge formation was the latest tactic, and it often degenerated into a shoving match over center, with Bill on the bottom.

One afternoon he had his moment of glory. On first down and goal to go inside the freshman five-yard line, the varsity hurled three plays directly at him. Two gained only a yard each, and on the third, he slipped past a blocker and tackled the halfback behind the line. The freshmen got the ball. As he leaned over to snap the ball for a kick, he felt a slap on his rump and looked up to see Walter Camp, the Stanford coach, standing there. "Good boy, freshman!" said Camp.[16] However trivial the triumph, it was one Bill would remember with pride the rest of his life.

What gridiron fame awaited him would never be known. In a scrub game he tackled the leader of the Stanford band and twisted his ankle as they both went down, their combined weight upon it. The result was a fracture with painful complications, three months in a heavy plaster cast and on crutches, the end of his football career, and an opportune introduction to an immature looking senior named Herbert Hoover.

Hoover, in his capacity as student body treasurer, stopped by Bill's room to assess the cost of the injury. He stood framed by the yellow door, tall, lean, broad-shouldered and slightly stooped, in a double-breasted blue suit. He had straight, mouse-colored hair and contemplative hazel eyes in a round face, and as he appraised the cast, he carried his head slightly to one side, standing with one foot forward, jingling keys in his pocket. Bill's broken ankle hurt terribly, and Hoover cracked a joke to keep up Bill's courage and chuckled. Then, turning to go, Hoover said, "I'm sorry." It seemed like a whole speech, coming from the shy, taciturn Quaker. "Then and there, I suppose," Irwin later wrote, "I put myself under his leadership."[17]

Under Hoover's leadership Bill became enbroiled in campus politics. Since Hoover was a senior engineering major and Bill a freshman English major, they shared no classes, but as residents of Encina Hall they were both "barbarians," members of the country element. The refined city element lived in fraternities and monopolized student offices. Bill regarded fraternities as undemocratic, and in the spring student body elections he helped Hoover line up freshman class opposition to the city element.

Hoover, Irwin, Herbert Hicks, Lester Hinsdale, and Ray Lyman Wilbur led the "barb" campaign against the snobbery, favoritism, and loose accounting methods of the frat coalition—and their reform ticket won. Hoover, a Republican even then, was elected the first financial manager, without pay, and the victorious barbs gained control of campus politics.

After Hoover received his degree in May 1895, he worked in San Francisco and would come down to Stanford on weekends to see his fiancée, Bill's classmate Lou Henry. Hoover often slept in Encina Hall, and sometimes he stayed up almost until dawn with Bill and his friends exchanging campus lore for talk of mines. Over the gulf of their intellectual interests, Bill continued to admire Hoover and to appreciate his "keen though delicate sense of humor."[18]

Bill devoted more time to extracurricular activities than to his studies. He would bluff through his classes most of the semester and then cram for forty-eight hours at a stretch for final examinations. In his freshman year he passed romance history, modern French, Latin (Horace), and English composition; he won a prize for a poem and wrote for the student newspaper. When the reigning theatrical producer was put on probation for a comic opera displaying too much calf of coed legs, Bill, who had been running errands for him, was put in charge of student theatricals. In his sophomore year he won twenty-five dollars for his senior farce script and picked up a few more badly needed dollars by producing and directing the show. He also organized the Fencing Club, joined the Euphronia and Philolexian literary societies, and served as secretary-treasurer of the Press Club and on the executive committee of the Intersociety Debating League. A fluent talker, witty, given to joking, he loved to orate at the meetings, gesturing dramatically. He was a gregarious leader who enjoyed playing at life.

After three semesters in assistant and associate editorships of the student newspaper, the *Daily Palo Alto,* he was promoted to managing editor. He supervised coverage of campus events and university financial developments and tried to carry out the tabloid's policy of earning the "good will and esteem of the students by giving them the news they want."[19] Many nights he worked late putting the paper to bed.

Despite his growing interest in journalism, he was still a poet at heart. His poetry tended to reflect two sides of his character, one the moody, melancholy Irwin and the other the cheerful, genial Irwin. Death was a favorite theme, as in his sonnet "To a Summer Moon": "O mighty Death, O healer sweet, I pray/Leave doubt and care but take not love away." Other poems, such as "Christmas in Encina," reflected his high spirits. In it, he and some friends prefer a holiday feast to a pre-Christmas dance in the parlors of Roble Hall, the women's dormitory, and "With a flagon of rarer old juice of the vine/That e'er sprang from Massica's loam," they toast the girls and the folks back home.[20] Several poems, including the first stanza of his high school piece about the Mount of the Holy Cross, were published in the *Sequoia.*

Sandwiched between activities and studies were whatever jobs he could find to supplement his loan from Sara Graham. In the summers he cut wood near Santa Barbara and picked fruit in the Santa Clara Valley, but most of his earned income during his freshman and sophomore years came from working in the Encina Hall dining room, where he advanced to assistant steward and head waiter. Midway through his years at Stanford, the dining room closed. Bill then found irregular jobs, including stringing sports and other local news for San Francisco newspapers.

He was more interested in work and activities than in his courses in ethics, economics, elementary Greek, and English drama, novel, and poetry. To him, formal education was "a thing to dispose of early in life, and with as little interruption as possible." He needed the university to put him "on the track of exact, detached thinking" and to eliminate a few of his "romantic Victorian illusions," but he rebelled against "the idea that life, at no matter what angle you tackled it, was a very serious and difficult undertaking wherein only the resolute and consecrated had much chance."[21]

Bill was ranked among the noisiest and most genial of the wild westerners, and his irrepressible spirit made him one of the most popular men on campus. To unwind, he would lead his friends to the wide-open little town of Mayfield, about a mile's walk south of bone-dry Palo Alto. In the back room of Anzini's or The Little Vendome, they would gather around the big round table carved with initials, Greek letters, and nicknames, and, pounding the table with their beer mugs, render a few verses of "Here's to Stanford College." Then Bill would offer up his irreverent lyrics to an old Irish drinking song, "The Son of a Gambolier," not only praising beer and hard liquor, but also making personal and anatomical references to the faculty Committee on Student Affairs, otherwise known as the "Firing Squad."

Other students added their own ribald verses, blurring the authorship. In one verse students referred to a professor as "the mathematical son-of-a-bitch," and in another they celebrated the traditional rivalry with the University of California.

> Oh if I had a daughter, I'd dress her up in green
> And send her up to Berkeley to coach the Berkeley team;
> But if I had a son, by God, I'd teach him to be true
> And to yell to hell with Berkeley! like his daddy used
> to do.[22]

The Irwin reputation was indelibly established by the time Mick joined Bill at Stanford in the autumn of 1896. To earn money for college, Mick had worked as an assayer in the Brodie Gold Reduction Company in Cripple Creek, Colorado, where their father was a bookkeeper. Now Bill eased his brother's transition to student by warning the sophomores to go easy on the hazing and by leading him to Mayfield.

The Irwin brothers' notoriety spread quickly. Whenever anything improper happened, one or both were liable to be blamed for it. Professors' wives told their babies that if they weren't good, the Irwins would get them. A girl in Roble Hall said of Bill, "He is supposed to be the most dissolute man in the university."[23] With a characteristic perversity, Bill gloried in the appearance of evil.

Bill's junior year was his busiest yet. Besides frequently "beering up" in Mayfield and occasionally studying, he remained active in the Philolexian Literary Society, served on the executive committee of the Sword and Sandals dramatic club, and was treasurer of his class and president of the Press Club. Unable to play football, he led cheers at the Big Game against Berkeley and helped create a yell honoring Stanford's tall lumberman's axe, symbol of the California rivalry. "Give 'em the axe, the axe, the axe!" it began.[24] Among all these activities, as well as work on student publications, he somehow found time to participate in the national presidential campaign.

He had only a hazy conception of the free-silver issue on which William Jennings Bryan, a Democrat and free-silver advocate, was opposing William McKinley, a Republican. But free silver sounded fake; besides, his roommate, John M. Switzer, was organizing the Stanford Republican Club. Switzer got him elected vice-president and talked him into campaigning, though Bill doubted his ability to speak on economic issues. Nevertheless, at five to ten dollars a speaking engagement, he raked in about fifty dollars, a small fortune. It was his introduction to campaigning in the hustings.

That autumn he reached the top of the hierarchy of the *Daily Palo Alto,* reigning as editor in chief. On the editorial page he criticized college men for their apathy toward national politics, opposed fast bicycle riding on campus, welcomed new clubs to campus, advised the freshman class, and boosted football. At last, in December, all the writing and editing and late hours putting the paper to bed were over. With the effect of a weary sigh, it was he, probably, who wrote in his last issue: "Journalism is always fascinating, even though it be amateur journalism, and sandwiched in between huge slices of University work."[25]

During his junior year he also wrote the class farce, helped put out the *Stanford Quad* yearbook, contributed poetry to the *Sequoia*, and wrote fiction. What was probably his first published short story and the winner of a story prize combined his two interests of football and Greek. In "The Making of a Greek," which the *Sequoia* published in the spring of 1897, Jack Denton, a Stanford senior, wins back his girlfriend by playing football. In the Big Game, Jack is irresistible, and at halftime she gives him a scarlet ribbon, which he wears on his uniform. Stanford wins, but in the last play Jack is injured.

> One hand was over the cardinal knot as he looked up and saw her gazing, with the light that used to be in her eyes, for she looked somehow through the soiled canvas, the mud and grime, and saw not the victorious athlete or the injured man, but the glory of her dreams — Marathon, Thermoplae, Discobolus, Belvidere, the Greek.[26]

Any resemblance of persons or events in the story to Will H. Irwin's private fantasies was not coincidental.

Advancing to upper level courses, he enjoyed his studies more. His favorite courses were Greek, with Professor Augustus Taber Murray; Chaucer, under Professor Ewald Flügel; and philosophy, under Professor Edward Howard Griggs. The study of evolution under President Jordan and Professor Vernon Lyman Kellogg would influence some of his significant journalism. On the projects he liked he worked hard. With Professor Edward Alsworth Ross he studied the American city as a social phenomenon, and in Professor Melville Best Anderson's seminar on Shakespeare he constructed a text of *Hamlet* from replicas of the quartos and the First Folio. Studying English literature and history, he began to appreciate his heritage.

Despite increasingly difficult courses in his senior year, he continued many of his extracurricular activities. He became president of Sword and Sandals and worked on the *Sequoia*, where he contemplated graduation in a poem, "Alma Mater," saluting "the world's new knighthood . . . the old A. B."[27] Busy as he was, his devotion to campus organizations was much less frantic than it had been his junior year, and he had more time for "girling."

Bill had a case on Harriet Sophia Hyde of San Francisco. Although she was two and a half years younger and a mathematics major, they had much in common. When he was writing, directing, and producing college theatricals, she was acting, and when he was on the board of editors of the *Quad,* she was a staff artist. They were both redheads and temperamental.

As commencement approached, Bill considered two careers, theater and journalism. He felt more confident about theater. His interest lay in directing, like Augustin Daly, the New York dramatist and theater manager, rather than acting. He doubted that he could make good on a newspaper. Fiction writers, such as Richard Harding Davis in *Gallegher*, depicted the newspaper reporter as a kind of superdetective who wrung secrets from crooks, society women, and magnates to score sensational scoops, and Bill was skeptical that he could do that. Whichever career he followed, it was certain to be an exciting new experience, and with that prospect, he felt an unusual contentment.

His euphoria was short-lived. One April day, when he returned to his room from a walk in the fields, a summons was awaiting him from the Firing Squad. The Committee on Student Affairs consisted of faculty members appointed by President Jordan. The liberal-minded professors avoided this disciplinary body, and its task fell to the Victorians. When the students got out of hand, the committee suspended or expelled the ringleaders. There was no appeal from the committee's verdicts.

In the crusade against drinking, the committee's Victorian spies had gathered a fat dossier on William Henry Irwin. Now, as he stood stiffly before his grim judges, he learned that the baseball team had recently broken training at Anzini's in Mayfield and had afterward serenaded one of the most rigidly Victorian members of the committee with some rowdy verses from "The Son of a Gambolier." Yes, Bill admitted, he was the author of the original stanzas and he had often sung them publicly, but campus wits had added ribald verses of their own and he could not rightfully accept credit for every line. The committee was not impressed by his modesty. The members disagreed over his punishment. One faction said the university would be rid of him in a month, anyway, so let it ride. The other faction held that he would disgrace his degree, if granted it. Finally they compromised. Four weeks before commencement, they summoned Bill and gave him an alternative to the supposedly lasting disgrace of expulsion: he could voluntarily withdraw from the university. He chose the less dishonorable course and was given thirty-six hours to pack up and get out.

And so one pleasant morning Mick and a group of friends courageously risked the displeasure of the Firing Squad and escorted Bill to the Palo Alto station and saw him off on the train to San Francisco.

Bill's first reaction was to enlist in the First California Regiment, bound for the Philippines to fight in the Spanish-American War. The country blazed with patriotism. He passed the vision test without his spectacles by memorizing the sight card in advance, but was rejected for varicose veins.

He went back to his small furnished room on Kearney Street and appraised his position. Alone now, rejected by the Army, he realized that he had acted impulsively, and that he had no right to. Going off to war and getting his head shot off would leave his college debts unpaid. The degree meant little to him personally, but since he had borrowed money from Sara Graham, he concluded that he must go through with it, if not at Stanford, then at some other university. Before he could decide what to do next, he received a letter from President Jordan saying that if he refrained from using "smutty language" he eventually could be readmitted and, after completing his courses, graduated.[28]

While the matter of his degree dragged along, he lashed up his nerve and went looking for a job in San Francisco. He approached the Grand Opera House, home of melodrama, and the Lyceum Theatre, home of a stock company, applying for any job, no matter how menial. They laughed at him. He tried the newspapers with similar luck. He seemed to talk himself out of jobs. Whenever he asked for anything for himself, he gave, as he later realized, "the impression of incompetence, insincerity, and downright criminality."[29]

Economic hard times in California only compounded Bill's problems and he could find no steady employment. He spent his many leisure hours between odd jobs helping a friend who was custodian of the Sutro Library and browsing through the 200,000 rare books and manuscripts, stored from public use while heirs wrangled over the estate of Adolph Sutro, the late Comstock Lode millionaire. He discovered incunabula, illuminated manuscripts, rare poems and Bibles, and Shakespeare First Folios. A thrilling intellectual experience, it was like a postgraduate course. He later remarked, "Probably I owe to it more essential education than I would have got from a year in any university."[30]

Despite his uncertain future, he and his college sweetheart, Hallie Hyde, who had graduated on May 25, were married before Justice of the Peace Frank H. Kerrigan on July 7, 1898.[31] The groom, the eldest of three brothers, was twenty-four and the bride, the youngest of three sisters, twenty-two, and neither was sufficiently mature to undertake the matrimonial venture under the prevailing conditions. He was in debt to his high school teacher, had yet to complete college, and had only intermittent income and no regular job in sight. He was still undecided whether to pursue a career in journalism or theater. And Hallie's mother was suffering from pernicious anemia.

What would Aunt Gussie have said! Mrs. David Bixler, Hallie's wealthy paternal aunt, had become the head of the family since the death of her brother and the illness of his widow, and the Irwins, realizing that it was hardly a propitious time to get married, may well have feared her disapproval. The marriage was a well kept secret.

Within a few weeks Hallie left San Francisco for Ottumwa, Iowa, to teach mathematics. Bill went on living like a bachelor. A hungry one. At the Sutro Library he filled his hours between jobs by answering occasional inquiries from scholars and by looking up Hallie's family genealogy. One month he wrote geneologies for prominent families in San Francisco at fifty cents an article; one week he made three whole dollars. He publicized a charity bazaar at the Pavillion, directed amateur theatricals, and contributed poetry to the *Sequoia* and *Quad.* The fall of 1898 was "one long hunger for grub, not knowledge or sympathy—grub—chow—filling—nutriment," he told fellow Stanford writer Dane Coolidge. "But I played in devilish good luck on the five yard line, and the third meal always came in somehow on the hungry days."[32]

On Sundays he picked up dinner at the Hyde house. Mrs. Marietta Butler Hyde and Mable and Helen regarded him as Hallie's suitor. He ran errands for them and helped around the kitchen, though with his jointless thumbs he seemed to drop everything he touched. Mrs. Hyde wrote Hallie: "The girls feel a moral responsibility in looking after him . . . he is a happy go easy individual and I guess there have been many days when the bean pot has contained his only food."³³ Undoubtedly, he would have been an acceptable son-in-law and brother-in-law.

In October, President Jordan granted Bill permission to make up his unfinished course work. The faculty agreed to graduate him if he passed his final examinations and if he promised not to attend commencement. While he was studying, his mother-in-law died. Late in February he took his last examination, and with unintentional prophesy, he told Coolidge that he would get his degree unless the "faculty finds new particulars wherein I am not nice." Buoyed by his reinstatement, he resumed his assault on San Francisco newspapers, complete with a suit of clothes made, on credit, to "paralyze City Editors with my style."³⁴ However stylish his approach or his suit, neither landed him a job.

Since the fall of 1898 Bill and Charles K. Field, an insurance executive, had been writing a book about Stanford, and now they had plenty of time to work on the stories, thirteen mood pieces and twisty plots linked by the university atmosphere and campus characters. Romances, student pranks, mistaken identities, spiritualism, and flights of fancy abounded. A dead fullback hero returned in a mediocre substitute's body to defeat Berkeley in the Big Game. A fraternity put a professor who looked like a pledge through a rough initiation by mistake.³⁵ Sparkling with campus slang, the stories entertainingly reflected the aura of Stanford life, though Bill professed to think they were "bum."³⁶ By spring the manuscript was almost finished.

While confidently awaiting graduation, Bill continued to eke out a precarious existence, partly by directing the junior show at Berkeley. As a matter of honor he resisted temptations to participate in Stanford plots to retrieve the lumberman's axe, which the Californians had stolen. But once his Berkeley job was over—

Oblivious to his parlous relations with the Stanford faculty, he devised one last attempt to rescue the axe. The faculty had prohibited any more raids to get it back but had said nothing about Berkeley's traditional senior fence, and Bill plotted to capture and hold it hostage for the axe. Only seniors could sit on the sacred block C fence and carve their names in it for posterity.

A month before commencement, on the dark and rainy night of April 24, 1899, Bill and nineteen other students made their way stealthily around the bay in three wagons and stole the fence.³⁷ Hundreds of students welcomed the conquering heroes back to campus in a triumphant procession worthy of Roman generals returning from Gaul. Students cut classes to rally in the quadrangle, and the band played "The Son of a Gambolier." The axe was avenged!

The Berkeley seniors, however, haughtily ignored the theft of their fence and refused to surrender the axe in exchange. The success of the daring raid faded into failure.

On campus now, Bill turned to directing his own musical extravaganza, "Atalanta in Stanford," a burlesque of classical subjects for Commencement Week. He was directing the final rehearsal when he received a summons to President Jordan's office.

William Henry Irwin had been a bad boy again. At the final meeting of the Committee on Student Affairs, that august body had opposed granting him a degree on the grounds that he had broken probation by leading the riotous escapade of the fence, thereby disrupting instruction for an entire day. It was reported that Mr. Irwin had perched atop the load waving a bottle, and when either Irwin waved a bottle everyone knew what was in it. Championing the accused, Jordan had inspired a motion to refer Mr. Irwin's case to a committee that he had carefully appointed and the committee was now awaiting Mr. Irwin's presence.

Bill presented himself before Jordan's special committee, and the professors solemnly examined him. After due consideration of their foregone conclusion, they decided that he was worthy of the degree. He ran back to the gymnasium, exonerated.

On Wednesday, May 24, 1899, he finally received his Bachelor of Arts in English.[38] The faculty capitulated and even allowed him to appear on the commencement platform with the rest of the graduating class and receive his diploma in person.

During the next month he catalogued the library of the San Francisco Chamber of Commerce, no permanent job yet in sight, although now that he had the A.B. degree the potential looked a shade brighter. A fellow Stanford writer, William J. Neidig, heard that J. O'Hara Cosgrave wanted a cub subeditor on his weekly San Francisco *Wave* to replace Frank Norris, who had gone East to literary fame. In behalf of his reluctant friend, he talked Cosgrave into offering Bill two weeks' probation and, if he made good, a permanent job. For two days Neidig labored to get Bill to accept the offer, but Bill, lacking confidence, repeatedly refused, until, worn down, he finally agreed at least to see the editor. He put on his good suit and last clean shirt and remembering Neidig's advice to be taciturn lest he talk himself out of the job, went to the *Wave* shop.

Cosgrave was in a small office writing copy on a pad upon his knee. He stared down his long, intellectual nose at Bill and confirmed the offer. "As for salary," he said, "I'm afraid I can't pay very much. There are too many weeklies in this town, and we've been through hard times. I will give you exactly the salary of a cub reporter on the dailies—six dollars a week. When you make good and we get on our feet, we'll see about raising you. Want to go to work?"[39]

Bill liked that part about *when* he made good. It gave him some confidence. He was ready to go to work.

Cosgrave, a tall man in his middle thirties, led him to another tiny office, swept a bale of exchanges from a rolltop desk, and slapped down a sheaf of clippings. "Write me a thousand words from that," he said, and left Bill alone with the job.[40]

Thus at the age of twenty-five Bill shelved his theatrical aspirations and embarked on a career in journalism.

CHAPTER TWO

Newspaperman

IN JULY 1899 the *Wave* was one of five weeklies in San Francisco. A ten-cent tabloid with literary leanings, it carried alongside its news features the works of Jack London, Gelett Burgess, Frank Norris, and other outstanding young California writers. Halftone illustrations abounded but unfortunately advertisements did not, and it was a constant struggle for Cosgrave to keep the *Wave* afloat. He wanted to make it the *Collier's Weekly* or *Harper's Weekly* of the Pacific Coast.

A skeleton crew manned its quarters on the upper floor of an old building on Montgomery Street. Cosgrave, the business manager and supervising editor, had been born in Australia, educated in New Zealand, and trained as a journalist in San Francisco. He was "an acute judge of copy" and "an indulgent nurse of young talent," as Bill would find out.[1] The staff also consisted of a lawyer who worked part time as the editorial writer, a printing shop foreman, two women compositors, and two photoengravers. A commercial firm printed the weekly.

Bill spent long hours doing a variety of editorial work. He wrote and edited copy and read proof and supervised the locking up of the last chase one night each week. Between writing captions and reading proof on those long nights he read files of the *Wave,* especially those issues which preserved the prentice work of Frank Norris. Finally, the foreman would pound the last quoin into place and draw the last page proof, and Bill, after reading it, would go home in the dark hours of the morning as the milk wagons made their rounds.

He wrote the paper virtually from cover to cover, including occasional sonnets, feature stories, most of the theatrical criticism, interviews with passing celebrities, and covers of the big event each week. Writing in diverse forms on many topics, he continued to develop the literary versatility that had characterized his writing at Stanford. The variety of assignments challenged not only his reportorial ability but also his imagination. When Cosgrave handed him clippings from the foreign exchanges, he had to concoct articles and columns on a vast range of subjects as if he were the foreign correspondent on the spot instead of a mere rewrite man in the *Wave* office. He routinely faked first-person observation.

This copy frequently appeared under noms de plume of both genders. As Katriona, he wrote regularly under a London dateline, reviewing plays, analyzing fashions, and covering society events. As Amos Sheldon, he usually played an exiled American dwelling in London, "not a lover but an admirer of the English."[2] As Etienne Marcel, he interviewed a German count and a French playwright, observed German military maneuvers, and covered *L'Affaire Dreyfus*. Faking the first person under noms de plume was good practice in presenting facts authoritatively and interestingly, hallmarks of his best journalism.

To supplement his meager salary, he free-lanced for other local weeklies. He sold humorous paragraphs and light verses to the *News-Letter*, which criticized the arts and commented on politics, and to the *Wasp*, which covered art, finance, politics, society, and theater. This sideline often yielded two or three dollars a week. The *Argonaut* occasionally bought a short-short story with a local setting for ten or fifteen dollars. He also completed his share of the Stanford stories.

To stretch his income, he shared a room in a house with four other young men, all Stanford "graduates by request," including Wallace.[3] Except for majoring in Latin, Wallace had followed in his older brother's footsteps in college: winning literary prizes, writing class plays, editing publications, and raising hell. After his expulsion for stealing a chicken, he had followed Bill to San Francisco, where he was reporting for William Randolph Hearst's *Examiner* and making a whopping twenty-eight dollars a week, almost five times his older brother's salary.

Bill ate inexpensively but well. He had breakfast at a German restaurant where he could buy coffee and rolls for ten cents and lunch at a bar where food was free with a glass or two of steam beer. For dinner he frequented the Hotel de France, a dilapidated wooden mansion on California Street, where he met drifters, sailors, cub reporters, starveling poets, struggling young painters, unemployed minor actors, French cab drivers, and other denizens of the city. For fifteen cents he could buy a banquet of soup, boiled beef, potatoes, carrots and turnips, salad, fresh fruit, and red wine pressed from native grapes. Despite the necessity of economy, it was a good life.

*****

In the spring of 1900 Cosgrave caught typhoid pneumonia, just when the *Wave* had sunk to one of its periodic financial lows. Bill was the only other staff member, except in the mechanical departments, and during Cosgrave's long convalescence the duties of art editor, business manager, and editor in chief were added to his usual functions of staff writer, makeup editor, and proofreader. He worked long, frantic hours to keep the weekly going and to put out a special issue Cosgrave had planned before his illness.

Realizing the pressing need for funds, Bill advanced publication of the special issue by two weeks. Cosgrave had selected the theme to take advantage of a local boom in the raising of Belgian hares. Contributions came in from breeders, chefs, and professors. Owners of blooded bucks or fancy warrens and dealers in equipment contracted for display advertisements, providing promise of temporary albeit future solvency for the *Wave*. What it needed now was money.

Before the advertisers' bills came due, the *Wave* had to meet debts of its own for printing, rentals, and salaries, so Bill borrowed from a Cosgrave who was cashier of the *Post*, a San Francisco daily. In making the payments, Bill miscalculated and left only two dollars for himself. To eat, he was forced to borrow from the prosperous Charlie Field, his collaborator on the Stanford book, which Doubleday, Page and Company of New York planned to publish.

Near the end of May "The Belgian Hare in Northern California" issue came off the press, replete with articles, photographs, and advertisements on the care, feeding, and eating of the rabbits.[4] The issue turned out to be a financial success, and the *Wave* was solvent again.

Soon after the proceeds were in, Cosgrave returned to work, ending three months of illness and convalescence. During his absence he had thought things out and raised some capital, and upon his return he made improvements in the weekly. He invested in a new typeface and with Bill planned a makeup similar to that of the *Saturday Evening Post*, a bright new star on the eastern horizon. He rewarded Bill for pulling the *Wave* through by promoting him to titular editor, with a raise doubling his salary to a substantial twenty dollars a week and with an assistant, James Hopper, a budding short-story writer. Things were going well.

Suddenly and happily he was a full-fledged author. *Stanford Stories: Tales of a Young University* by Charles K. Field and Will H. Irwin was published in June of 1900, culminating almost two years of writing and waiting, and the authors received their royalties on advance sales. Bill used his windfall to make his first payment on his college debt to Sara Graham and to buy some needed clothing. But that was nothing compared with the thrill of seeing his book in the stores. Bound in flaming Stanford cardinal, the book reached the shops on a Saturday, when the beauties of San Francisco made Market Street blossom. "I was watching this show," Bill later wrote, "when I saw approaching a pretty, well-upholstered young woman in a lavender foulard dress. Across her ample abdomen she held a square of inharmonious red. Was it—yes it was—our book! I was not only a published author but I had a customer. I felt almost as proud as I did when Walter Camp said, 'Good boy, Freshman!' "[5]

The *Wave*'s financial condition was really not so rosy as it had appeared. The promised support turned out to be illusory, and the weekly foundered again in late summer. Just then Cosgrave received an offer to become editor of *Everybody's*, a magazine published in New York, and seeing no hope for the *Wave*'s eventual success, he accepted. He sold the mechanical equipment, paid off the debts, and went to the San Francisco *Chronicle*, where he had worked, and persuaded the managing editor to hire Bill as a cub reporter. Accepting with misgivings, Bill went to work on the morning daily in October 1900.

With a population approaching 400,000 San Francisco was enjoying a period of great prosperity. Hard times had faded with the Spanish-American War, the prosperity of the nation, and the growing recognition of the future importance of oriental trade. The city was romantic yet had its own brand of hard, grim realism. It was amoral yet had its puritanical aspects. It was bohemian, tolerating anyone's personal eccentricities, yet had its exclusive social set. It was careless, yet the financial center of the Pacific Coast. It was also the center for daily journalism.

At the turn of the century, newspapers were casually started and just as casually killed. Among evening newspapers only the *Bulletin* seemed permanent. Morning newspapers reigned, and the city had three: the *Call, Chronicle*, and *Examiner*. The *Chronicle* occupied a downtown building ten years old and ten stories high, the first steel skyscraper in San Francisco, at the corner of Market, Geary, and Kearny streets.

Bill went to work on Tuesday, October 9, 1900, feeling he had to prove himself all over again. Working for a weekly, which had been mostly desk work, was one thing, but reporting for a daily, which entailed a lot of legwork, was quite another brand of journalism. Boastful anecdotes by reporters he knew had strengthened his impression that daily journalism required "qualities of nerve, persuasion, aggressiveness, and ingenuity in intrigue" that he neither had nor could acquire.[6]

He was sitting in the local room worrying about his ability to make good when the city editor, Ernest Simpson, bawled out, "Irwin!"

Bill anxiously entered the city editor's enclosed sanctum and received an assignment to cover the trial of a young Spanish girl charged with disposing of two trapped rats by scalding them to death with boiling water. "Take an artist," Simpson ordered.[7]

Bill inquired his way to the art room, where he picked up Harry Bunker. Out on the sidewalk he threw himself on the mercy of Bunker, and in court the artist sat beside him, sketching and calling his attention to salient features in the trial that would read well in print. When Bill looked at the *Chronicle* the next morning, he was relieved to find that his first story had been printed virtually intact. Although he had successfully completed his first assignment, it had been with the artist's assistance, and he still lacked confidence.

Two weeks later he was returning from an assignment at Golden Gate Park when he caught a glimpse of a crowd gathered on a corner two or three blocks away. He jumped off the trolley, investigated the scene, discovered that a cable car had collided with a truck, and got the story, complete with names of the injured. When he reported to star reporter Eddie Bowles, doing a Sunday trick on the city desk, the elderly, quizzical newshawk looked up at him and said, "You showed good news sense, kid!"[8]

With that compliment Bill began to gain confidence.

By this time his secret wife was back in town. Hallie had hated teaching in Ottumwa and had threatened to go on the stage, which was no proper profession for a young lady. Aunt Gussie and other members of the family disapproved of such rash action, and they settled for sending her to the Mark Hopkins Institute of Art. Hallie and Bill tried to continue their marriage in secret, but eventually Aunt Gussie discovered it.

Horrified, the grand dame of the family insisted on a formal wedding to make the marriage moral. Since David and Elizabeth Augusta Bixler were the Hyde sisters' closest living relatives, the Bixler residence was a logical setting. Aunt Gussie laid plans to begin the New Year properly, with a January 1 wedding. The Bixlers sent an invitation to David Irwin, who declined with regrets and wished Bill and Hallie happiness. He probably could not afford the journey from Colorado. In his reply he commented that Herman talked a great deal about the wedding.

After Edith Irwin's death, Aunt Susan had reared Herman, who upon completion of high school in Denver had joined his father at Cripple Creek. Herman was nine years younger than his oldest brother and interested in mechanical things rather than in the literary arts that bound together Bill and Wallace. There was a close, warm bond between David and his youngest son, closer than with his older sons, who had been strongly influenced by their mother. In a letter to Hallie, David lamented that his sons in

California never wrote to him, and he worried about Bill's health.[9] It was true, they were not dutiful sons.

For the wedding the Bixler salon at 2845 Pierce Street was decorated in Stanford cardinal and white. David Bixler escorted his niece to the bower, and the bride and groom were united in holy wedlock by the Reverend David McClure, an Episcopal minister, as they stood under a canopy of cardinal silk. The bride wore her mother's wedding gown of creme crepe de chine trimmed with Honiton lace, without a veil, and carried a bouquet of roses. Grace A. Luce was maid of honor, Wallace best man. Few people knew that this was the second time around for the bride and groom. In another room were displayed gifts of cut glass and silver and, from artist friends, castings and paintings. After the wedding the Irwins left on a short honeymoon to southern California. Upon their return, they moved in with Hallie's sisters.

As Bill gained experience and confidence on the *Chronicle* staff, he discovered that daily journalism in San Francisco was "a gay turmoil with a touch of melodrama."[10] The sensational, yellow journalism developed by Hearst's *Examiner* had affected the other newspapers, even the conservative *Chronicle*. The scoop, or beat, was the key to circulation, prestige, and prosperity, and the dailies played up any big exclusive story out of proportion of its real news value.

Competition in the local rooms of the three morning dailies was "murderous," Bill learned, but on beats reporters from competing newspapers frequently cooperated. On night police, the traditional training ground for cubs, Bill and his competitors routinely divided their news-gathering chores and pooled their results. About once a week one reporter, by the agreement of all, would scoop the others. To prevent too rhythmic an arrangement, the reporters were on their own—no cooperation—for a night now and then. On a big story all cooperation was called off, and there was usually a turbulent quarrel or a fist fight. The police helped to maintain this system, apparently believing that if they allowed reporters free access to witnesses, suspects, the corpse, the murder room, and all other sources of information, the journalistic competition would make less police work necessary. Sometimes the reporter not only competed against opposition newspapers, but also against the police.

After Bill passed his apprenticeship he was assigned to space and detail. Unless he was given a morning detail, or assignment, the night before, he would go to the office at one o'clock in the afternoon and wait until the city editor called his name. Then he would be handed a detail, which he would go investigate. On returning to the local room he would check with the city editor, then write his story, including the headline, to economize on copy desk help. This earned him two dollars. After dinner he was supposed to receive another detail, for which he would collect another dollar. If he received a morning detail, in addition to his afternoon and evening assignments, he might make four dollars a day, a rare occurrence. For an exclusive story he originated, without a detail from the city desk, he would earn five dollars a column, excluding the headline; but the editors saved expenses by cutting such stories to a few sticks of type. If he enterprised a story for the important Sunday supplement he received fifteen dollars. Only the star reporters were paid regular salaries. Bill regarded this arrangement, a common one among the morning dailies, as "calculated to extract the last ounce of energy in return for the first dollar of wages."[11]

Although he was writing in fewer forms than he had for the *Wave*, he was covering a wider range of events, and consequently, expanding his versatility. Events ranged from public appearances by such visiting dignitaries as Vice-President Roosevelt and President McKinley to prize fights by such champions as James J. Jeffries and Bob Fitzsimmons. Once he even covered a society wedding. The variety suited him well, for he was interested in almost everything except electricity, mathematics, and philosophy and had an inextinguishable passion for experience. He relished his daily adventures reporting for the *Chronicle*.

Bill had been fascinated with the Chinese for years, and while working for Cosgrave he had begun to make himself an authority on Chinese-American culture. As a reporter, he wrote about the highbinders and tong wars in Chinatown. As an amateur dramatist, he attended the Chinese theaters on Washington and Jackson streets with Dr. Arnold Genthe, a photographer, and other friends. One winter evening he witnessed a play that left a lasting impression on him.

It was *Pi-Pa-Ki, The Story of a Lute*, written by Kao-Tong-Kia two hundred years before *Hamlet*. Bill was struck by the similarities to Elizabethan drama. To the right of his proscenium box lay a bare platform, much like an Elizabethan stage, on which two male acters in beautiful rose and cream robes, like the boys who had played female roles in the Globe Theatre, carried on a falsetto dialogue. Elizabethan style, the audience sat near the stage, almost crowding upon it. Bill believed the play had beauty, charm, humor, irony, pity, suspense, and deep understanding of character—universal appeal. As he watched and listened enraptured, a Chinese friend whispering an explanation in his ear, he resolved that someday he would adapt *Pi-Pa-Ki* for the American stage.

*****

On the *Chronicle* Bill covered big crime stories with star reporters Eddie Bowles, an old-school reporter without a college education, or Archie Rice, a Stanford graduate in Hoover's class. Bill eventually became a star reporter himself, but when a big, sensational crime story broke he dropped to the grade of Bowles's assistant. One of the big stories he covered with Bowles was the Nora Fuller mystery.[12]

The Fuller case began in January 1902 with a classified advertisement in the *Chronicle* for a nursemaid. The applicant was to meet a man at Johnson's, a popular low-priced restaurant on Geary Street, less than half a block from Lotta Fountain and Newspaper Corners. On the same day a man rented a vacant house at 2211 Sutter Street. Miss Fuller, a sixteen-year-old unemployed nursemaid, answered the advertisement with her mother's consent and never returned home.

A week after she disappeared, the *Chronicle* published a missing-girl story with a photograph. Two weeks later her naked, decomposing body was found in the rear, second-floor bedroom of the vacant house by the rent collector. Her clothes were neatly folded on a chair and the shades were drawn, but the windows were wide open. A search by police and reporters revealed few facts beyond the identity of the girl.

Since the *Examiner* had bought exclusive rights to information from the principals in the case, including Mrs. Fuller and her surviving children, the *Chronicle* and *Call* were put in the intolerable and humiliating position of depending on the police for all information. This was the situation when on Monday, February 10, the third day of the investigation, Simpson handed Bill a digging detail.

In the excitement of the mystery, reporters and detectives had neglected the fact that the small table, chair, and bed in the room were secondhand. Bill went to the secondhand district, which began on the south side of Mission Street between Third and Fourth streets near Newspaper Corners, to find out if any store had made deliveries to 2211 Sutter Street. It was an intelligent shot in the dark.

To conceal his interest in the Fuller case, lest the opposition be tipped off, he invented a lie to account for his curiosity. He went from one secondhand store to another, inspecting their daybooks for the crucial period. At the third place, the Standard Furniture Store, 945–947 Mission Street, tingles went down his spine as he read in the daybook that a bed, a set of springs, and a chair had been sold to a customer on January 10. Here was a beat!

Concealing his excitement, he interviewed the clerk who had made the sale, Richard Fitzgerald. Fitzgerald remembered the transaction because it had been a rush order and because the customer had refused to give his name, but he only vaguely remembered what the man looked like. "I can remember only that the man was very well dressed, and I was a little surprised when he asked for a cheap bed," he told Bill. "I do not remember his clothes in detail, except that it seems to me that they were rather light rather than dark. I do not think he wore a tall hat. I should say that it was a Derby." The chair sold matched the description of the chair in the back bedroom, even to a burned area on the seat.

Watching for competitors, Bill slipped into a drugstore, called Simpson, and advised him to send a photographer to take a picture of the daybook entry. Then Bill looked up the free-lance express man who had delivered the furniture. A stalwart young bullet-headed Irish-American, he was parked in his rickety wagon, with one anemic horse at the traces, before the entrance to the *Examiner* building—dangerous territory for a *Chronicle* reporter. Bill asked him to drive down Mission Street, and they stopped in a quiet block, where Bill began asking questions about deliveries to 2211 Sutter Street.

"What do you want to know for?" Thomas Tobin, the delivery man, asked suspiciously.

Bill thought that Tobin suspected that he was prying into the business secrets of a customer. It seemed best to speak frankly, and he told Tobin the truth. Tobin produced a small, battered notebook in which he recorded his deliveries, and turned to a penciled entry similar to the one in the daybook at Standard Furniture.

Suddenly he understood. "Holy saints, to think I was mixed up in that delivery!"

Like the sales clerk, Tobin remembered the rush order more than he did the customer. The man had met him at the house and ordered him to carry the furniture upstairs and to put together the bed. "He did not help me at all," Tobin told Bill, "and I remember that I was put out about it." The only thing the delivery man could remember about the customer's appearance was that he had been of average height and weight and had worn an overcoat and a Derby. He clearly recalled that the man had refused to sign his name and only after persistent urging had he consented even to make a little mark on the delivery slip.

With the three silver dollars in his pocket, Bill offered to hire Tobin for the rest of the day and evening. Tobin accepted, provided he could go home to eat supper and to put up his horse. He would come to the *Chronicle* after supper. Bill phoned the city desk and Simpson approved the arrangement.

When he returned to the local room, he found the staff flowing with excitement and bubbling with rage. Bowles had found that handwriting on the mattress in the back bedroom corresponded with the signature on the lease, and the excitement had arisen with the realization that the *Chronicle* had a beat. The rage arose over an *Examiner* man giving the elderly, slender, unathletic Bowles a black eye. Pending arrival of the delivery man, Bill sat down to write a lead on his story.

"This paper doesn't usually brag," Simpson said, "but here's where we turn loose. Sock it to the *Examiner*.

Bill did. The opposition was trying to pin the murder on a politician, and Bill sneered at the *Examiner*'s false lead about the suspect, sarcastically mentioned Hearst's practice of locking up witnesses, and gloated over the *Chronicle*'s beat. He was still slinging adjectives when a copy boy informed him that the delivery man was in the outer office.

Sitting beside Tobin, who looked subdued, was a broad-shouldered young man whose clothing, manner, and accent branded him as a South-of-Market tough. Under his arm he carried a photograph album bound in blue plush. Speaking first, he broke into a diatribe against the *Chronicle*. A bunch of cheap bums they were. The *Chronicle* had paid Tobin only three dollars for a big story while the *Examiner* was paying twenty dollars for any story. A lot of guys he knew had collected just that, and as Tobin's partner, he was here to get his friend his rights. By vague half promises, Bill managed to edge the pair into the local room and to seat them at a remote desk. Then he conferred with Simpson.

The main question was, had Tobin and his friend already sold out to the *Examiner*? The certainty with which the friend continued to mention twenty dollars as the going rate for a story seemed to prove that he had. But what about the photograph album?

A woman reporter worked her wiles on Tobin's business partner and discovered that he had brought along the family album because he was afraid that a newspaper flashlight would make his friend look like a bum. He opened the album and there was a picture of Tobin, his hair slicked down and cowlicked. The photograph which should have occupied the opposite page was missing.

Simpson decided that all the *Chronicle* could do was give Tobin and his manager twenty dollars, but the cashier had gone home and it was the night before payday. Bill went around the office collecting spare change from the staff and down to the all-night cigar stand in the lobby where he borrowed five dollars. Then he approached Tobin, money in hand.

"We're going to pay you twenty dollars on two conditions," he said. "One is that you stay in this office until two o'clock in the morning. The other is that you give me your word that you haven't gone to the *Examiner* with this story."

"Course we ain't gone to the *Examiner*!" the manager broke in. But before handing over the money Bill waited until Tobin solemnly nodded his confirmation.

Bill turned his desk to face the two men and resumed writing his story.

When he looked up they were whispering earnestly. Suddenly Tobin jumped to his feet and with his protesting friend following, headed for the door. Bill sounded the alarm and six reporters rose up and blocked their path. He leaped in.

"I didn't go to the *Examiner*," the delivery man told him in a faltering tone that betrayed a stricken conscience. "The *Examiner* come to me."

"But you sent for them," Bill said, "you or your side-kick here."

Without another word Tobin poured the twenty dollars into Bill's hand, and departed.

The deadline was approaching rapidly. Should the *Chronicle* play the story straight, killing the boasts in Bill's lead, or play it up as a beat? Simpson called Central Police and established that no one else had photographed the handwriting on the mattress. The *Chronicle* reporter at 2211 Sutter Street reported that the *Examiner* was still trying to pin the case on the politician. Simpson decided to tone down Bill's braggadocio but otherwise let the copy stand.

The story began on the front page of the Tuesday, February 11, 1902, paper with three related stories accompanied by illustrations of the principal characters and documents, all in the splashy tradition of yellow journalism. The two-line banner over the full-page spread announced:

ONE MORE IMPORTANT STEP TOWARD
SOLUTION OF FULLER MURDER MYSTERY

In the story Bill told how the *Chronicle* had uncovered another step "on the road that led Nora Fuller to her death," how another day had been "wiped from the blank between the hour when she left home to seek employment and the day when her strangled body was found decomposing in a vacant house." He bragged about how the *Chronicle* had scooped "detectives and other investigators," the latter obviously an allusion to the *Examiner*. Then he reconstructed in detail the unknown murderer's transactions with Fitzgerald and Tobin.

When the first edition of the *Examiner* arrived, he discovered that Tobin's narrative had been cut to a four-inch trailer on an inside page. The *Chronicle* had a beat, after all.

For three or four weeks there were no major developments. Then for once the police beat the press. The mistress of the man who had signed the rental agreement and marked the mattress talked. The man had run out on her, leaving her broke, and in a vengeful mood, she identified him. Bill was amused to learn that the suspect had been an employee in the business office of the *Examiner*. To Bill's knowledge, he never was found.

Although Bill enjoyed reporting, he was unable to resist the regular, high salary of an editorship long. He and Hallie were renting a place of their own, and he was still paying his debt to Sara Graham. Eventually, he accepted a promotion with a raise to editor of the Grand New Year's Edition. John P. Young, the portly, white-bearded managing editor, told him: "I want you to fill it with bright, snappy, sparkling statistics."[13]

Although Bill disliked arithmetic and lacked any interest in commerce, he was able to please Young by finding untapped sources of information and by getting good color pages out of the art room. In seven-column headlines the *Chronicle* praised the matchless resources of northern California. Pride in the port city impelled merchants and town boosters to purchase "the prune edition" by the thousands for distribution East. The edition was so successful that Young decided to publish a similar section each week, and he appointed Bill development editor.

Each Saturday, Bill filled half a page or more with information about the natural wealth and unlimited opportunities in "the great interior valleys" of northern and central California.[14] Reporting had been play, but editing the development section was work, and dull work at that, except for excursions that took him off the desk and put him in contact with back-country Californians. This legwork made his job tolerable.

On one of these excursions into the back country, his sense of journalistic ethics faced a stern, if not altogether unpleasant, test when a young inheritor of an old Spanish grant took a liking to him.[15] The wealthy playboy entertained him on a vast ranch with hundreds of acres of prune and orange orchards surrounded by expanses of wheat fields and grazing lands. He took Bill to dinner with some riotous friends, drank liberally, and afterwards insisted on playing stud poker.

Bill had no interest in gambling, knew little about stud poker, and could not afford to lose.

"Got no money with you?" asked the young host. "Here, take this." He slid two double eagles across the table.

Bill politely tried to refuse.

His host became angry.

Bill knew that to get the story he wanted he would have to placate his host.

"All right, I'll play this—for you," he said finally, and took the money, fully expecting to lose and to have it done with.

To his dismay he won and kept on winning. By the time they quit playing that night his pockets were sagging with more than two hundred dollars in gold. He tried to explain tactfully that a reporter simply could not accept financial favors from a news source, an interested party. That only made his host quarrelsome again.

When Bill mentioned the matter the next morning, his host waved aside his protest and refused to bother with such a trifling matter.

Two days after the poker game, Bill departed with his story. In a bureau drawer he left behind a parcel containing the two hundred dollars in gold and a note restating his professional position.

In September 1902 Bill succeeded Mable Craft as Sunday editor. To his previous editing chores were added such new duties as seeking tips for special stories, buying features from free-lance writers, supervising a corps of artists, and producing two color pages each week. As editor, he helped the Sunday supplement attain "a wide distinction for originality of matter and mode of presentation."[16]

Breaks in the usually "sober routine work" on the desk were too few to suit Bill; rarely was he pulled away from the paste pot and shears to cover an important story.[17] On the side, he worked on a novel, wrote verse and short-short stories for local weeklies, and submitted articles to national magazines. One important national periodical, *World's Work*, bought a piece about Stanford.[18] For a while he helped a young reformer try to revive the *Wave*, but when the politican's money ran out, the weekly foundered for the last time.

Then Frank Gelett Burgess returned to town.

Gelett Burgess, a civil engineer who had turned to art and literature, had been one of Bill's predecessors on Cosgrave's *Wave*. After building a reputation as an artist and writer by editing *The Lark*, a clever little periodical, he had moved to New York and London. He became nostalgic for San Francisco, and shortly after his return, Bill met him.

Bill's awe of his reputation was no barrier to an immediate friendship. Burgess, who was seven years senior, listened to Bill's stories of odd characters and curious occurrences in San Francisco with interest. Why not write a local version of Robert Louis Stevenson's *New Arabian Nights*? They tried turning episodes Bill had witnessed into plots for stories and found they worked smoothly together.

They devised a series of short episodes within episodes, bound by a larger story that began with the accidental meeting of three picturesque drifters in "Coffee John's," a thinly disguised Coffee Dan's, a cheap hangout for reporters on the Hall of Justice beat. The topical trio consisted of an "ex-Medium," a composite of the faking spirit-evokers infesting the city; a "Harvard Freshman," based on Bill's debonair Stanford friend, Billy Erb; and the "Hero of Pago Bridge," a cowboy out of his element. Coffee John staked them to a dime each and sent them out to parlay it into a fortune or what fate willed. In individual bizarre adventures each drifter ran his dime up to a thousand dollars.[19] Bill and Burgess named their tales within a tale "The Picaroons," after the petty rascal, or adventurer, who lives by his wits.

Their manuscript was rejected by *McClure's Magazine*, the best market for young writers, but accepted by *Pearson's Magazine*, a national monthly, where it was serialized in 1903 and 1904.[20] Before it was published, the authors had begun writing another novel in the same genre.

This story was based on a reporting detail. Just before Bill had become Sunday editor, the *Chronicle* had sent him to cover a fiesta in the Santa Clara Valley, and Burgess had gone along for the ride. From this experience emerged the fictional tale of a fiesta embellished with episodes revolving around the disappearance of the reigning "Queen of Youth and Beauty." Her rival, Isyl Shea, crowned in her absence, is suspected of engineering the elected queen's kidnapping. In the climax the missing queen appears, announces that she does not want the crown, and exonerates Queen Isyl, who keeps it.[21] And all's well that ends well.

Cosgrave, who was building *Everybody's* into a leading national magazine by publishing noteworthy American writers, bought "The Reign of Queen Isyl" for serialization in 1903. That November McClure, Phillips, and Company published it in book form. Five months later the same house brought out the *The Picaroons*, which was also published in London by Chatto and Windus.[22] Their publication encouraged Bill to continue writing fiction.

By the time *The Reign of Queen Isyl* was sold, Bill and Hallie had become members of the artists' community of actors, editors, novelists, painters, poets, and stage directors who were exercising their talents in the permissive atmosphere of San Francisco. The Carmel Crowd was forming, and the Irwins met Ambrose Bierce, Porter Garnett, Jack London, Joaquin Miller, and George Sterling, among other authors. With red hair and a temper to match, Hallie, herself a painter, was known as the "Red Cyclone."[23]

Those were days—and nights—that Bill would cherish all his life. Sometimes the Irwins dined with friends such as Waldemar Young and Maysie Griswold at Sanguinetti's or Lucetti's, or went slumming along the Barbary Coast, or caught Johnnie and Emma Ray's knockabout comedy act at the concert hall. One evening the Irwins had dinner downtown, drank a bottle of chianti, and went to a vaudeville show, a fortune teller, and a shooting gallery, where Bill liked to test his marksmanship; Hallie walked two blocks along Market Street smoking and causing a sensation. They often partied all night Saturdays, perhaps getting "sizzed," and ending up at the Cliff House for breakfast. "What parties we had—simple, sauced with wit, ballasted with ardent discussion!" Bill would remember.[24]

The Irwins and their dachshund lived at 104½ Vallejo Street, a tiny house on the cliff side of Russian Hill, overlooking the bay. You got there by walking up the weedy cobbles of Vallejo Street and climbing a zigzag of ladders or by taking a roundabout route and riding the Hyde Street cable car and walking to a short flight of steps and up to where the hill flattened out into an area the size of a city block. It was dotted with cottages whose doors and sashes were trimmed in white and with little gardens, fringed by weathered redwood fences, where Shasta daisies bloomed in sheltered spots. At the very top lived a colony of artists and writers, including Wallace and the Bill Irwins.

During this period, two arrivals added to the Irwin clan in San Francisco, which with Wallace's departure for New York made a net gain of one Irwin. The first addition was the youngest Irwin brother. Herm, as his brothers called him, had been an apprentice tinsmith in Denver; moving to California, he went to work for a hardware firm. He and Bill occasionally attended prizefights together. The other new arrival was William Hyde Irwin, a son, on October 14, 1903.[25] The first thing the father looked at was the baby's thumbs, and he was relieved to find that they had the normal joints and would not be stiff like his own. The birth was difficult for Hallie, and for a year afterwards she was ill and frail.

Having a son did not cement a tenuous relationship between the mother and father; Bill was wary of babies. Around their cottage he helped her with such chores as washing windows and dishes, but she complained that he always left a mess. Their volatile temperaments were hard on their marriage. She could be headstrong, and he sometimes threw tantrums. Bored with his desk job, he took it out on her. "As usual," she noted in her diary, "Will gives me hell for something I know I didn't do and he is blue and depressed about his work . . . all my happiness and joyness and optimism is being crushed and turned sour. Wish I were dead!"[26]

In a city where hospitality was almost a vice, the Bohemian Club was a center of male conviviality. Since its founding in the 1870s by a few newspapermen, its membership had grown to several hundred businessmen and amateur and professional actors, authors, musicians, and painters. The Bohemians entertained and teased writers and other visiting celebrities of the arts, and Bill found it a delightful vent for the perennial college prankster in him. On different occasions, he helped "guy" William Butler Yeats, who was insulted, and Samuel Hopkins Adams, who guyed back.

Adams, a former star reporter on the New York *Sun*, was a literary talent scout for the thriving enterprises of S. S. McClure—among them a feature syndicate, the magazine that had rejected the *The Picaroons*, and the book house that had published Bill's collaborations with Burgess. Adams and Bill struck up a friendship, and before leaving town, Adams asked if he would like to work for the New York *Sun*. Would he! Charles A. Dana's morning *Sun* was "the newspaperman's newspaper, the ambition of half the reporters in the United States."[27] It might be arranged, Adams said, and went on his way, leaving it at that.

While the *Sun* job dangled, Bill continued to edit the Sunday *Chroni-*

cle, to free-lance stories and articles, and to cavort with the Bohemians. In 1904 the club honored him by asking him to write the twenty-seventh annual High Jinks for the Bohemian Grove encampment in August. The play would give him an opportunity to vent his Shakespearean imagination and to write poetry and drama, two of his favorite literary forms.[28]

While he worked on his script, Cosgrave commended him to the *Sun*, but the newspaper had nothing for him in the winter of 1904. The more he despaired of landing the job, the more determined he became to venture East, where literary glory awaited the talented, even if he had to gamble at free-lancing. He wanted Hallie, who was still in frail health, to accompany him, but she did not want to go.

On the day after she rented a house for the summer near Boulder Creek in the Santa Cruz mountains south of San Francisco, he received a telegram from the *Sun* offering him a reportorial position at space rates with a liberal guarantee—if he would come to work within a month. Most of his play was written, and he could complete it in New York. He accepted.

After a round of farewell dinners in San Francisco, Bill took the train out to Boulder Creek for a few final days with Hallie. He worked on his High Jinks and read them to her; she thought they were "darned good." They got along wonderfully for four days. Then on Thursday, June 2, he took the seven o'clock train for San Francisco, leaving behind his wife and eight-month-old son. "Feel blue," she noted in her diary. "Wish Will were nice all the time."[29]

On Friday evening he boarded a train east, feeling as though he was going there for the first time. Now thirty, he was going to try his luck in the literary mecca like the late Frank Norris had done and like Wallace was doing now, both successfully. He felt that this pilgrimage was crucial to his literary career; leaving behind his wife and son was a necessary sacrifice. A greater wrench was leaving behind the "bonny, merry city—the good, gray city" where he had "mingled the wine of her bounding life with the wine of his youth."[30]

CHAPTER THREE

Reporter

AFTER a long trip with stopovers in Leadville, Denver, and Chicago, partly to contend with chronic tonsillitis, Bill arrived in New York on Wednesday, June 15, just as a big story broke. An old excursion steamer, the *General Slocum*, had caught fire and run aground in Long Island Sound. The decrepit side-wheeler, its safety equipment useless, had been overloaded with two thousand mothers and their children on a church picnic. Early reports indicated that the list of dead might reach a thousand, mostly children.

At Grand Central terminal Bill was met by Wallace and a friend, Chris Bradley. They took his baggage to Wallace's apartment, and Bill headed directly for the *Sun* in Park Row.

Founded in 1833, the New York *Sun* had been the first successful penny newspaper in the United States. After the Civil War and its acquisition by Charles Anderson Dana it became a newspaper of peerless literary standards. It was still shining, seven years after Dana's death, under the management of some of his closest associates.

The *Sun* had three direct rivals in the conservative morning field. The *Press* was declining toward collapse. The *Tribune*, once great under founder Horace Greeley, had become a stodgy sheet. And the *Times*, under publisher Adolph Ochs, was improving. Flamboyant in comparison were the sensational *American, Herald*, and *World*, all of which used many illustrations and colored inks. The *Sun*, read by artists and intellectuals, depended on colorful writing.

Bill had heard that the *Sun* inhabited an old, dilapidated building, but he was not prepared for what he saw when an office boy admitted him through a gate on the second floor.[1] The local room resembled a small public hall, with dingy iron pillars supporting a low ceiling; time and smoke had streaked the walls a dingy brown. The wooden floor and the sashes of the two antique twelve-paned windows overlooking City Hall seemed about to distintegrate. Down the middle of the room ran two rows of long tables at which men in shirt-sleeves were writing by hand.

Bill marveled at the quiet. Had an event so great as the *Slocum* disaster happened in San Francisco, the *Chronicle* local room would have been a riot and the *Examiner*'s a madhouse. He was surprised to learn that a man giving orders at a desk over by a window was the city editor. Here he sat in the same room with his reporters. In San Francisco the city editor was enclosed in a sacred inner office. Bill learned that even the managing editor sat among his minions here.

He was led to a roll-top desk before another window where Chester S. Lord, in shirt sleeves, was talking softly on the telephone. He was a large man with "a fine face, an air of old-fashioned gentility." When Lord hung up, Bill introduced himself.

"This seems like a very big story, and I thought you might be needing men," he said. "So I've come straight from the train."

"In other words," said Lord, "the war horse smells the battle from afar. Thank you for reporting. But Denison is handling this, and we've got all the points like the morgue and the police stations covered. We don't believe in putting too many men on any story. It only causes confusion."

Lord then introduced Bill to the city editor, George Mallon.

Mallon, who was not so large as Lord, had the steady, alert eyes that Bill associated with ability. Between telephone calls, Mallon explained that although the story was covered, Bill could stick around in case any new angle broke.

Around six o'clock Lindsay Denison came in, followed by a rush of other reporters. Denison was a big, plump man with Byronic black locks of hair and prominent eyebrows over inquisitive brown eyes. Bill had met him in San Francisco. Denison recognized him, welcomed him to New York, and reported to Mallon. Then he sat down at a table and began to write furiously.

Bill realized that he had not heard a single typewriter. All the reporters were writing by hand. Lord believed that the typewriter contributed to a diffuse style.

After a while Mallon came over to dismiss him.

"Everything's going nicely," the city editor said. "You'd better settle yourself and get a night's sleep. I'm giving you a morning assignment—the temporary morgue at Bellevue Wharf, where they're identifying the dead. Smith covered that today. Ask him how to get there and whom to see.

"You don't know your way about, of course. Just throw yourself on the mercy of the reporters for the other papers. They'll tell you all they know."

Mallon's last statement surprised Bill, fresh from San Francisco where trading information on big stories was an unpardonable sin. He would soon discover another surprising departure from San Francisco journalism: in New York reporters had to depend entirely on the police for their basic information. Bill afterwards wrote, "I had a feeling that all my values were turned upside down."

The next morning he began covering the aftermath of the *Slocum* disaster. Police officers, firemen, and coastguardsmen recovered the bodies of those who had burned to death or drowned and laid them out in two long rows on the covered wharf at Bellevue Hospital. The first corpse Bill saw was that of a baby not more than six months old dressed up for the holiday in a lace cap and a muslin dress with bows of blue ribbon down the front. The baby's lips were blue and his eyes staring. Bill could not help crying. Then he gained his composure and became the detached reporter again.

The police allowed the relatives of the missing, mostly German-Americans, through the lines, and a curious trait of these people impressed Bill. A German couple would pass along the line peering at the bodies and stop, and the mother or father might say:

"Das ist Gertie."

"Ja, das ist Gertie," the other would respond calmly.

The father would turn to the attendant, confirm the identification, and sign the necessary papers. Then the undertaker would come to settle other details. Throughout this gruesome business the bereaved parents would maintain a stolid indifference, and then without warning and often in the middle of a word, one of them would burst into torrential tears and both of them would abandon themselves to explosive, abject grief. It was Bill's first lesson in what he would come to regard as a peculiar trait of the Germans.

From Bellevue, he was assigned to the tenement district where most of the dead had lived. Every hour he had to pass Saint Mark's Church where, he would recall twenty-three years later,

> a committee was keeping check on the latest arrivals from Bellevue Morgue. Somewhere behind a window above, a girl was crying. It seemed to me that for four days she never stopped. Her voice had an odd, catarrhal tone. In the second day I crossed the area behind the church no more, but went clear around the block; and to this day, whenever I hear that tone in a woman's voice, the world goes for an instant a little black.[2]

Upon the fourth day of covering Saint Mark's parish, he successfully completed his first series of assignments for the *Sun*.

New York was a hard, brutal contrast to good-humored, easy-going, gregarious San Francisco. The city of success was hot, humid, crowded, and indifferent. Bill was just another one of "its thousands of middle-class argonauts—men and women who want to break lances on newer and greater fields," who flashed into the metropolis, got acquainted, and were seen for a time in the restaurants, the clubs, and the shops. How long depended entirely upon whether they made good and multiplied their incomes. The chosen half went up, multiplying their income to meet multiplying desires.[3] Which half, Bill wondered, was his fate?

Homesick for San Francisco and his gregarious Bohemian friends, he strolled the sidewalks of New York. New Yorkers were living complaisantly under corrupt Tammany rule. Harlem was still a middle-class residential district, and Greenwich Village was a community of Irish-Americans living in three-story brick houses built by their fathers or grandfathers, much as he had read during his childhood in H. C. Bunner's *The Story of a New York House*. The social aristocracy of Fifth Avenue and Washington Square rode in carriages pulled by prancing black horses and driven by arrogant top-hatted coachmen. Financial, literary, and theatrical celebrities paraded up and down "the line," a stretch of Fifth Avenue between Twenty-third and Forty-second streets. Victorian taboos still were impressed upon the "good" woman, and only in the lowest dives of the Bowery might any woman smoke a cigarette publicly. On Broadway the first of the moving electrical signs advertised Heatherbloom Binding, a necessity for skirts that swept the pavements to conceal fully the unmentionable limb. At the foot of Broadway, steamers dumped waves of strangely dressed immigrants lugging bags and bundles; most of the newcomers were bound for the crowded lower East Side. Bill played the machines of Adolph Zukor's penny arcade and walked about town and observed life whirling around him but never touching him.

He sent money to his wife to pay their debts and urged her to join him, but she was making plans of her own. Upon doctor's orders, Herman had moved to the mountains to recover from an illness, and Hallie was making plans to turn seven acres of new redwoods at Brookdale into a chicken ranch to provide Herman and his father a business. What had been a temporary move into the Santa Cruz mountains was becoming permament. Bill objected. He wanted her with him in New York.

He was extremely unhappy. Except for the expansive, generous Denison, his colleagues shunned him, barring his entrance into the *Sun* fraternity. *Sun* men considered themselves the aristocracy of journalism, and new men, with or without college diplomas, had to "fit in." Bill did not, and their coldness hurt him deeply.

Not that there were any disagreeable episodes, for the *Sun* was a gentleman's shop. But his colleagues erected a wall against any approaches toward friendship. Deskmen answered him in monosyllables, and after a while he responded in kind. Behind his back he was the butt of the office.

When he ate at the Hippodrome or Jack's, newspapermen's hangouts, *Sun* men would walk past his table, ignoring him. Selah Merrill Clarke, the night editor, was cold, too. "Boss" Clarke's wide reputation as a stickler for well-written copy and as an outstanding teacher of newspaper journalism made his aloofness all the harder for Bill to take. Eventually, an overheard conversation revealed why the staff disliked him.

Sam Adams had oversold him to the *Sun*, getting him not only space but also a guarantee, and the only other guarantee went to Denison, who had been friendly. The staff considered Bill a fiction writer trying to play reporter, and it deeply offended him. Hadn't he served his apprenticeship in daily journalism on the *Chronicle*? Did he have to begin all over again on the *Sun*? "All this brought a practical anxiety," he afterwards wrote. "I was expected not only to make good but to make very good."[4]

The first opportunity to make good came on his third Sunday in New York.[5]

It was a beautiful morning and he could not sleep, so he got up, ate breakfast, and went to the office early. Young Kenneth Lord, son of the managing editor, was alone, holding down the city desk for the first time. He jumped up and hurried over to Bill and poured out his troubles.

There was a train wreck on the Erie Railroad at Wanaque-Midvale, New Jersey. A big one. He'd tried by phone to get Denison, Frank O'Brien, Lawrence Hills—the *Sun*'s best men—but couldn't reach them. The only chance of getting to the remote scene of the wreck was to appeal to the Erie Railroad itself. Perhaps they'd send Bill in a locomotive or with a wrecking train.

"At any rate, try!" urged Lord. "Don't waste time with the lists of the dead and injured. That will come automatically from the hospitals and police. But hurry!"

Bill ran to the Erie station and caught a ferryboat to the terminus on the other side of the river. Invoking the name of his Uncle Arad Smith Irwin, who had been a passenger engineer on the Erie, he wheedled a ride on a locomotive taking a claims agent and a railroad attorney to the wreck. By the time they arrived, the dead and the injured had been removed.

Bill crawled into the engine wreckage and determined by a damaged clock the exact minute of the wreck. He got the brakeman's gruesome story and interviewed uninjured survivors, getting accounts of the wreck with dramatic details. It reminded him of the *Slocum* disaster. The crowded train of old wooden cars packed with picnickers had stopped at the station; a fast freight, coming from behind, had plowed through the rear cars, telescoping two or three others, leaving about fifty people dead and three times that number injured. Something had gone wrong with the signal system.

He cleaned up the story before any rival reporter appeared and waited until a relief man arrived from the *Sun*. When he reached the office about seven o'clock that evening, the night editor was at his desk, spectacles pushed up on his forehead, reading copy. He greeted Bill with his regular one-word formula, uttered truculently under his drooping mustache. "Well?"

Bill summarized what had happened.

"Let it run," Clarke said, and asked if Bill thought he could finish in time to scan the casualty list for any discrepancies. Deadline for the first edition was midnight.

"It's good for three or four columns," Bill said, "and I'll have it finished by eleven-thirty. That will give me half an hour to edit the casualty list."

Clarke nodded.

Bill sat down at a table and began the narrative he had constructed in his mind on his way back from the train wreck. As the deadline rapidly approached he wrote with fierce intensity.

At the *Sun* it was etiquette to keep away from a man working, but Clarke was having one of his chronic attacks of big-story jitters. They were worse than usual that night because he had no confidence in this new and unproven reporter. On assignment from Mallon, Irwin had been writing short descriptive features about New York and comic episodes of the polyglot East Side, good enough as assignments in themselves, but they had left some important questions unanswered. Was he really a newspaperman? Could he handle a big news story on his own? Knowing what Clarke was thinking, Bill tried to ignore him.

Tall, stoop-shouldered, Clarke hovered over him, breaking in with questions.

"How do you know when the crash came?"

"Saw the clock in the engine, Mr. Clarke," Bill said meekly. "And statement of the train men."

He went on writing.

Clarke was soon back at his elbow. "How do you know how fast the freight was running?"

"Statement of the train crew. Condition of the indicator in the engine."

It went on like this for almost three hours. Clarke was "like a sticky, persistent fly when one is trying to sleep." Near eleven o'clock he started bugging Bill for copy.

"When are you going to give me that casualty list?"

"I'll finish the story at half past eleven," Bill replied, his patience thinning out. "Gives me half an hour to edit the list. Plenty of time."

Ten minutes later Clarke was back, asking the same question, receiving the same answer.

Then he did it again.

Bill's temper burst. He rose up from his chair and, looking Clarke square in his large grey eyes, said: "Mr. Clarke, that story will be in your hands, to the last line, at a quarter to twelve. Now for God's sake, will you let me work!"

Abruptly, without a word, Clarke turned and went back to his chair. Bill cursed himself. What a fool, he thought. Well, back to San Francisco.

He finished his story on time, complete and clear, then edited the casualty list. When he laid it on Clarke's desk, the night editor did not deign to look up. That night Bill slept fitfully.

When he read the newspapers Monday morning, he discovered that his early arrival at the train wreck had enabled him to beat the competition on evidence indicating the cause of the collision and on enriching details. At the office young Lord was bubbling with happiness; he had made good on his first day on the city desk. When Bill returned to the *Sun* at six o'clock in the evening to report the second-day story, Clarke actually smiled at him. The night editor opened his mouth, as if to say something, then clamped it shut.

After the train-wreck story, Clarke and Bill got along fine. Bill even discovered that they had something in common. Clarke had come from Canandaigua and had some memory of Bill's mother when she was a girl and knew of her eccentric artist father. Bill actually got on gossiping terms with the reserved, reticent Clarke.

Clarke, who preferred to praise or blame by manner rather than speech, even paid him a compliment once, though it was a slip. After interviewing Sarah Bernhardt, Bill returned to the office shortly before the deadline, and Clarke went over his copy in takes. He read one page while standing at Bill's side. Wondering if anything was wrong, Bill looked up just in time to catch Clarke's whisper to himself: "Fine!" Clarke realized that Bill had heard and scurried away to his desk.[6]

With Clarke's support, Bill was overcoming his reputation as a literary dilettante in the local room.

By the autumn of 1905, Bill had earned recognition as a skilled, journeyman reporter. He covered highbinder wars in Chinatown, exposed spirit mediums, and interviewed visiting celebrities. In one week he interviewed the archbishop of Canterbury, actress Anna Held, and boxer Bob Fitzsimmons. Covering the East Side, he wrote comic and pathetic stories about fires, riots, school disturbances, and stray cats. Reporting still satisfied his desire that each day bring something new, preferably delightful, but most of all unexpected.

Sun reporters were expected to exercise skill and enterprise in getting the news, but a beat did not necessarily justify the means. There were limitations, as Bill learned during the Equitable insurance scandal, a big financial story in which two *Sun* men competed against hordes of opposition reporters.[7]

One day the insurance company's board of directors held a meeting from which the press expected important news. Upon adjournment, however, the secretary announced that there was nothing for publication.

That afternoon Bill was in the local room when Mallon received a mysterious tip. If a reporter would meet a certain eminent director at a subway entrance at 5:15 P.M., the *Sun* might learn something to its advantage. It sounded like the director might spill the story, giving the *Sun* a beat. A few days before, Bill had interviewed the director, and Mallon gave him the assignment.

Instead of spilling the story, the director told Bill that his lips were sealed. "But the whole thing's in a mimeographed report drawn up last week," the man said. "All we did today was to endorse it. A dozen extra copies are piled up just behind the door of the main office. When the scrubwoman comes in at six to clean up, slip her five dollars and she'll shut her eyes while you lift one of them."

Bill took the director's proposition to his city editor.

"Well!" Mallon said sharply.

"Well," Bill said, "I don't like the idea, myself."

"It's just as well you don't," said Mallon. "If you'd have turned such a trick I'd have fired you."

Many newspapers would not have hesitated to take advantage of any opportunity to lay hands on an important, exclusive story. In the highly competitive climate of daily journalism in New York, the *Sun* was a rarity. *Sun* men considered themselves professionals.

While Hallie, Herman, and David Irwin, who had moved to California, built the chicken ranch in Brookdale, Bill shared an apartment with Burgess on East Twenty-third Street in New York. He hoped that his wife would eventually join him, and he sent her a pretty buckle and three pairs of silk stockings for Christmas. In the meantime, he had met another woman, who impressed him.

In December 1904, Burgess had given a tea at their apartment for a friend from Boston. She was a Spanish-looking woman a few months older than Bill. She had been born on March 2, 1873, in Rio de Janeiro, but of New England stock that could be traced back to a colonel in Cromwell's army. An ancestor had married an American Indian maiden, and the Spanish cast to her aquiline features was actually derived from her Indian heritage, of which she was quite proud. She had black hair and high cheekbones and looked stunning in a flowing dress and bold earrings.

One of seventeen children in two marriages, Inez Leonore was the eighth child born to Gideon Haynes of Waltham and his second wife, Emma Jane Hopkins of Boston. In Rio de Janeiro, Gideon, who had been an actor and a state senator, was engaged in business; when it failed, he returned to Massachusetts. Later he became the first reform warden of the State Prison at Charlestown. Inez was strongly influenced by her father, an intellectual man and an author, who read Shakespeare to his children when they were very young.

In her childhood she lived in the west end of Boston and attended public schools. After graduating from the normal school, she taught in the Charlestown public schools for three of four years and saved her money for college. In 1897 she married Rufus Hamilton Gillmore of Boston on the condition that she could become a writer instead of a mother. Mrs. Gillmore kept house in Arlington, wrote persistently, and studied English as a special student at Radcliffe College. By the turn of the century she had completed her studies with high honors and was writing with increasing success.

At the tea in her honor, Bill devoted all of his time to her, and she found him very attractive. To her, he was a typical westerner: tall, broad-shouldered, muscular. His gentian blue eyes "were sometimes deeply meditative in expression, sometimes extremely mischievous, but at all times gentle. His teeth were close-set, regular and white. His face was strikingly mobile." The gold of his hair had a glint of green, and his curls rushed "at a furious speed and in an almost uncountable—certainly in an entirely uncombable number—from the nape of his neck, up over the crown of his head, to his forehead." He had small hands and slim ankles. She had never met anyone like him before.[8]

They had much in common. Both of their marriages were held together by a long, frayed thread. Both actively supported women's suffrage, Bill's interest in the issue going back to his mother's influence and the hue and cry he had heard for it in Colorado. Both were boxing fans. Both admired Shakespeare. Both enjoyed history and literature. And both were struggling writers with a mutual need for sympathy, understanding, and encouragement. Each regarded the other as uniquely unconventional, a "sulphite."

Soon after the tea, Bill accepted her invitation to visit Boston. She showed him Bunker Hill, Concord, Lexington, and other historic sites, and he amazed her by describing battles and pointing out the avenues of approach, attack, victory, and defeat. They talked about their writing and found in each other the sympathetic companionship they craved. After his visit they continued their discussion of personal and professional problems in frequent letters.

Although the public already recognized him as a writer of fiction and journalism, he felt frustrated in his desire to make a living as a fiction writer. Discouraged, he considered giving up the "story game." There was "a lot of rot" stacked up on his desk at home, he told her. Oh, if he could only write as well as he could talk. He had no confidence in his story-telling ability with a pen and he had no set writing habits at all. He wrote during his one day off a week and at odd times when he could snatch a few hours, morning or night, but on no regular schedule.[9]

In his letters he revealed a melancholy side that few people perceived behind his facade of easygoing congeniality. Hallie had suffered its slings and arrows, and it had intensified in his lonely, trying early months in callous, puritan New York. He reacted bitterly, as though life had cheated him. He sometimes felt that death would be a relief; there were days in the winter of 1904–1905 when he contemplated suicide.

But he felt that he must go on living, struggling, fighting—and must do it blithely. He must face life, failure, even the supreme evil of age with a laugh on his lips, he wrote, feeling old beyond his thirty-one years. He must play at happiness. He did not want to give "the infernal gods" the satisfaction of seeing his misery.[10]

In the spring of 1905 he tried to purge himself of what he felt was a deep-seated cowardice, a fear of both life and death, and Inez's letters bucked up his courage. He told her he did not know which he admired most, her mind or herself. She reminded him of the sweet sadness he had felt a month before his anticipated graduation from Stanford in 1898. After his expulsion, he told her, he had known no happiness until he had met her.

To him she was "a lark, singing on a morning when the brown earth wakens . . . a white pinnace that steals across a sea of dreams . . . the voice of gentle beasts calling out of the twilight for joy . . . the spirit-softening fog which makes cities of toils into cities of beauty. . . ." She was a "Daughter of the Gods."[11]

On June 15 Bill marked his first year in New York by moving into his own apartment at 530 West 123rd Street and writing to Inez that the year had been totally wasted except for meeting her. She had invited him to visit the Haynes family summer home at Scituate in July, and he was impatiently looking forward to seeing her again. He wanted to stay a week, if she would allow it. "Will the good people of Scituate talk scandal, New England town fashion," he asked her, "if a married gent, without his family along, makes an extended call?"[12]

He had a very important matter he wanted to discuss in person. For two or three months he had seriously considered leaving newspaper work. Although he was proud of his profession, he did not intend to remain a reporter any longer than he could help, and he wanted to know what she thought of his working for the *Sun* another year and then going back West to the Brookdale ranch for a year's straight trial "at the writing game."[13] He was not certain that he had the nerve to take the gamble.

During his visit, Inez undertook to convert him from western chauvinism to an appreciation of New England. Around Scituate, a small harbor town and artists colony thirty miles south of Boston, she showed him points of historical interest. The New England antiques and the story of the Pilgrims fascinated him, and he began to collect antiques for his New York apartment and to gather books on the Plymouth Colony. Gradually, he became impressed by the solidity and permanence of New England life, two attributes missing from his own experience. Inez's campaign to win his affection for New England was effective.

Soon after he returned to New York he was rewarded for his dependable performance on the *Sun* with an assignment to cover the Portsmouth, New Hampshire, peace conference to end the Russo-Japanese war. He was to write color sidebars for the news coverage by the *Sun*'s Washington correspondent, Richard V. Oulihan. Mallon told Bill to write anything that would read well. *Sun* editors liked colorful writing "decked mainly with those details which the trained eye of the good reporter comes to perceive."[14] They required that reporters' writing be concise and lucid, with an easy style that avoided stock phrases and flamboyant language and emphasized human interest and color—attributes of Irwin's best writing throughout his career. The techniques of writing for the *Sun* resembled those of writing fiction, and the newspaper spawned essayists, novelists, and playwrights. Bill would remember the *Sun* as "the best-written newspaper ever issued in the English language."[15]

With the assignment to cover the peace conference, he felt he would have to prove himself again. He would be covering for both the newspaper and its Laffan News Bureau, which competed against the exclusive and much larger Associated Press, and he dreaded the heavy responsibility. Every major newspaper in the world would be represented at Portsmouth by crack correspondents, many of them so versed in international affairs that Bill thought he would feel like a "child" in comparison.[16] It was his most important assignment yet.

The peace conference began August 8, 1905. Although it was "the most newsless news event" Bill had ever covered, he managed to write a color story of more than a column's length almost daily.[17] He reported the Russians' attendance at a high Episcopal Church and described the Japanese delegates. He portrayed a local Chinese laundryman who had been a rum runner and a Portsmouth patrolman whose usually peaceful job was disturbed by the crowds coming to gawk at the peace envoys. When life around the Hotel Wentworth headquarters became intolerably dull, he reported the doldrums and the debate on the possibilities of peace.

Bill and the roving international correspondents covering the conference, the "Lost Legion," were bored. In a letter to Inez he complained of his regular schedule, with meals and activities at the same time day after day. His life had been so irregular that a regular schedule disagreed with him. The drinking water did, too. Ever since his arrival he had felt ill; after three weeks, he had a cold. He lost eleven pounds.

In his depressed state, he was feeling desperate about being stuck in journalism. He had met so many first-class men covering the peace conference that he wondered if Inez did not like the reporter type instead of himself personally. He discovered that he was much more like the typical reporter than he had ever suspected. On the surface the reporters were pleasant, witty perhaps, magnetic in talk, and artists at telling stories orally. Together, they were overly merry, yet underneath their congeniality was a sadness, a persistent haunting melancholy and a sense of failure, a fear of the future, a hatred of life. Their happy-go-lucky facade often masked a chronic sadness and despair. Liquored up, one might confess that he was trying to get out of journalism but could not and probably never could. By one's thirties, what else could a man do?[18] Bill would be thirty-two in less than a month, and it worried him.

The peace conference suddenly ended with an accord on August 29. "It is all over but signing the treaty, and the lost legion is packing to leave," Bill wrote the next day. "Weird, foreign looking baggage, spotted with labels of hotels from Cape Town to Skagway, is going away by the truckloads. There's a babble of farewells in the lobbies—Russian, French, English and Japanese running in streams. . . . This was the greatest convention of the international correspondents ever held in this country—ever held in any country under one roof. . . ."[19] Plainly, the Lost Legion had impressed him. One day he would become a member.

Shortly after Bill returned to the *Sun* from the peace conference, Lindsay Denison resigned. Denison had received the most picturesque assignments and the highest guarantee, and Bill regarded him as one of the best reporters on the newspaper. On the day Denison resigned, Lord summoned Bill over to his desk and offered him Denison's place and a 50 percent increase in guarantee. "You fit in," the managing editor said. Bill later wrote: "I almost choked up, not so much over my good luck as over appreciation of the manner in which he conferred it. Chester Lord has always stood as my ideal of the gentleman in journalism." It was the honor even more than the money that pleased him, he wrote to Inez. Now he would make ten dollars more than Denison had, and only two other men in the history of the *Sun* had been paid so high a guarantee: "Jersey" Chamberlain and Sam Adams. He felt proud, extremely proud.[20]

Yet there were drawbacks to his promotion. He would be taken off the East Side and the picturesque crank stories he loved to write. Also, it would make leaving the *Sun* for a full-time trial at writing fiction more difficult. Despite the honor, he was still disenchanted with daily journalism.

Even as the *Sun*'s star reporter, he received assignments that were often unchallenging and sometimes downright discouraging. Sent out to

Columbia University to report on new dormitories, he was given the run-around for two hours and finally loosened his temper on the university president. On the next evening, he was getting ready to go home at nine o'clock when Boss Clarke sent him to the Imperial Hotel to interview a Kansas City man about an unimportant bank deal. It was a cub's job, but Bill happened to be the only reporter in the local room. At the hotel he waited, and waited, and waited; it was maddening. At 1:30 A.M. he phoned in that the man had never arrived and went home, swearing that the newspaper business was "no craft for a man with the slightest sparkle of ambition."[21]

Some of his discontent focused on the city editor. George Mallon was the most conventionally minded "bromide" he knew, and Bill had little respect for him intellectually. The *Sun*'s conservative editorial policy spilled over into the local room, where it took a satirical tinge. The city desk seemed to classify as fakes most progressive movements, the good with the bad, and as the staff color writer, Bill was often assigned to guy causes like socialism, free love, the single tax, and Populism, all of which Mallon thought funny but Bill thought had elements worthy of respect. These assignments increased his resolution to leave the *Sun*.

He envied those people who could live and write for themselves. Depressed, he regretted spending the five productive years from twenty-one to twenty-six going through the conventionalizing process of the university. If he had devoted himself to writing he might be a fiction writer now.[22] As it was, he occasionally sold a story or article to a magazine, but his modest success failed to match his ambition.

Soon after New Year's, 1906, Hallie came east without their son, urged by her family to try a reconciliation. Bill regarded her as a "queer mixture of artistic temperament and aristocratic instincts," of conventionality, fantasy, and high-bred gentleness, "a regular Alice in wonderland."[23] The tension during her visit was exhausting, and the longer she stayed, the more he looked forward to her leaving. Straining to please her and covering his assignments filled his days from early one morning to the next.

He disliked more and more of his assignments, he told Inez in letters he wrote during Hallie's visit. Covering the funeral of Gen. Joe Wheeler, he walked and ran alongside the procession for miles, only to have the copydesk butcher his story. To cover the strike of a grand opera chorus, he had to sit through one and a half acts of *Tristan und Isolde*, and the music made him melancholy. On one afternoon he almost lost his life.

Covering a fire, he climbed up into the action despite a fear of heights. For a moment he was ready to die. The wall of a building began falling and he and a fireman dove under a heavy dump cart. At least he would not die

in bed, he thought. He heard a roar and a rattle, saw darkness, and choked
on rising clouds of foul dust. Then he realized the cart had held.

He crossed the street to a saloon, swigged four whiskies like water,
went into the back room, shook out his clothes, exchanged information with
other reporters, and returned to the local room.

He was trying to organize his thoughts when Clarke swooped down
on him: "What the hell's the matter, Irwin? You're getting as slow as
the rest."[24]

That night Bill covered another fire.

Hallie's visit ended in February, after slightly more than a month.
Wanting to settle their situation, Bill had asked her to rejoin him permanently, and she talked of returning to New York in the autumn, but their
relationship remained strained and essentially unchanged. When he put her
aboard a westbound train he felt like he was beginning a vacation.

Oppressed by his marriage and his job, he felt incapable of either
affection or ambition. He sometimes thought that death would provide a
convenient escape, but he rarely contemplated suicide anymore. Despising
newspaper work, he kept his eyes open for an appropriate avenue of escape
from daily journalism.

Publisher S. S. McClure opened a way out. In San Francisco, Bill had
met and liked the compact, mustachioed dynamo whose book house had
published his collaborations with Burgess. Since moving to New York, Bill
had sold a story to *McClure's Magazine*, which had attained national
prominence for its fiction and its recent muckraking. Now McClure wanted
him to edit either a new Sunday newspaper or a new mass-circulation
magazine, two of the publisher's latest brainstorms, and to write on special
assignment.[25]

The salary they discussed was substantial, around $125 to $150 a week.
But more important to Bill was the opportunity to do something big and to
produce works of greater literary value than daily newspaper reports. Should
he accept?

When he actually had to decide whether or not to leave the *Sun*, he
realized how much the newspaper really meant to him. He would miss his
daily adventures, the running around town and seeing people. It would be
a terrific wrench to leave.

Yet there was no financial risk involved in moving to McClure's organization. Although he had no executive ambitions and desk work bored him,
it would be a painless transition from newspaper reporting to more literary
forms of writing. He noted that muckraker Lincoln Steffens had begun on
a desk and evolved into a staff writer.

Finally, "with mental reservations," he accepted an executive position with McClure, though what his duties would be were not clear.[26] When he had taken the *Sun* job he had promised Lord that he would stay at least two years, but McClure, always in a rush, persuaded the managing editor to set back that release date to May 15. By mid April, Bill was working for the *Sun* afternoons and evenings and learning the ropes at McClure's offices in the mornings.

He was at McClure's on the morning of April 18, 1906, when an office boy laid an early edition of an evening newspaper on his desk. The headlines caught his eye and he snatched up the paper. An earthquake had wrecked San Francisco. Fires were raging unimpeded. A thousand people were reported killed. He grabbed his hat and rushed to the *Sun*.[27]

Questions raced through his mind. Were his wife, his son, his brother, his father all right? What had happened to his friends and the old familiar places? Surely, he thought, the *Sun* would send him to the city he had known so intimately.

In the local room he found the city editor, the night editor, and the Laffan Bureau manager grouped around the managing editor's rolltop desk; it was the first time the executives had held a morning conference. A telephone call came for Bill from Wesley Beach, a Stanford alumnus with whom he now shared a walkup flat. Beach had assumed that Bill would be sent to San Francisco on the earliest train and had packed his suitcase. He offered to meet Bill with it wherever and whenever he designated. Bill joined the huddle around the desk. "I'm ready to start to San Francisco whenever you say," he told the executives. "All packed."

Lord shook his head. "I know how you feel, but we want you here." Then he explained that the morning and evening *Suns* had received their news flashes of the earthquake and fire from government sources in Washington, indicating that the Laffan Bureau's stringer in San Francisco, George Hamilton Fitch, might be dead or injured, for it was unlikely that so reliable a newspaperman would fail to send even a flash. And the Laffan Bureau needed coverage immediately.

The little Laffan agency competed against the mighty Associated Press (AP) on a shoestring, serving young newspapers trying to establish themselves in competition with newspapers owning exclusive AP franchises. In San Francisco, AP had a corps of newsmen, and the Laffan Bureau could not afford to wait the four days it would take Irwin to get there by train. If the bureau stumbled on this, "the biggest story since the Spanish War," Lord called it, the news service was finished.

The closest wire open originated in Oakland, across the bay from the ravaged city, and it was jammed with messages from government officials, influential individuals, and AP reporters. For the Laffan Bureau the wire was useless. Bill sat down with his editors and planned alternative coverage.

They decided that he would telegraph the many small-town editors he knew in northern California, asking each to send any news he had and to name his price. Urgent messages went to Palo Alto, Santa Rosa, and other towns. Larry Hills was stationed at the wire head in New York. In Washington, Dick Oulihan's staff gathered information from the Red Cross, army, navy, and other governmental sources that had precedence over the overworked wire. From the local room, about three thousand miles from the holocaust, Bill would write the running account as if he were a witness, if nothing was heard from Fitch soon.

When one o'clock passed without a word from the stringer, Bill began writing. The editors ordered that no one should speak to him or venture near him except when absolutely necessary. Office boys answered "out" to all telephone calls for him and stood off his California friends besieging the outer office in the pathetic hope that he would obtain for them what he could not obtain for himself—family news.

Between one o'clock and the deadline for the last edition he wrote fourteen columns of copy based on frustratingly fragmentary dispatches from California. Smoking cigarettes, drinking coffee, and eating at his table, he avoided alcohol. That night he slept in his clothes on a couch in the office.

In the morning he resumed writing his anonymous front page reports of the fire from fragmentary dispatches. Under the strain of putting together long coherent running stories for the *Sun* and its Laffan Bureau, he worried about his family and friends in California. It took all of his will power to control his emotions. Ordered not to let him become emotional, the staff acted casual and unsympathetic. By the deadline, in the dark hours of the next morning, he felt numb. His adopted hometown was gone.

Too tired for the long journey home on an elevated train at three o'clock in the morning, he went quaking and drooling like a senile old man to a Turkish bath. He awoke at breakfast time with a head that felt like a hangover from a three-day debauch and with uncontrollable little jerks agitating his muscles. After a vigorous rubdown he felt better and returned to the local room.

That morning of April 20 he completed forty-eight hours on the story, with insufficient sleep. He was on the verge of nervous collapse when his former city editor on the *Chronicle* slipped through a brief telegram from Oakland. It consisted of a dozen names, including those of his family and dearest friends, and the closing words, "All well and safe."

The sudden end of his anxiety released a strange flood of consciousness. No longer tired, he stoked in food with his left hand while with his right he continued writing. Every faculty seemed to function with preternatural acuteness. Especially his memory. When a news source mentioned a locality, he envisioned it with the accuracy of a photograph. "The information from which I was writing would carry the name of a locality—as, say, 'Mission Street between Third and Fourth'," he later explained.

A week or two before or a week after, I could have remembered of that
locality only a church, a saloon where sometimes we used to resort after
the paper went to press, and—dim in detail—that row of secondhand
stores where I discovered the evidence in the Nora Fuller case. Now it
seemed that I could enumerate each establishment on either side of the
street, could often remember the number of stories in its building and
even the legend on its sign.

As if having an hallucination, he could even discern individual houses and
count the trees on Russian Hill.

By noon the fire was still burning but the story was settling down and
there was a lull in the running account. Mallon asked him to take on an extra
job. The *Sun* had not printed any general description of San Francisco.
Would he write one?

He picked up a sharp pencil and without consulting a book or map
began writing:

> The old San Francisco is dead. The gayest, lightest hearted, most
> pleasure loving city of the western continent, and in many ways the
> most interesting and romantic, is a horde of huddled refugees living
> among ruins. It may rebuild; it probably will; but those who have known
> that peculiar city by the Golden Gate and have caught its flavor of the
> Arabian Nights feel that it can never be the same. It is as though a
> pretty, frivolous woman had passed through a great tragedy. She sur-
> vives, but she is sobered and different. If it rises out of the ashes it must
> be a modern city, much like other cities and without its old atmosphere.

He went on to describe vividly the old city, its hills and waters and woods
and winds and rains, taking his readers on a tour in mood-creating scenes:

> Yet the most characteristic thing after all was the coloring. For the
> sea fog had a trick of painting every exposed object a sea gray which
> had a tinge of dull green in it. This, under the leaden sky of a San
> Francisco morning, had a depressing effect on first sight and afterward
> became a delight to the eye. For the color was soft, gentle and infinitely
> attractive in mass.

He remembered in detail the steep flight of stairs up Vallejo Street to the
winding path to the summit where he had lived among artists in small villas
whose windows overlooked the bay; and he recalled that "loud bit of hell,"
the Barbary Coast, which had intrigued him. In two hours he wrote four and
a half columns of copy, concluding with a paragraph about an old

> sixty foot cross of timber. Once a high wind blew it down, and the
> women of the Fair family then had it restored so firmly that it would
> resist anything. As it is on a hill it must have stood. It has risen for fifty
> years above the gay, careless, luxuriant and lovable city, in full view
> from every eminence and from every valley. It must stand tonight above
> the desolation of ruins.

Bill's copy went to Franklin P. Matthews, who edited it and wrote the headline, "The City That Was."

While Bill returned to the running account for page one, eating at his desk, drinking coffee, and smoking cigarettes, compositors set the type and locked it into the page five chase for the April 21 edition. Although his story carried no byline, in accordance with the *Sun*'s practice, the identity of its author quickly spread.

On the fourth day, Bill was still working under intense strain, feeling he could write at high speed indefinitely, when a crisis arose. Toward midnight a copy boy laid on his table a sheet of flimsy, and Bill routinely picked it up. Under a Washington, April 22, dateline the War Department was announcing that the peninsula, with San Francisco, had sunk out of sight under the Pacific Ocean. The big muscles at the front of his thighs "jumped like frogs." Somebody handed him a glass of whiskey.

About five minutes later Clarke came over with another sheet and laid it on the table. Bill's fingers trembled. He could hardly pick it up. "Washington April 22," he read. "War Department report a canard. Kill."

The shock of the War Department's report had broken his mood. After that he wrote without the mystical, superhuman power of recollection that had characterized his creation of "The City That Was." At the end of eight consecutive days on the job, usually with time out only for catnaps on an office couch, he had written about seventy-five columns of copy from the fragmentary dispatches and his own nostalgic memory. On the last night he did not feel at all tired. He had gone beyond weariness.

Instead of going home to bed, he went to Atlantic City for the New York publishers' annual party for their authors and sang, laughed, and larked until three or four o'clock in the morning, when he caught a train back to New York. At one o'clock that afternoon he reported to the city desk feeling fine.

After the fire, Fitch returned to his part-time job as a Laffan stringer, and Bill learned why the California journalist had failed to wire a report. Having critical professional and personal responsibilities in San Francisco, Fitch had ordered an assistant to "cover for the New York *Sun*." The assistant had marked his reports for that newspaper instead of for the Laffan Bureau, unaware that the harried telegraph clerks were filing newspaper dispatches on the floor and sending only press matter marked for the news bureaus. If the assistant had marked his copy for the Laffan Bureau, it might have been transmitted to the *Sun*.

Bill had sent out almost a hundred telegrams to possible new sources, and he had written for six or seven hours at a stretch. At one sitting he produced eleven columns of news about the fire. His handling of the running accounts and of the bay city's obituary, all anonymous, had enabled the *Sun* to excel against tough competition in New York and the Laffan Bureau to weather the storm against the larger AP. Suddenly he was famous in the profession.

Congratulatory telegrams poured in from around the world, many of them from foreign correspondents he had met at Portsmouth. A rival newspaper called his achievement "an unusual example of that imaginative reconstruction of the truth of an event which, whether based upon his own observed facts or the reports of others, every great reporter achieves at his best."[28] His feature on the old San Francisco was recognized as a *Sun* classic, and he polished it for publication between hard covers, his first book without a collaborator.[29] As the congratulations poured in, he was torn between tears and pride. What a way to end his newspaper career!

On the afternoon after the publishers' party, when the big story was over, Bill glanced up from his table to see the managing editor looking at him. Lord gestured with his little finger, and Bill went over to his desk.[30]

"Don't leave us," Lord said quietly. "We'll make it worth your while to stay, if that's what's eating you."

He told Bill that he had done the most remarkable thing in the history of American journalism.

"You've made yourself one of us now," Lord said. "Have you got to go? I'll do this for you now. If you'll stay with us, I'll sign a contract for two years at $125 dollars a week."

He concluded by saying he considered Bill the greatest of all the great *Sun* men and that he thought his feat was of enduring quality. No other compliment ever touched Bill so much. But he tried to harden his heart.

He lay awake at night, worrying about leaving the *Sun*. Was he doing the right thing? Lord's offer to raise him to a salary included vacation and sick leave, each with pay, which he did not receive working on a guarantee. Should he change his mind? he wondered. Should he stick with the *Sun*?

Added to this concern was his sadness over the loss of his beloved San Francisco. The earthquake and fire had left 250,000 people homeless and 490 blocks in ruin, for a loss of around $500 million. The death of the city marked for him the end of a significant intellectual period.

Fortunately, his own material losses, at least, were insignificant. His family and friends had survived, the place in the Santa Cruz mountains had not suffered, and his personal property loss ran to no more than five or six hundred dollars, mostly silver, Japanese paintings, and "junk" destroyed in the fire. Contemptuous of property, he was not greatly concerned about the loss of his possessions.

His earnings for the San Francisco stories more than compensated for his losses. At a space rate of eight dollars a column, he collected more than six hundred dollars above his guarantee. With part of that money he paid for the removal of his tonsils, which had become inflamed under the eight days of strain.

By the end of April, McClure had changed his plans, leaving Bill a way to graciously change his mind and remain on the *Sun*. But he finally decided to accept a revised offer, this one to edit the publisher's latest brainchild, *Public Opinion Magazine*. At last his break with daily journalism was definite.[31]

CHAPTER FOUR

Muckraker

BEFORE Bill completed his transition from the *Sun* to McClure's organization, the erratic publisher changed his plans again. Over the years the chief's temperamental personality and disorganized editorial policy had ripened revolt in the ranks, and when he fanatically insisted on a grandiose expansion of his publishing organization and diversification into banking, housing, and life insurance, the nucleus of his talented *McClure's* staff deserted him. Lincoln Steffens, Ida M. Tarbell, Ray Stannard Baker—all leading muckrakers—and three others went with John S. Phillips, McClure's longtime partner, to the *American Magazine*. McClure painted a glowing picture of what he and Bill could do with *McClure's* and on May 10, 1906, Bill was officially hired as the new managing editor, apparently at a lower salary than he had expected.[1]

From the beginning, his job was exasperating. Witter Bynner, who with Viola Roseboro and Burton Hendrick remained with *McClure's*, had been appointed managing editor upon the old guard's exodus, but had not realized that it was temporary until he walked into his office one morning late in May and found Irwin established there. It was an awkward situation for them both. Crestfallen, Bynner was moved to another position.

Snapping orders around the office in a sharp, high voice, McClure was soon interfering in Bill's editorial management. The magazine was overstocked with 180 stories, and one day the chief gave Bill 21 to read overnight, which he did. The files also contained two major factual works, one on the reign of the copper kings in Montana and one on Mary Baker Eddy and her new religion. McClure gave the Christian Science series to Willa Cather, another new staff member, to edit, although Bill apparently wanted to edit it himself.[2]

Thirty-three in September, Bill sank to one of his mental lows, what he called "sourballs." Although Californians ranked him with Jack Cosgrave of *Everybody's* and other accomplished magazine editors from the state, behind the spectacles and bow tie he still felt like a failure. It seemed that age was rushing upon him and time running out.

A $40 a week raise to $140 in November and possibly at this time a promotion to editor failed to assuage his feeling that success was eluding him. Even though he was making more than twenty-three times his $6 cub reporter's salary of seven years ago, his raise gave him no thrill. Sale of the short stories he was writing on his own time meant more to him than his work at *McClure's*.[3]

The job was not turning out as he had hoped. He had expected to edit half time and write half time. Instead, he was spending most of his time fighting McClure's follies. Short, blond, smiling through a yellow mustache, the chief was a dynamo of nervous energy. Everyday he sprang something new. He might generate twenty ideas—always big ones—in a week. Eighteen of them might vary from impracticable to fantastic, and two might be good, but all struck him with equal impact. The chief needed somebody to supplement his magnificent, uncontrolled genius with judgment, to balance the scale, to throw cold water on his bad ideas, as Phillips had done. But Bill was not the man. "As a curb on genius," he realized in retrospect, "I was not a success."[4]

He fought McClure during the day and dreamed about him at night. One night in December he saw the yellow beady eye of the chief fixed upon him like the eye of a snake, holding him in a spell. McClure said: "We will run thirty-two pages of editorial after this!" In the recesses of Bill's sleeping mind, the message sounded like the voice of doom, and he woke up crying.[5]

On top of his frustrations at *McClure's* was added a visit by Hallie and little Billy in the winter of 1906–1907. The attempted reconciliation, again urged on Hallie by her family, was strained at best. Nervous around children, Bill shyly and awkwardly tried to get to know his three-year-old son. Billy did not fully trust him and would not let him close the door to the room where Mother was sitting. Hallie was as strong willed and outspoken as ever. Although she read few of his works, she told an acquaintance within Bill's hearing: "I don't care especially for the things he writes."[6] A slap in the face would have stung less.

While Bill tried to cope with strained family relations at home, conditions grew worse at the office. He suspected that McClure's wife, Harriet, who liked to meddle, was working against him and that Willa Cather was intriguing for his job. He told Inez that Cather and the chief were having a love affair and McClure's wife knew it. He believed that his own days with the magazine were numbered.[7]

Finally, after months of the McClures' meddling in editorial decisions, Bill revealed his dissatisfaction to the Board of Directors, and they urged him to stay. He took a relaxing eight-day steamer cruise to Bermuda to think it over, and when he returned the situation was still intolerable. One day McClure agreed to turn over the magazine's editorial management to him and the next day the chief, prodded by his wife, was raging to take back control. Bill demanded his own way, or else. "It was a case of win or get out," he wrote afterwards. "I lost."[8]

In March 1907 he resigned, ending less than a year of unhappy association with the magazine. Although he had risen from managing editor to editor, as long as McClure was around either position was largely titular. The experience would leave a deep scar on his memory.

Serving his last month on the editor's desk, he considered his next move. The *Sun* tempted him to return, but he feared that entering daily journalism again might forever eliminate any opportunity to devote more time to his own literary efforts. Working on *McClure's* had extended his interests, and he longed to join the muckrakers. "Hitherto, I had taken little real interest in politics," he later reflected.

> Usually I voted the Republican ticket, but with many scratches. The glimpses of Wall Street and state politics gained from my work on the *Sun*, had given me considerable sympathy with the muckrakers then expressing themselves in the magazines; but it was sympathy without enthusiasm. The job at *McClure's* changed all that; I wanted to wield a muckrake myself.[9]

The problem was making a living by muckraking.

That was soon solved by an arrangement with Robert J. Collier, a magazine publisher he had met through McClure. They agreed that Bill would contribute regularly, but not exclusively, to *Collier's Weekly*. Assured of a financial safeguard, he at last made the plunge into free-lance writing.

Collier's ranked with *McClure's*, the *Saturday Evening Post*, and *Everybody's* as a popular national periodical. Exerting a strong influence on national affairs, the magazine covered news events in a more leisurely, comprehensive, and literary manner than the press bureaus and filled a gap in American journalism by backgrounding and interpreting events. Editor Norman Hapgood, a reformer who disliked rant and fustian, held *Collier's* on the periphery of the muckraking movement.

Ready to rake muck, Bill went to Hapgood with a sheaf of ideas in the spring of 1907. To his disappointment, the editor chose one of no political significance: an exposé of professional mediums. Hapgood wanted it national in scope. It was Bill's first assignment as a full-time free-lance writer. With his brother, already an established contributor to *Collier's*, looking on, he once more felt the pressure to make good on a new job.

About this time his attempted reconciliation with Hallie ended. Thin, bitter, and depressed, she took Billy back to California. Their departure left Bill free to devote all of his time to working on his séance series.

At first he followed blind leads, attempting to break into the inside organization of the fakers and especially the "Blue Book" system for exchanging intimate personal information on habitual dupes. His first important break came in Chicago. Posing as one "Professor Beach," a California clairvoyant, he shopped for a pair of rigged slates in a bookstore that was a blind for a shop in spiritualist apparatus. There he met a middle-aged, plump, expansive woman medium who needed a platform worker for the public séances she conducted in her parlor on Cottage Grove Avenue. Accepting Professor Beach on sight as a member of her profession, she offered to hire him. Bill was slightly ashamed of himself when he decided to take the risk and accept.[10]

That afternoon he moved from his hotel to a furnished room, cut all identification marks out of his clothing, had business cards printed, and reported to "Martha" for rehearsal. The act was easy.

While in the parlor Bill began with "a vague hocus-pocus" and asked each sitter to place a ring, glove, locket, or other personal object on the table. In the hall Martha went through the sitters' coat pockets looking for letters, cards, and other objects that might contain useful information. Even an out-of-town clothing label could be exploited. On a piece of paper she would jot down brief notes, such as: "Red dress, r. front comes Peoria. Agnes bad cough. Family stationery business. Jimmie, Bill."

Then she entered the room and made an inspirational address, dropping the paper, tightly folded, among the objects on the table. Bill fumbled among them to get their "aura" and, as he did, palmed the paper. In the hall he quickly memorized the notes before returning for a half-hour demonstration of spirit power.

After their second show, she began telling him her troubles and ambitions. He encouraged her to talk, and she spilled the story he was after. He learned that as the typical dupe went from medium to medium, information was exchanged by telephone through a central card index, the "Blue Book" in Chicago.

Bill had the information he needed. He worked once more with Martha two nights later and failed to appear for the next performance, leaving her to suspect that the police had caught up with him. He also left her with his promised share of the profits as compensation for his subterfuge.

Not all mediums were complete fakes. On his travels he discovered two back-street mediums who seemed to have genuine flashes of extrasensory perception but who found it necessary to "water the milk" because they could not depend on a flash of second-sight during an important sitter's appointment. Bill himself believed in extrasensory perception, telepathy, and clairvoyance.

Sitting down to write the medium articles, his first major magazine series, he struggled to compose his large collection of facts, illustrative details, and anecdotes in an interesting form. When he submitted his manuscripts, Hapgood insisted that he tighten his prose and eliminate carelessnesses. Repairing here, pruning there, he sacrificed some of his best material to make the articles concise. The result was a compact four-part series exposing the illegitimate methods of "those humble, unsung adventurers who gain an easy living by playing upon the deep pieties of the human heart."[11]

For the next major *Collier's* series, Bill investigated "a sudden storm of hatred and resentment against the Japanese on the Pacific Coast."[12] It was his first free-lance investigation of a critical social and economic problem. The assignment gave him an opportunity to return to California.

Traveling up and down the coast, he visited San Francisco for the first time since the earthquake and fire. Once familiar sections looked bizarre. At Market and Powell streets he found a pile of mortar, a sheet-iron shack, and an excavation which he remembered had been the entrance to the tenderloin and the exit to the Columbia Theatre, "from which nightly the stalwart gay-gowned, tropic women used to troop." On Market Street, pipe-smoking loafers around a new building site reminded him how men used to stand and watch the matinee parade pass in the old days. It was home, he told Inez, but it was a nightmare.[13]

From Russian Hill the city looked white, instead of the gray he remembered, but beyond still lay the shimmering bay. Gradually he began to like the new city . Seeing old friends and visiting relatives with Hallie, who came up from Brookdale, he found San Franciscans "the same easy, lovable, open minded sulphites." In spirit the city was essentially unchanged. As he watched the people enthusiastically rebuilding, he wondered how he could have ever called San Francisco "the city that was."[14]

In the backcountry he had been familiar with as development editor of the *Chronicle*, he interviewed the officials of a Japanese sardine canning factory, visited old friend Jimmie Hopper, and spent several days with his family on the seven-acre ranch nestled among young redwoods in the Santa Cruz mountains. His wife, young brother, father, and son were trying to become self-sufficient in the rustic setting. Hallie was good at arts and crafts, Herm handy with wiring and plumbing. Dad helped with carpentry and odd jobs, and Billy fed the chickens and watered his cow. He was cute, even pretty, and took an intelligent and conversational interest in the ranch. Almost four, he had suddenly grown from a baby to a boy, and his father was impressed.

Herm, nine years Bill's junior, also impressed him. Herm was an avid hunter and fisherman and superb horseman, a skill Bill could especially appreciate. Muscular, compact, with deep, violet blue eyes set wide apart in a sun-bronzed face, Herm dressed in khaki and wore high boots and a sombrero. To Bill he looked like a Greek god.

Astride a horse for the first time in seven years, Bill rode until he was saddle sore. He wrote to Inez that he "climbed mountain trails where the great ferns, still with last night's dew brushed our flanks & soaked our hair." He rode under the redwoods and slept out under the stars and awoke with the low-lying mist caressing his face. He told Inez that he could not blame his wife for wanting to stay on the ranch, with its clear streams, wooded hills, and mysterious canyons. It was like a Garden of Eden. If he had no ambition, he could be as content as Hallie to live this way.[15]

But he felt that he did not belong there.

After several weeks of exhausting hospitality in northern California, Bill left for Los Angeles. He would soon be thirty-four and he was feeling worn out and old. He dreaded aging.

Taking snapshots to illustrate his articles, he continued to study the Japanese situation. The attitude of native, white Americans had not changed since he had seen the two Chinese, their pigtails tied together, threatened with lynching and railroaded out of Leadville. But however forcibly the Anglo-Saxon passion for racial purity might block social assmiliation of other races, it could not restrain economic forces. Able, industrious, proud Orientals created antagonism by competing successfully against the white Americans; that was the root of the racial conflict.

The situation was complex. It was not the kind of story Bill was used to writing. His specialty was the single incident, the flash of life, not the proportionate description of a whole phase of life. "I have painted Flemish paintings on a thumbnail canvas," he wrote to Inez, "and the technique of heroic painting on a great canvas eludes me."[16]

He finally captured the technique of heroic painting in four articles packed with anecdotes, quotations, and details. Although he revealed some prejudice, calling the Japanese "childlike" and "children" and "approximately our equals," he wrote about their economic and social plight with sympathy and understanding. He condemned racism, but saw no way the Oriental could be either segregated or assimilated into white culture. Like many muckrakers, he concluded his series with no answers, only questions.[17]

Before he completed his Japanese series, his first medium article appeared in *Collier's*. It happened to run on his thirty-fourth birthday. About this time he suffered two "sick headaches," perhaps migraines.[18] Severe headaches recurrently plagued him but never diminished his fortitude.

By October he felt that he had made a successful beginning as a free-lance writer. Three installments of "The Medium Game: Behind the Scenes with Spiritualism" had appeared and his series about "The Japanese and the Pacific Coast" had begun. The appearance of two articles, one from each series, in the September 28, 1907, *Collier's* made him feel especially good. He was now a bonafide member of the influential "Collier group."

The group consisted of liberal writers who regularly contributed articles and editorials to Robert Collier's magazine. Among Bill's colleagues were his brother Wallace, a humorist; Frederick Palmer, a specialist in war and politics; and Arthur Gleason, a writer on sociological problems. Other members included his friend Sam Adams, who had effectively muckraked patent medicines. Together, they exerted a wide influence on social and political affairs.

While writing on a wide variety of subjects for *Collier's*, Bill contributed articles and stories to other magazines and worked on a book. His standard rate was $300 an article; at one time he had orders totaling $1,250 from *Collier's, Everybody's,* and the *Saturday Evening Post*.[19] From San Francisco, Arnold Genthe sent eighty artistic photographs of Chinatown before the earthquake, and Bill prepared a reflective text to accompany a selection of them in a book. Then he investigated another major social problem for *Collier's*.

Hapgood assigned him to study the national trend toward prohibition. The country was gradually going dry, at first in towns, then counties, then whole states. "See what it is all about, what's at the bottom of it," the editor ordered.[20]

Glad to escape the northern winter of 1908–1909, Bill headed south to begin his on-the-scene investigation. On his way to Leland, Mississippi, Judge Harris Dickson of Vicksburg tipped him off to a detail the judge could not use in prohibition articles he was writing for the *Saturday Evening Post*. It was a pornographic trick label on cheap, sweet gin.

Bill believed it was a myth of the prohibition forces until he saw it for himself in Leland. With knowledge of Black Belt slang, you could translate the name, device, and motto on a bottle into four-letter Anglo-Saxon obscenities. If you turned the lithographed picture of the blonde in extreme décolleté upside down and covered part of it with one hand, you saw an obscene picture. Cards and circulars distributed with this cheap gin carried similar suggestions of sexual relations with white women.

Whites believed that the widely distributed "nigger gin" and other liquor contributed to the so-called characteristic crime of the Negro—rape. In Louisiana Bill heard of a drunken Negro who had raped and fatally shot a white girl. Although an isolated case, it provided ammunition for the white southern temperance movement. Southern voters, whatever their personal drinking habits, thought that the only feasible way of taking the gin away from the Negro was general prohibition.

The key to the prohibition question eluded Bill until Arthur Gleason, crusading against the evils of the liquor traffic, pointed out the unsavory alliance between the great brewers and distillers and the saloonkeepers. Gleason had discovered that the brewers and distillers set up too many saloons, which created severe competition. That forced saloon proprietors to ally with criminal gangs, prostitutes, and corrupt politicians or go into bankruptcy. It was not just a southern problem; it was a national one. The saloon was the base of the political bosses ruling many American cities. Now Bill was working with a favorite theme of the muckrakers: the collusion among big business, corrupt politics, and vice.

After several months of rounding up the story in southern and western states, Bill had a conference with Hapgood, who favored prohibition. Bill told him that only a crusading minority of the people thought drinking was sinful and that the state could never enforce a law against it.

"Then what's the answer?" Hapgood asked.

"No single answer," Bill replied. "It's too complex. Honest regulation for one thing. Some method of getting the saloon out of politics. And scientific temperance education, not the hysterical pseudo-science which our children are getting through the W.C.T.U. 'A dry America by 1920' is the nubbin of this story. As for us, inform the liquor interests that, unless they stop overdoing their salesmanship and obey what laws we have, this dream is going to come true."

That was the slant Bill gave his series. In six articles, published in the spring of 1908, as well as in subsequent pieces, he showed how the alliance of bad politics and lawless saloons controlled by the distilling industry was driving the nation toward prohibition. Although he vaguely proposed some regulation, he left the ultimate solution in the hands of the brewers and distillers. Like many a muckraker's solution, it was no solution at all.

Although "The American Saloon" series was extensively circulated by prohibitionists, an unobtrusive, brief postscript appended to the final installment attracted the most fervid reaction. "Who Killed Margaret Lear?" was the rape story Bill had heard in Louisiana. Writing it, he dropped his usual pose of the detached reporter and let his emotions run.

According to testimony, a Negro drunk on cheap gin had raped then shot the fourteen-year-old white girl on her way home from Shreveport High School. The girl lived long enough to crawl to the gate of her home, where, as Bill reported, "clutching the pickets, she died." The governor ordered out the militia, and the suspect was caught, convicted, and hanged within nine days.

Bill could not blame the mob that "howled for the blood of this poor black beast" as much as he could blame those who trafficked in the liquor with the obscene labels. He named companies, with addresses, and the only offending brand whose name was not obscene, then brought his postscript to a close with these two paragraphs:

> Is it plain now—the secret of many and many a lynching and burning in the South? The primitive negro field hand, a web of strong, sudden impulses, good and bad, comes into town or settlement on a Saturday afternoon and pays his fifty cents for a pint of . . . gin. He absorbs not only its toxic heat, but absorbs also the suggestion, subtly conveyed, that it contains aphrodisiacs. He sits in the road or in the alley at the height of his debauch, looking at that obscene picture of a white woman on the label, drinking in the invitation which it carries. And then comes—opportunity. There follows the hideous episode of the rope or the stake.
>
> And neither this black brute, dying in agony, nor these whites, temporary brutes in their mob anger, can see this vision: A—gentle-man—of St. Louis taking his fat, after-dinner ease, sitting on plush, decked with diamonds, lulled by a black cigar, and planning how he shall advance his business through his membership in the Model License League, which has been formed to chastise abuses in the retail liquor traffic![21]

Here was the single incident, the kind of story Bill had frequently handled as a newspaper reporter. However flawed by his racial prejudice, it was like many of his other "Flemish paintings on a thumbnail canvas." The new ingredient was his personal indignation.

Southerners in districts under pressure by the prohibitionists reacted with indignation, too, but for their own reasons. Wets called Irwin "an apologist for the black brute," and some threatened him with bodily harm if he again ventured South.[22] Drys reprinted the Lear postscript for propaganda. The controversy led to the arrest and conviction of the leading disseminator of the gin with the trick, pornographic label. His punishment was a mere fine, but the bad gin disappeared. The San Francisco *Call* commented that Will Irwin's " 'Who Killed Margaret Lear?' is said to have done more toward making it hard for the negro to get the sort of gin that maddens him than any orator or organizer the prohibitionists have ever sent forth."[23]

With publication of the prohibition series, Will Irwin emerged as a full-fledged muckraker, not in the genre of David Graham Phillips, Steffens, Tarbell, and other pioneer pliers of the national magazine exposé, but in the milder style of latter-day entrants into the movement. Although he was making good money now, his success did not satisfy him.

Vowing he would make good as a fiction writer, he filled in time between articles by writing light, entertaining short stories for *Everybody's*, the *Saturday Evening Post*, and *Munsey's Magazine*. Inez encouraged him. He must, she wrote, "learn to mint all that gold of temperament into coin."[24]

In the early months of 1908 he needed her encouragement desperately. While he was working on his prohibition series, Hallie filed suit for divorce on grounds of desertion. Bill wanted a divorce and did not contest the suit, but the actuality of the break with Hallie hurt his ego. His reaction was reflected in letters to Inez, who was irked by his chronic complaint of senility. "You go through life like a man with a decaying corpse hung to his shoulders," she wrote, "and you can't resist showing the face at intervals to the passers-by." She was determined to extirpate that dead weight. "And as for letting a great over-grown boy with blue eyes and curly hair, bubbling over with life, joy, genius, charm, magnetism and physical health make a noise like a psalm all the time," she wrote, "before I get through I'll make a gentleman, a scholar, a muckraker, a reformer and an Easterner out of you!"[25] Notably, she did not say fiction writer; since reading in so many letters how inadequate he felt writing fiction, she had changed her mind about that. Now she advised him to concentrate on muckraking because a writer could not do both well at the same time. But he was driven too fiercely by ambition to heed her advice.

In the autumn of 1908, Bill's fifth book, *Pictures of Old Chinatown,* was published. Like his previous four, the setting was northern California, and like three of them, it was a collaboration, this time with a photographer. A New York *Times* reviewer thought Genthe's forty-seven full page illustrations were remarkable but considered Irwin's text chauvinistic.[26]

Bill was soon at work on his sixth book. Personal experience stories, providing realistic accounts of everyday life in America, were attaining a vogue as a backdrop for muckrakers' themes, and one day he met just the character for this kind of story. A. B. Stafford, a reformed confidence man who looked like a benevolent grandfather, was quite willing to reminisce for publication for half the take, providing his identity was kept secret. Writing in first person to capture the flavor of Stafford's "personality of mud-and-rainbows" and vocabulary of Latinate words, Bill told how for twenty years the con man had operated shell games at the back doors of cheap circuses, bilked country bankers with gold bricks, and played crooked three-card monte on transcontinental trains. In February and March 1909 the *Saturday Evening Post* serialized "The Confessions of a Con Man," and in September, B. W. Huebsch published the book.[27] The skeptical public did not believe that they were the real confessions of an actual confidence man.

In May the *Saturday Evening Post* published another of Bill's serials, this one featuring a heroine who would turn out to be his most captivating fictional character. Called Rosalie Le Grange, she was based on the medium he had assisted in Chicago. Mme. Le Grange applied the wiles of her trade to helping police Inspector Martin McGee capture thieves who stole the big and famous McGregor Rose diamond and six matched diamonds.[28] She was so well received that Bill began writing a novel-length mystery around her.

In the summer of 1909 Bill traveled to Colorado to work on articles about early Leadville for the magazine. It was difficult for him to write about his childhood home, it had changed so much; it looked like a dying mining camp. Visiting Denver, where he had spent an unhappy part of his life, was another emotional experience. He visited Sara Graham, who had mellowed, and attended high school commencement, which moved him to "inner tears."[29] Old friends feted him and reporters interviewed him.

In September his first book of fiction written without a collaborator was published by Doubleday, Page. *Warrior, the Untamed* was a brief, wildly humorous tale based on a publicity stunt from his *Sun* days. A circus press agent, who narrates the story in his own patois, hides a gentle, "motheaten and decrepit" old lion in a remote shed, announces that it has escaped, and milks the lion hunt for all of its publicity value. The story reflected Bill's own zestful sense of humor, which was rarely apparent in his writing. Wallace was the professional literary humorist in the family. It was just as well. Sales of *Warrior, the Untamed* were disappointing; in its first six months the slim little book garnered Bill only $114.10.[30]

His luck was almost as bad with his Rosalie Le Grange book, *The House of Mystery*, his first full-length novel without a collaborator. Genial and kind-hearted Mme. Le Grange again applied her unethical occult skills for righteous ends, this time to rescue a young woman from the unscrupulous clutches of her aunt, a high-class medium.[31] In the novel Bill demonstrated that he could create suspense, manipulate plots, and mold engaging characters—if not write a best seller.

A month after its publication in March 1910, *The House of Mystery* looked like a flop. Many reviewers found it commonplace and banal. Bill was satisfied with Century's promotion and blamed only himself when sales stopped late in April at 3,100. His dim, remaining hope was to sell the dramatic rights.[32]

In *The Readjustment*, a novel published in December 1910, he displayed both his weaknesses and strengths as a literary artist. His story was sentimental, his plot shallow, his characterization one-dimensional. But his writing was occasionally vivid, particularly in his recreation of scenes around San Francisco, which were reminiscent of his powerful description in "The City That Was."[33] Both his best fiction and best journalism reflected his ability to appeal to the visual sense.

Since leaving *McClure's* in 1907 he had been doing what he most wanted to do: write. He had muckraked, written other magazine pieces of fact and fiction, and produced five books, three of them fiction. Although he had not achieved the literary eminence he sought, his high productivity had earned him wide recognition in the writing game.

Even as his three novels appeared in the book stores, he was working hard on a third series of social significance, which had evolved from an assignment from Rob Collier to muckrake the American newspaper. Recently several books about newspapers had been published, but no mass magazine had yet muckraked the daily press, although it had occasionally been implicated by writers exposing corrupt business and political practices. Writers had uncovered the silence of local newspapers in cities where machine politicians "were stealing the shingles off City Hall," and Progressives had accused "the interests" of adversely influencing editorial policies through control of advertising. It was about time that a magazine writer muckrake the American newspaper, but by September 23, 1909, when Bill began his investigation, the original assignment had been broadened into an analytical, historical, definitive study. The magnitude of the job appalled him.[34]

Few written sources were helpful, and Bill relied mostly on interviews with publishers, editors, and reporters. The power of the press, he found, lay in the news columns, not the editorials. Colonel William R. Nelson, publisher of the Kansas City *Star*, agreed. So did Sam Chamberlain, Hearst's trouble shooter, and E. W. Scripps, head of the newspaper chain bearing his name. Thirty years before, Bill had heard C. C. Davis say the same thing in Leadville.

There was no shortage of muck to rake. Editors and reporters talked off the record with astonishing candor, revealing scandals that Bill subsequently documented. Records of deceased corrupt newspapers showed that the downfall of a newspaper often began with its acceptance of a direct subsidy or by permitting advertisers to dictate policy. When a newspaper lost its independence, it began the downhill road to oblivion.

In March 1910 his investigation took him to San Francisco. He wished that somebody else could do the California research. Once out there, he felt obligated to see his family, and they revived unhappy memories. There were new tensions, too. Shortly after he arrived he heard a rumor that his former wife and his younger brother had been intimate, even before her divorce. Bill wanted to avoid them, but he had made plans to see Dad and Billy.

He saw Hallie for a minute when she brought Billy to spend a day with him at an amusement park. His six-year-old son was growing up articulate, an only child among adults, with an adult way of talking. His favorite expressions were "by the way" and "I imagine," and he called his father "Will" and bossed him around. He impressed Bill with his curiosity and practicality. The boy had brains, Bill bragged in a letter to Inez.[35]

Soon after his day with Billy, he spent some time with his father, who was sixty-six. Dad was living at Brookdale, and Bill tried to discover what he knew about Hallie and Herm. His father thought that their relations were pure, but Bill believed the malicious gossip.

Shortly after he left California, Inez went on a visit, curious about the state whose praises she had often heard from Bill and Burgess. From San Francisco she went down to Stanford and visited Bill's room in Encina Hall and his other old haunts. It was no secret that she intended to marry him, once she was divorced from her estranged husband.

The frequent letters exchanged between Inez and Bill were sometimes curtailed and cautious, as if the lovers feared they might be discovered in a secret tête-à-tête. At other times their letters were effusive. He often addressed her as "Beautiful" and signed his letters "Rose Lover," and she addressed him as "Rose-Will." In one letter she wrote, "Get busy and marry me, kid."[36]

Traveling, Bill missed her. Occasionally, local hospitality or an hour in a shooting gallery alleviated his loneliness, and sometimes he addressed local groups. A reporter covering an address to a church group described him as "bright-eyed, rosy cheeked with the brisk manner of a college graduate who has had some of the bookishness rubbed off."[37]

By late June he had virtually completed his exhaustive and exhausting research on the newspaper series. While Inez planned with Burgess a summer home of her own at Scituate, Bill stayed at her brother Walter's house near Peggoty Beach and wrote in the mornings and played tennis in the afternoons.

In his introductory articles he established his theme, that only religion was a more influential institution than the press, whose power was based in the news columns, and summarized the history of American newspapers from their English origins through the extreme sensationalism of yellow journalism in the 1890s. Pointing out the crucial necessity for unbiased and untainted news, he got to the muckraking nub of his series. He had drawers full of provable instances of newspapers that had abandoned reform policies under the pressure of unscrupulous interests. Some publishers had bowed to the demands of bankers, who provided the capital that gave birth to new ventures, while others had succumbed to the threats of advertisers, who supplied the lifeblood of newspapers in those highly competitive times. Although a minority of newspapers were edited from the business office, it was in Bill's opinion a large enough minority to endanger the foundation of American journalism.

Bill was writing about one corporation that frankly subsidized a newspaper when a "pleasing young newspaperman" appeared in Scituate, got himself invited to play on the Haynes tennis court, and joined Bill in a double's match.[38] After the match, the guest revealed that he had heard of Bill's intentions to write about the corporation's journalistic subterfuge.

Did Bill know the head of the corporation? the young man inquired. Splendid fellow. The guest suggested that the life of this young Napoleon would make a big magazine article, much better than a mere incident in the press series.

"If you want to write it," the guest added, "you won't have to do any digging. He'll give you the dope. And if you'll take your article to him when you've finished it"—here an impressive pause—"I shouldn't wonder if he'd give you five thousand dollars!"

Bill was flattered. No one had ever before offered him a bribe. He afterwards recalled: "I felt as a debutante must feel when she gets, from a man whom she doesn't much like, her first proposal. She's going to turn him down, of course. But oh, the compliment of it!"

What right would he have to criticize unethical segments of the daily press for failing to live up to the tacit franchise of the First Amendment if his own ethics were tainted? Of course he declined the bribe.

Early in his series, he had decided that honor compelled him to make only one major compromise. If he found any evidence of unethical practices by the San Francisco *Chronicle* or the New York *Sun*, he would not mention it. To muckrake those two newspapers would be like biting hands that had fed him.

He saw no ethical conflict, however, in biting the hand of William Randolph Hearst, whose newspapers included two Bill had competed against. Threats from the publisher did not deter him, either. Hearst, hearing of impending attacks on him, sent his secretary over to *Collier's* to warn Collier and Hapgood that the magazine would be held criminally and civilly responsible for false statements published. Hearst's attorney also wrote a letter to Bill, but confined his threat to criminal libel without hope of recovering pecuniary damages. Collier wondered publicly why Hearst considered it necessary to yell before he was hit and said that the articles were not libelous, anyway.

Completion of the series was delayed for six weeks when Bill needed a decision from Rob Collier. He could arrange no appointment with the publisher, who now rarely appeared in his office and refused to delegate authority, and he received no answer to letters or memoranda. Finally he located the playboy publisher at his country estate in the Adirondacks, where, between sets of tennis, they settled the question in three minutes.

Since Robert Collier had inherited his father's publishing empire in 1909, it had been sliding downhill. Rob Collier spent money recklessly, sometimes drawing on the magazine's funds, delaying payments for manuscripts for weeks. As he slipped deeper into debt, his banker friends were gaining control of the magazine. Bill saw what was happening and wanted out.

Hapgood aggravated the irritations of working for *Collier's*, demanding that Bill rewrite parts of the series and do more research. His incessant demands angered Bill and possibly contributed to the severe headaches he was now suffering every four or five weeks. One morning he awoke with a terrific headache, went back to sleep, later vomited, and then slept the rest of the day. Working for *Collier's* had become more irritating than it was worth.

He was losing money, he figured. He wrote to Inez that from November 1, 1909, to November 1, 1910, he would make only $5,200, actually a comfortable sum in those days. He would receive about $320 for each of the fourteen articles he planned in the series and the balance mainly for a tribute to his friend, the late William Sidney Porter, for *Cosmopolitan*, and for a short story, set in a wild west mining camp, for *Everybody's*. This was his lowest rate of income since he had quit the *Sun*.[39]

On January 21, 1911, after more than a year in research and writing and rewriting, Bill's series on "The American Newspaper" began running in *Collier's* and he braced for Hearst's reaction. Bill had laid the foundation for the criticism Hearst had feared by attacking the sensational tactics of the San Francisco *Examiner* and New York *Journal* and by declaring that "Hearst's task was to cheapen the product until it sold at the coin of the gutter and the streets." Trying to balance his report, Bill admitted that over the years Hearst had responded to a sounder public opinion. The part that Hearst had objected to appeared in the tenth installment. In it Bill appraised both the positive and negative contributions of Hearst to American journalism in a parenthetical paragraph written "not because *Collier's* fears his rather ridiculous threat of arrest for criminal libel, but just that we may keep our sense of proportion." Hearst had lowered the tone of news reporting by making it more sensational and less accurate, but more than any other journalist he had helped revive the newspaper as a "tribunate of the people." He had trampled on private feelings, but "carried the standard of public rights." He had lowered public taste, but had been a "plowman for culture" among the masses. He had been immoral in many of his methods, but he also had been an "inspirer of the larger public morals." A balanced appraisal given, Bill then presented his documented exposé of Hearst's collusion with advertisers.

Bill showed that in 1908 and 1909, Hearst's newspapers had exchanged editorial matter for advertisements. Under one plan, Arthur Brisbane, a close associate of Hearst, would write a favorable editorial on a play— though only if he liked it—in exchange for a full-page, $1,000 theater advertisement. For $500 an advertiser could get a half-page advertisement and a feature story by Nell Brinkley or other special writers. With Bill's words Hapgood boldly ran illustrations of the offending Hearst copy.[40]

Over the weekend after the article appeared, Bill and Hapgood waited to see if Hearst would have them arrested for criminal libel. Hapgood knew Hearst's penchant for blustering with libel actions his attorneys never pressed to a conclusion. There was no arrest, but Hearst filed a civil libel suit for $500,000. It would never reach open court.

The fourteenth installment most resembled the archetype muckraking article. Unannounced in the original schedule of articles, it apparently had been an afterthought, stretching the series to fifteen installments. In this article Bill exposed the politically controlled press of Cincinnati and Pittsburgh.[41]

"No one more than the reporters of Pittsburgh awaited the number devoted to our politically purged city," George Seldes, then one of them, would remember. "I cannot begin to describe the fury, the enthusiasm, which pervaded the journalistic corps the day *Collier's* arrived telling our sundry citizenry the fact that Pittsburgh's Prostituted Press was about the worst in the nation. It was a harlots' holiday."

It was also a surprise. Bill told them facts about themselves they had not realized. "In Will Irwin's story of Pittsburgh," wrote Seldes, himself a budding critic of the press,

> I learned that the exposure of municipal corruption had been made despite a conspiracy of silence among the seven newspapers; that, in fact, the Voters' League had been forced to issue pamphlets and bulletins for a long time because the press individually and collectively had refused to publish a line about the city's corruption until the League forced them to do so.

Bill accused some reporters of compromising their integrity by accepting money for political jobs. When they read his accusations, they complained angrily. They said,

> "Irwin is also a newspaper man, he is fouling his own nest, he is disloyal, he is just a muckraker," but the majority helped spread *Collier's* through the town, made it town talk, hoping both to clean up the rotten situation and shame the publishers into paying decent wages. But naturally nothing happened.

Venal reporters were exceptions, just as the press of Pittsburgh provided extreme examples of corruption. Bill himself identified with the reporter and editor, who worked close to the news, and placed in them his hope for the future of the American newspaper as an organ of public service. The publisher, with his big business bias, seemed beyond redemption.

Despite all the effort Bill had put into the series, Hapgood considered it mishandled, a failure. His opinion sent Bill tumbling into a mental depression. Two years of his thirties wasted. He told Inez he felt "like a man who has gone into bankruptcy."[42]

But Hapgood's opinion seemed to be in the minority. A more representative reaction to Irwin's series was expressed by the San Francisco *Call*, which called it "remarkable, instructive and entertaining." The Palo Alto *Daily Times* depicted Irwin as a Stanford boy who had made good, praise that particularly pleased him.[43] *Collier's* published many of the compliments.

Bill's mordant account of "kept" journalism in an age of rampant commercialism was remarkable especially because it reflected his personal integrity and his concern for professional standards. His experience in daily journalism and his immense research of the topic led him to three general conclusions of enduring significance. One, the newpaper's influence had shifted from editorials to news. Two, the commercial nature of the newspaper was responsible for many shortcomings. Three, establishing new papers had become very difficult. Thus in "The American Newspaper" he drew the lines for criticism of the press for many years to come.[44]

Tired of living in clubs and hotels, Bill rented the top floor of an old red brick house at 59 Washington Square South in New York. At the front was a spacious, square room with a table by a window where he wrote articles or stories for the *American, Century, Collier's, Lippincott's*, the *Saturday Evening Post*, the *Masses*, and other magazines. Shortly after the sinking of the *Titanic* on April 15, 1912, he sailed for a two-month vacation motoring with friends through France and Italy before covering the Olympics for *Collier's*. Watching the opening procession in Stockholm, he felt a warm thrill of patriotic pride when his countrymen marched by with "the gait of the plainsmen who tamed our wilderness, of Jackson's 'foot cavalry', of Sherman's army of athletes." The Olympiad was the best managed and most picturesque event he had ever seen. Signs of international tension were overlooked, and not until later would the Olympics seem to him "like the funeral game of an epoch."[45]

Afterwards he went to London, where he visited Herbert Hoover. During a three-day wait for a steamer, he and Hoover reminisced at Red House, the Hoovers' eighteenth century home in Hornton Street, Campden Hill, about their college days. Since then, Bill had dined intermittently with Hoover when the independent consulting engineer had passed through San Francisco or New York to and from obscure, remote corners of the globe. Hoover had laid the foundation for a personal fortune with "interests spread from the Yukon to Tierra del Fuego and from the Altai Mountains and the Irtysh River to the Sierras."[46] Now, nearing forty but looking thirty, he was contemplating retiring from business and moving back to the states permanently. On the last evening at Red House together, they talked about his future.

Hoover believed that a man who had earned enough before forty to

ensure his family a comfortable living ought to do something for his generation. When Bill pressed him for details, he said he thought that many of the
world's problems would yield to common sense, honest intention, and cooperation—the method an engineer used on any big job. There should be a
place for a man of his experience somewhere.

"It sounds to me a little like politics or government work," Bill
commented.

"Well," Hoover said, "I've always been interested in government and
all that sort of thing. You remember Stanford. I don't know yet what it will
be—but something."[47]

Bill himself waded into the political mainstream upon his return to the
United States, joining the Bull Moose campaign of Theodore Roosevelt as
an unpaid volunteer. He may have agreed with the former president, who
had given the muckraking movement its name, that economic concentration
was irreversible and the bigness of business should be offset by enlarging
the authority of the federal government, but his support was more personal
than ideological. He had met TR at the White House several years before
and had been impressed by the toothy dynamo. From Bull Moose headquarters Bill directed a syndicate offering pro-Roosevelt copy free to newspapers. Among the contributors were Inez, Wallace, George Ade, Edna Ferber,
William Allen White, and Richard Harding Davis.

During the campaign, two novels by Bill were published. One was his
second Rosalie Le Grange mystery, *The Red Button*.[48] With the lost shoe
button of the title, a clue, the reformed medium used spiritual fakery to help
Inspector McGee solve a murder. Reviewers particularly liked the engaging
Mme. Le Grange and the suspenseful plot. The other was a sentimental
story previously in the *American*, "Where the Heart Is: Showing that
Christmas Is What You Make It."[49] Neither book gave Gene Stratton Porter's *The Harvester* or Zane Grey's *The Riders of the Purple Sage*, best
sellers in 1912, a run for the money, but the Rosalie Le Grange story was
later adapted for the stage.[50]

As a veteran of the writing game with eleven books and dozens of
magazine pieces to his credit, Bill was a leader in the authors' battle against
copyright laws that gave all the rights to publishers. Some minor magazines
bought short stories for fifty dollars and sold them to the fledgling motion
picture industry for as much as two thousand dollars without paying the
author one cent. Angry over this injustice, Bill, Burgess, Rex Beach, Rupert
Hughes, Ellis Parker Butler, and Jesse Lynch Williams met in Arthur
Train's law office to organize the Authors League of America, a trade union
for writers to lobby for immediate and drastic change of the copyright law.
Bill was an active charter member from its beginning on December 18, 1912.

The year 1912 marked an important transition in Bill's magazine commitments. After Mark Sullivan succeeded Hapgood at *Collier's*, Bill switched

his primary allegiance to the *Saturday Evening Post*. It would become the most profitable free-lance connection of his career.

George Horace Lorimer of the *Post* was the ideal editor, Bill thought. Other magazines might hold an unsolicited manuscript for six weeks while subeditors wrote reports and held conferences and then, like as not, finally reject it. Lorimer seldom kept a contributor, even of a long manuscript, waiting for more than two days. And within a week after an acceptance, a check and the proofs arrived in the author's mailbox. Lorimer rarely asked Bill for rewriting, and he edited a manuscript only to change a word here and there to conform to the magazine's Victorian standards.

Although the *Saturday Evening Post* never was really a muckraking periodical, Lorimer accepted articles and stories with reform themes. His own conservative brand of muckraking blended the fictional form with factual accuracy but required as much investigation as a standard exposé for any good magazine. A typical series of this kind grew out of Lorimer's suggestion that Bill expose the tinplate trust, whose watered stock was receiving unfavorable publicity in 1912. Blending factual data with fictional form, Bill contrasted the rise of a smug, hypocritical tinplate tycoon with the futile struggle of a hard-working wage earner.[51] Bill obviously sympathized with the laborer.

One day he stumbled onto a subject for another kind of series. The subject was Al Jennings, who had been a cowboy, land boomer, lawyer, train and bank robber, and life-termer in the federal penitentiary in Ohio. Pardoned by President Roosevelt, he returned to his old robbing grounds in Oklahoma and without hiding his prison record waged a reform campaign for prosecuting attorney of Oklahoma City, fighting the crooked politicians of both parties and losing by a narrow margin. In the summer of 1913 Bill and Jennings spent several weeks at Scituate, guests in Inez's new home, collaborating on an autobiographical narrative of Jenning's life.

Financed from Inez's literary earnings, her summer home had been built near Peggoty Beach on two slanting lots next to her brother Harry's summer home. A marsh and a woods came up close to the piazza in back. There were six bedrooms, a maids' wing, a library, and a large living room with an oversized fireplace. Rustic and spacious, the house accommodated perfectly the constant stream of guests, including Franklin P. Adams, Sam Adams, Jane Peyton, Viola Roseboro, A. E. Thomas, Jesse Lynch Williams and, of course, Jennings.

That autumn "Beating Back" was serialized in the *Saturday Evening Post* and book publication arranged for spring.[52] The collaborators agreed to split the proceeds of the two publications and of the dramatic rights for a motion picture, but the impulsive Jennings later reneged on his agreement to share the film royalties, and Bill had to take legal action to get his 3,000 share.

Although Lorimer raised the rates he paid Bill, sales to the *Saturday Evening Post* alone provided insufficient income to pay for food, clothing, shelter, and alimony. So he continued to free-lance for other magazines. An article about Dr. Genthe in the *American* coincided with the reissue of their Chinatown book by another publisher, this time with better reproduction of the photographs.[53]

Bill would look back on the years before the Great War as "good days, full of honest work, and innocent play, and secure comfort without luxury."[54] Since he had begun spending summers in Scituate in 1907, other New York authors, as well as actors, artists, and musicians, had discovered the picturesque Yankee town off the beaten path of the automobile, still a rich man's toy. They established retreats from the heat, humidity, and formality of the metropolis or, like Bill, visited the summer residents. When summer green turned to autumn reds and yellows, they migrated back to New York.

In Manhattan one of Bill's favorite pastimes was the theater. In Greenwich Village, Eugene O'Neill, Susan Glaspell, and other bohemians were producing original one-act plays in a converted grocery, while most of Broadway imitated itself. The Great White Way glittered with jewels and furs. Bill frequently ducked into friends' rehearsals or caught their first nights with a vicarious nervousness. Someday, he hoped, it would be his own first night on Broadway.

He still cherished the idea of an American adaptation of *Pi-Pa-Ki*, the ancient Chinese play he had seen years ago in San Francisco. The Broadway success of *The Yellow Jacket*, a play with a Chinese theme, stimulated his active interest, and he even discussed an adaptation with impressario David Belasco. Why wouldn't a play that ran five-hundred years on the Chinese stage run a season on Broadway? But few Chinese actors could read and write their own difficult language (they memorized their plays), and Bill could find no suitable text in the United States.

Not everything was good about those good old days. In April 1914 a friend told him that Hallie had married Herman, and the news hit him hard—on account of Billy, he told Inez. Better Hallie marry Herman, he thought bitterly, than to live in "open adultery." Well, he tried to console himself, he would no longer have to send her alimony checks. Two days later he learned that the report of her marriage to his younger brother was merely another unfounded rumor.[55]

Between severe headaches, Bill kept busy in the spring of 1914 fulfilling writing assignments. In two *Harper's Weekly* articles he extended his reputation as a critic of the daily press, assailing the reactionary, publisher-owned Associated Press and commending the younger, privately-owned United Press. On assignment from Lorimer, he touted a congressional bill for frequent government reports that would enable industry to use labor more efficiently. This compassionate three-part series on the plight of the "floating laborers," who worked in road gangs summers and somehow existed winters, was his last major work in the muckraking tradition.[56]

By now, muckraking was virtually dead. Most muckrakers had branched out into other forms of writing. Like many writers, Bill had found magazine exposés a profitable means of expanding his social conscience, of meeting interesting people, of experiencing new adventures, of making good as a magazine writer. And like many other muckrakers, he wanted to make his living writing fiction.

He got his chance in the summer of 1914. While Europe reacted to the assassination of Archduke Francis Ferdinand, heir to the Austro-Hungarian throne, Bill conferred with Lorimer in Philadelphia. "Why don't you have a sustained go at fiction?" the editor suggested. "Write me another batch of short stories. I won't guarantee to take them all, but your batting average with us is high."[57]

For the first time in a busy career, Bill paused to review his past and to appraise his future. Every major mass magazine and eight American book houses (and some abroad) had published his works. He had written many short stories and eight novels, his last five without a collaborator, but most of his work had been reportage. For more than seven years he had roved the country for magazines, lodging in hotels in forty-five states, associating with every kind of man from hobo to bishop, writing in an art gallery, in a brewery, and on cross-country trains. "But reporting is a boy's job, whether you're doing it for a newspaper or a magazine," he told himself. "Time to settle down."[58]

At Scituate he arose around six o'clock in the morning, ate a light breakfast, and then wrote until noon. But writing at a desk, day in, day out, was almost as boring as editing had been at the *Chronicle* and at *McClure's*. As it became apparent he could not sustain his daily pace, he began to realize that he liked reporting better than creating.

Newspaper reports from Europe added to his restlessness. On July 23 Austria-Hungary delivered its ultimatum to Serbia, and five days later declared war. Offers from the New York *Times* and the *Sun* to become a European correspondent tempted him, but he declined, partly to write fiction full time, partly to watch over Wallace, whose wife was slowly dying of cancer, and partly to get his share of the film royalties to *Beating Back*.[59] When Belgium began her heroic defense against the German juggernaut, he reconsidered going abroad.

He had never covered a war; it would be an exciting new experience. Like many Americans, he believed that the war could last only six months because there was not enough money in the world to keep it going longer. He finally decided, "One campaign—just one—then back to my desk."[60]

Making the round of magazines in New York, he discovered that most editors had already commissioned writers to cover the war. By the time France and Britain joined the fray, however, he had made arrangements to send back articles from Europe to *Collier's* and the *American*. On August 6, 1914, he boarded ship, apprehensive and eager to cover his first war.

CHAPTER FIVE

War Correspondent

ABOARD the crowded *St. Paul*, American, British, and Belgian business-men, titled Britons, American military observers, conscripts for the French army, volunteers for the British army, and a few correspondents crammed into staterooms and slept in rows on mattresses in the saloons. Among the passengers were Irvin Cobb of the *Saturday Evening Post*, Arno Dosch-Fleurot of the New York *World*, and John T. McCutcheon, of the Chicago *Tribune*. On the crossing they anxiously received bulletins about the hero-ism of Liège, which was holding out against German siege guns.

London had changed since Bill's visit after the Olympics two years before. Reserves drilled in the parks. Transportation was limited. Few people bought luxury foods. Newspapers contained only scanty, rewritten official reports about action across the English Channel. Seeking war news, he went to the central hangout for correspondents, the Savoy Bar.

At the Savoy he met weary British correspondents who had been suddenly ordered home after one of them had published the exact location of the Belgian general staff. Liège, they told him, had probably fallen; if it had not, the Germans had masked it and moved on. No one knew exactly where the French were. And the British army? It had disappeared "somewhere in France."

The English sat in a "fog of ignorance and doubt," wondering where their army fought in Europe, Bill wrote for *Collier's*.[1] Censorship barred all but official news. Though the War Office barred British reporters from Belgium, he learned, no Yanks had been arrested yet, and with his American passport, he might see something there—until the authorities clamped down.

From Folkestone he crossed the channel to Ostend and from there took a train to Brussels. On the way he heard that the Germans' big guns had demolished Liège and that one German column was advancing toward the Belgian capital while it marched northeast toward Antwerp. In Brussels windows were shuttered, and refugees fleeing the German advance were streaming in from the east.

At the legation, United States Minister Brand Whitlock, a former muckraking novelist and reform politician, told Bill that he was the first American correspondent to reach Belgium since the invasion. On his heels arrived Cobb, Dosch-Fleurot, and McCutcheon. Despite the plucky defense of Liège, Whitlock told them, the Germans' main columns were headed straight toward Brussels through Louvain. To the four correspondents, it looked like an exciting opportunity to see some action.

Cleared through Belgian military headquarters the next morning, they naively headed east in a hired two-cylinder taxicab. Only Bill spoke any foreign language, a rusty textbook French learned some fifteen years before at Stanford; only McCutcheon had seen war; and none of them had been in Belgium. They were not even sure exactly where they were going that warm and pleasant morning.

Passing barricades, trenches, and barbed-wire entanglements, they came upon endless lines of refugees pushing and pulling their belongings in baby carriages, wagons, wheelbarrows, and dogcarts toward Brussels. Topping a rise, they saw Belgian cavalry and infantry spread out before them and beyond, in the hollows of the hills, artillery threading along the roads. The soldiers were dirty, bedraggled, many wounded. From the road, the correspondents could hear a distant thunder and the steady, rattling buzz of musketry. Thrilled by the first touch of war, even the horror of it, they went on.

When their driver, fearing that the Germans might commandeer his taxicab, adamantly refused to continue, they proceeded on foot, ignoring the warnings from a British film crew and a Belgian soldier. After walking awhile, they found themselves in Louvain, where they wandered around aimlessly until they came upon the passing German army.

"First came motor-cycles; then bicycles; then troop after troop of Uhlan lancers, dust-grey men on coal-black horses, riding as though on parade," Bill would report. "The knots of people in the streets began to press forward, as though drawn by a fascination of curiosity stronger than their fears; and we pressed on with them."[2]

Low overhead whirred a heavy grey biplane, the eye of the column.

When the cavalry had passed, Bill heard "a sound heavier than the ring of hoofs on the macadam roads; then—singing. Round the corner swung the head of an infantry brigade giving full voice to 'Die Wacht am Rhein.' They were singing in absolute time; they were singing in parts, like a trained chorus!" The heavy, knee-high cowhide boots struck the macadam "with a concerted shuffling thump which shook the earth."

The rattle of small arms broke out ahead, and a line of men in blue and red Belgian uniforms dashed through a gate. The correspondents, in the line of possible fire, leaped for cover. "Myself," Bill reported, "I damaged a hedge."

Recovering, the correspondents went back to the crowd watching the marching Germans. Bill approached a man and explained his predicament and asked for the town authorities. The man waved his hand toward the Hôtel de Ville, and with a sarcastic gleam in his grey, Flemish eyes, said in French: "A *grand* chance you have to live."

Of the four, only Bill realized at first how precarious their position was. The German army treated hostile correspondents captured within their lines as spies, and they were uncertain of their status. When the police in the station under the Hôtel de Ville couldn't help them, even McCutcheon, who had been optimistic, became discouraged. The sight of four Belgian youths with Red Cross brassards carrying a litter that bore a covered corpse, apparently a firing squad victim, followed by two priests, heads bowed, did nothing to raise the correspondents' spirits. Were they doomed to face a firing squad, too?

Finally, with the help of an instructor from the local Berlitz school, they found beds in the three-story Hôtel des Milles on the square before the railroad station. They were sitting in the open-air cafe debating whether to turn themselves in, while guns rambled in the distance, when a grey German automobile pulled up.

The three officers who descended looked congenial, especially a tall officer, who laughed as he stepped down; here was the correspondent's opportunity to turn themselves in. Bill approached the tall one and began to explain in French. The officer caught the word "Américain" and pointed out a captain who spoke English. Bill explained again. The captain looked at him severely.

"How did you get here?" he asked.

"In a taxicab," Bill replied.

"In a taxicab!" He burst into a roar of laughter. Gasping, he translated to the other officers. The room rang with their robust laughter.

After hearing of the Americans' adventure, the captain took them to the Palais de Justice, temporary headquarters of General von Bülow's army, where they learned they must wait until morning to see the adjutant. Since German orders posted on the walls of Louvain warned that if a single shot was fired at the troops from any window, everybody in that house would be immediately taken out and shot, the correspondents occupied the front rooms of their small hotel. Following orders, they slept with candles burning behind closed windows. When they awoke in the morning, the great grey machine was still passing through Louvain.

At nine o'clock the correspondents reported to German headquarters at the Palais de Justice. Cobb was elected spokesman because of his wit, cordiality, and disarming personality, and went in to see the adjutant while Bill, Dosch-Fleurot, and McCutcheon waited outside.

After a long interval, Cobb returned, grinning broadly. "Well, boys, we're still the joke of the German army!"

The adjutant—and all of headquarters—had roared over Cobb's tale.

" 'You know we have no correspondents with the German army,' " Cobb quoted the adjutant.

" 'Well,' " Cobb said he had retorted, " 'you've got four now!' "

The adjutant, who spoke perfect English interspersed with American slang, had told Cobb it was too dangerous to send them through the lines back to Brussels now. In an interview with them all, he politely issued orders:

> Remain quietly in your hotel. Go out to meals if you wish, go out for a drink if you wish, but show no curiosity about our movements, and talk as little as possible with our officers and men. Take no notes. Avoid out-of-the-way quarters of the town. You are our guests, but we are very busy. I shall send for you when it is time to go.

All that day and the next the grey columns of men and machinery rolled through Louvain. Each day a German sergeant searched Bill and his room. Usually the correspondents read, played cards, and waited in the sidewalk cafe, while opposite their hotel a German military court sentenced young men in civilian clothes to the firing squad at the railroad yards. The sounds of cannonading in the direction of Malines and Antwerp made it especially frustrating to be sitting virtually in the ring yet so ignorant of the fight. The greenish, ghastly gloom of an eclipse of the sun one day fit Bill's mood perfectly.

When Bill awoke on the fourth day of their captivity, the rattle of horse carts had replaced the rumble of motor transport. Outside, all that was left of the long grey line was the litter and reek that an army leaves behind and a few German soldiers. The townsfolk walked about their customary business, a little relieved of the strain. When McCutcheon sighted a Brussels taxicab, the correspondents figured the road must be open.

Having heard nothing from the adjutant, the four marched to the Palais de Justice, where the Germans were preparing to leave. Inside, the adjutant was putting his last papers into a case. "Gentlemen, you are free to go," he said. "The road is clear. . . ."

Exulting, the four correspondents set out for Brussels. As they went over a hill and Louvain dropped out of sight, an optimistic, joyful mood infected Bill. Perhaps, he naively thought, he had seen the worst of this war in Louvain.

*****

In Brussels, German soldiers were everywhere, and the American correspondents headed for the safety of their legation. Hugh Gibson, secretary of the legation, brought them up to date. Learning that the French and British planned to dig in at the Franco-Belgian border, the Belgian general staff had decided that a defense of Brussels would be futile and might ruin the old city. The Belgians decided to defend Antwerp, an important European port and a good base for attacks on the German flank. That city would soon be under siege. The French were fighting in Alsace-Lorraine, but there was no action to the south. If the correspondents wanted to see battle, they should follow von Bülow's army toward Waterloo.

The next morning Bill left with three other correspondents but had to turn back with a high fever and a very sore throat. After two days in bed, he was able to set out with correspondent Gerald Morgan for Mons. Walking down a road, they caught up with a German transport column that left a lasting impression on Bill.

"Amongst these men, as they sat stolidly bobbing up and down on carts, or lolled at ease on their horses, shone out, now and then, a fine, powerful, intellectual face," Bill reported.

> And it always revived in me the chief intellectual horror of war. In these ranks, and equally in the French ranks, march incipient Pasteurs and Ehrlichs, born with the genius to save suffering in our world; incipient Faradays, born with the genius to interpret the forces of this world; incipient Rodins and Sudermanns, born with the genius to bring beauty out of the world. There they go, on to the chance of death before guns.[3]

Bluffing their way deeper into the German lines, beyond the jurisdiction of their passes, Bill and Morgan suddenly came upon a sight that affected Bill more than all the brutality and destruction he had yet seen in the war.

Around a bend came a line of British prisoners, mostly in the sober brown uniforms and black-and-red checkerboard caps of the Highlanders, marching wearily but proudly in irregular ranks. Bill estimated two or three hundred. They looked tall and athletic beside their stubby German guards. The correspondents' clothes and features marked them as Britons or Yanks, and the expression of the sergeant heading the procession seemed to say: Who the devil are you?

When one Highlander turned around to regard Bill, a guard burst into a rampage of German and kicked him, and guards started kicking all along the line, but the Britons never flinched. Their cool British disdain impressed Bill. They marched on without missing a step, eyes straight ahead, one of them here and there uttering vehement and vulgar Anglo-Saxon from the corner of his mouth.

Bill's neutrality broke. He had come to the war mildly favoring France and Britain, whose people and institutions he preferred to those of Germany, but he had worked himself into an impartial reportorial attitude that he had managed to maintain in Louvain. Now that was all gone. "A wave of hot, primitive rage swept over me at seeing one of my own race and speech treated in a manner so brutally cowardly," he reported; "for the first time I felt the full call of the blood and knew where I must stand in this war."[4]

In Mons black crusts of blood spotted the paving stones, and everywhere were cavalry, wagon trains, artillery, warnings on the walls. Bill and Morgan found a place to stay overnight, and the next morning, learning that the Germans had crossed into France, returned to occupied Brussels.

At the legation Bill heard that the Germans planned to arrest all neutral correspondents in Belgium and deport them to Germany where, presumably, they would be imprisoned. That night he, Morgan, Dosch-Fleurot, and Mary Boyle O'Reilly, another correspondent, decided to give themselves up and take an empty troop train to Germany through Louvain with Richard Harding Davis, the only other American correspondent in Brussels. Louvain was burning, and the correspondents hoped to get the story.

Prisoners, the five Americans rode all the next day locked in a dingy third-class car with armed guards on the platforms, bound for Aix-la-Chapelle. At sunset they began to smell the heavy odor of smoke, and as the train came over a hill, they saw a city of desolation. Part of the town had already been burned, and the fires were down to lingering smoke. Windows of orderly rows of houses gaped empty and roofs were gone. Beside the intact six steeples of the Hôtel de Ville four ruined walls stood majestically, all that was left of St. Pierre's, a Gothic church that had survived for six centuries. A new moon illumed the darkening sky as the train stopped before the arch of the station.

While the correspondents waited, arc lights came on over the platform, revealing the German army in a satanic mood. From the distance came regular explosions, and when rows of houses flamed up, the soldiers shouted cheers that were half snarls. A soldier less excited than the rest yielded to the thirsty correspondents' pleas for a drink of water.

In a half-light of whites and blacks and greys, which reminded Bill of a Whistler etching, they saw through their open windows a group of men in white shirts, who by their posture appeared to have their hands bound behind them. Three shadowy figures rose high above the rest on the pedestal of the statue of the Liberator of Louvain. In the intervals of the soldiers' babble, the correspondents heard chanting. A Hollander explained that the three men, who were priests, were about to die as an example for the men in the white shirts, who had been caught in the town. Shortly after the captives were led away, Bill thought he heard the distant ragged volley of a firing squad.

After a wait of several hours the train pulled out for Liége. Twenty-four hours later the correspondents were in Aix-la-Chapelle, unexpectedly free; their guards had simply unlocked the doors and walked away. The correspondents made their way to Maastricht, where O'Reilly planned to sneak across the border back into Belgium. Bill headed back to London, and shortly after embarked for the United States to comfort Wallace and see Inez.

Aboard ship, he wrote about his recent "glimpse of Hell." Hell it was, but it also was a fascinating new adventure that infected him with a curious, exalted state of mind. "All of us who dodged about the rear, immune from its hardships, nearly immune from its dangers, felt that mood," he would write. "It was as though I were constantly and pleasantly a little drunk."[5]

Except for the opportunity to deliver articles to *Collier's*, the *American*, the *Ladies Home Journal*, and the New York *Times*, his return to New York was largely in vain. Grace Irwin was very near death, and he could give little comfort to Wallace. Inez was in San Francisco, seeking a divorce. After only three days ashore, he boarded the *St. Louis* with writer and old friend Jimmie Hopper. He planned his route to London by way of Paris, hoping he might get to the front or near enough to see some fighting with his own eyes.

In the autumn of 1914, French authorities permitted virtually no correspondents near the front, and Bill crossed the channel many times to seek permission in France and to report on conditions in England. Britons seemed imperturbed by the war. "It grated upon us Americans, sometimes, to come from stricken Brussels or Paris and see so many things running at their usual pace in London; to find the cafés open, the inhabitants dressing for dinner, the theaters running," he wrote in an article for the *American*. "I heard a large concert-hall audience, on the night after Antwerp fell, laughing at jokes about the war; and, fresh from mourning Paris, I liked it but little."[6] Yet he sensed that this imperturbability, which prevented the British from panicking in danger, might just sustain them to victory. And he realized after several weeks of German victories that it was going to be a long, long war.

In London he usually stayed at Red House. Mrs. Hoover had gone back to New York to put their two boys in school, while her husband completed helping 200,000 Americans stranded in Europe safely out of the war zone and untangled his own business affairs. "Herb" looked lean and worried.

One day he came home with the news that Walter Hines Page, the United States ambassador, had asked him to form an organization to purchase, sell, transport, and distribute food to the seven million Belgians, if he could talk Great Britain and Germany into permitting it. "Of course," he told Bill, "that means I must chuck all business, give up everything until after the war."[7]

Bill said he didn't see any necessity for that.

"I'll have to make enemies," Hoover explained. "Too many factions on both sides of the line won't want this job done. They'll believe that I'm doing it only to make important business contacts and get concessions when the war is over."

"And so?"

"And so—I don't know yet."

For three tormented days Hoover resisted steady pressure from the embassy, Belgian officials, and his house guest. Bill's bedroom was under his host's, and waking from nightmares of the war, he could hear the incessant tramp-tramp-tramp of his host pacing overhead. On the fourth morning Hoover came down to breakfast in the dining room, gravely bade Bill good morning, filled his plate from the chafing dishes on the sideboard, poured and sweetened his coffee, sat down, took his first sip, raised his head, sober of mien as usual, and looking Bill in the eye, said quietly: "Well, let the fortune go to hell."

Bill felt that he had witnessed a significant moment in history. It was also a significant moment in his own personal and professional life. His relationship with Hoover was entering a new phase.

While Hoover began to divest himself of his vast commercial interests, Bill moved into a hotel room in Calais, where he hoped to branch out toward the lines about forty miles away. The Belgians had completed their retreat from Antwerp to the Yser River, and six-hundred miles of trench lines were locked from the channel to Switzerland. Miserable refugees crowded the roads, and Bill saw Belgian women stagger into Calais with dead babies in their arms. Hearing of renewed and severe fighting on the British line, he set out by carriage and foot for Ypres.

By now he had learned how to see battle. You eluded rear guards at the war zone and kept going until arrested. Released, you went back to London or Paris and wrote your story. Coming to confused rear areas of a general action, he saw troops and ammunition going forward and ambulances and trucks loaded with wounded coming back from the front. From the east he heard the drum-drum-drum of artillery. Here was something worth taking a close look at.

Atop a rise on a side road he could see nothing specific in the light haze of battle but one battery firing. As he watched, he felt a tap on his shoulder; turning around, he was confronted by a British captain. The captain asked who he was and what he was doing there. Bill admitted that he was an American correspondent.

In custody, he was taken to a cottage and searched. A major behind a desk questioned him, then ordered him put on an empty train for Calais. "We've got you on the record now," the major warned. "If you're caught out of bounds in this sector again, it will go hard with you."[8]

On the dock at Calais, Bill encountered George Gordon Moore, whom he had met in September aboard the *St. Louis*. Moore was a tailored, debonair American in his thirties who had settled down in England. He had just come from British headquarters at the Ypres front, and he evaded Bill's attempts to pump him for military information.

To the north the fighting grew more intense. The Germans evidently were trying to break through the Allied lines. Belgian and British wounded began streaming into Calais, and Bill helped for two or three days as a volunteer stretcher bearer. He recalled reading in some old history book a line about Grant's operations in the wilderness campaign: "There was none of the pomp and parade of war; only its horrible butchery."[9] Bill had sobered up.

Hearing that the War Office was about to declare Calais out of bounds for correspondents, he returned to London. During his absence, Hoover, Hugh Gibson, and a group of American engineers had founded the Commission for Relief in Belgium, and Bill joined them as an unpaid volunteer. Early in December he embarked for New York to publicize Belgian relief. He had made enough money reporting to lay off for the winter, when there would be a lull in military activity.

The autumn of 1914 had been a dreary one, and he sailed, in his words, "hating war to the bottom of my heart, my dreams tormented with its miseries and with the downfall of all good causes which has followed the Madness in Europe."[10] He hoped that returning to his happy, peaceful homeland, then in the first flush of a war boom, would restore his old, laughing self.

Inez and his friends noticed that he never smiled. Sam Adams, with whom he shared an apartment, told him that he would sit up and gibber in his sleep. Sometimes he would wake up in the night "with a sense of black horror hanging over me and the world."[11]

On New Year's Eve he went to a stag party and sang Gilbert and Sullivan and pounded the table with a stein of beer. At least that was all he remembered when he awoke the next noon with a bad taste in his mouth. But his hangover did not matter. His melancholy had lifted, and he felt more like his old congenial self.

Once the publicity for Belgian relief was organized, he considered resuming his aborted career as a full-time fiction writer.[12] In August he had promised himself that in six months he would return to regular writing at a desk, and his time was up at the end of January. But he had thought that the war would be over by then. How could he be content in New York making up stories when hundreds of dramatic true stories were breaking every day during the historic crisis in Europe? As much as he hated war, he longed to return for a closer look.

He was brooding about his prospects when he received a long cablegram from George Gordon Moore. After encountering Moore for the second time, at Calais, Bill had checked out his background and discovered that he had made a fortune in street railway companies in Detroit and then transferred his business interests to London. Wealthy and influential, he ranked high socially. Moore's cable said if Bill would return to Europe, he could probably get him to the front.

About that time someone near Ambassador Page hinted to him that his presence in London would please Moore. Bill believed this because he knew of a personal letter in which Moore had written that some American reporter with a broad outlook, "like Will Irwin," should come to England to write about the situation.[13] Hurriedly, Bill began making arrangements to resume his war correspondence.

To get anywhere in Europe a reporter needed credentials, and Bill knew from experience that few people abroad recognized the importance of magazines in America. So in addition to making loose arrangements with two or three magazines, probably including the *Saturday Evening Post*, he arranged to write newspaper dispatches exclusively for the New York *Tribune*. At the end of January 1915 he embarked on the *Lusitania* for his third crossing from New York in six months.

To Bill's surprise, Page met him at the railroad station in London. The ambassador reassured him that Moore's cablegram was genuine and left him in a state of delighted bewilderment. That same night Bill dined with Moore at Lancaster Gate, the house Moore shared with Sir John French, the field marshal, and began to learn about the situation.

Censorship prevented news of British soldiers across the channel from reaching back home. Young Britons went to the front poorly trained, and the next thing their parents might learn came in a letter from a hospital "somewhere in France" or in the black-bordered notice from the War Office that their son had died "for King and Country." Through October and November residents of coastal Kent and Essex had heard at intervals the drumming of guns to the east, knowing that it came from the British front. But newspapers printed only brief official communiques: "We repulsed a heavy assault on the Ypres sector" or "Yesterday as a result of a German attack in great force we were obliged slightly to readjust our lines."[14]

No more. No atmosphere, no description, no episodes, and few stories of heroism that would help bolster civilian morale. People thought in details, in specifics, not in abstractions, Bill well knew, and the British public was growing restive.

What interested him most was that three months had passed since the battle of Ypres—the greatest of all British battles in numbers engaged and losses sustained to that time—and the public had not been informed of the details. From late October to middle November in the Belgian lowlands a thin British line had held against vastly superior forces trying to punch a hole between the French and Belgian lines to capture the channel ports. The confused action Bill had glimpsed before his arrest had been part of this engagement. Outgunned and outmanned, the Tommies had made a valiant stand, yet the public had been told only the bare facts of Field Marshal French's official report, significant chiefly for what it omitted.

Here was a big story, and Moore would help him get it. Moore had been at Ypres headquarters on the day the Prussian Guard had made its desperate final charge and during other crises, and he knew high-ranking line officers in the British army. With delays of copy for examination by the censors, beats were rare in war, but if Bill could penetrate the secrecy, he might get an exclusive report of this decisive battle more than three months after the fact.

If he realized he was being used by Moore for political purposes, it did not deter him, and he went eagerly sniffing after his big beat. He interviewed military officers, United States attachés, newspapermen, and every survivor of the battle he could find. He talked to men who had fought at Ypres, others who had watched the battle, and a few who had directed it. He pried open confidential, authoritative sources and gathered all available documents on the subject.

While writing the story he saw Hoover, who advised him against defying the censor. "You're new over here," Hoover said. "You'll get your fingers burned."

But he had no idea—in Bill's words—"how many hot irons a reporter will handle in order to get a big and true story."[15] Bill went on writing.

Near the end of February he met Alfred Harmsworth—Lord Northcliffe—in the London *Times* building. Northcliffe published the *Daily Mail,* which had the highest circulation in the British Isles, as well as the *Times,* the traditional bible of British journalism. Over tea, Northcliffe commented favorably on Bill's *American* article about British imperturbability, which had been reprinted in the *Daily Mail*. Bill learned that Northcliffe agreed with his own views about the censors: that their consistent refusal to allow any correspondent to see the front was diminishing enthusiasm for the war effort and stifling sympathy abroad. Also, he agreed that the small British army at Ypres had performed heroically. When Bill revealed his plans to smuggle out to the New York *Tribune* the full story, Northcliffe hesistated to commit his support.

After thinking it over, he proposed that they show up the censors and force them into a policy that would bolster civilian morale without revealing military secrets, like the Germans were already doing. He proposed to revise the story according to the censor's own rules, publish it in the *Times* and *Daily Mail*, and defy the War Office, which would dare not discredit a story reflecting such British valor. To get Bill's story for his newspapers he would join the *Tribune* syndicate. Because the censor might ruin or kill a cabled story, Northcliffe and Bill made plans to send it by courier on the next fast ship. Northcliffe would cable the *Tribune* to publish it in New York on the morning after its arrival.

"I want you to go into this with your eyes open," he told Bill. "We may face a jolly row, you and I."

"Let's go ahead, of course!" Bill said, disregarding the consequences.[16]

He had two days to finish writing and to put his copy aboard a British ship to the United States. To be near his principal source of information, he transferred his papers to Moore's house and worked at a desk beside the gilt showcase in which Sir John kept his gold field marshal's baton. Northcliffe, assisted by one of his military experts, edited the copy.

Bill considered his final version no extraordinary story. Gathering all his information second-hand at best, he could not inject the fine detail that an observer might have picked up, and his story contained few of the human details that would illuminate facts for the average reader. Otherwise, he considered it a typical New York *Sun* style of story, with a chronological structure, emphasis on clarity, and without sensationalism. As an omniscient observer, he narrated the retreat that turned into victory for the daring field marshal and his heroic Tommies. With the perspective of three months, he could effectively blend analysis and narrative. The paragraph in which he described the last desperate assault by the Germans was such a blend.

> . . . Ypres is the old historic capital of French Flanders; and the British observers noted a curious fact about the operations against Ypres. However heavy the German bombardment, the famous old Cloth Hall, the most beautiful building of its kind in Flanders, went unscathed by shells. It was saved, we know now, for a special purpose. Kaiser Wilhelm himself was moving forward with a special force to a special assault which should finally and definitely break the allied line at Ypres. To do this was to clear Flanders of the Allies; then, as by custom he might, he intended to annex Belgium in the Cloth Hall of Ypres. He came with his own Prussian Guard; it was that Guard which, on the 15th, led another terrible massed attack. It was no less vigorous than the attack of the 31st, but the English, reinforced now by the French, met it better. Again the dense masses poured in; again the very officers fired until

their rifles grew too hot to hold. When, that night, the strength of the German attack was spent, the better part of the Prussian Guard lay dead in a wood—lay at some places in ranks eight deep. . . . A fortnight more, and the line from La Bassée to the sea had been locked as thoroughly as the line from Switzerland to La Bassée. It had cost England 50,000 men out of a 120,000 engaged—a proportion of loss greater than any previous war ever knew. It had cost the French and Belgians 70,000. It probably cost the Germans 375,000. That is a half-million in all. The American Civil War has been called the most terrible in modern history. In that one long battle Europe lost as many men as the North lost in the whole Civil War.[17]

"The Splendid Story of Ypres," as Northcliffe's *Times* headlined the story, was the British public's first real news of the battle and it glorified their army. Published in the prestigious morning *Times* and the popular afternoon *Daily Mail*, the story created a sensation in London.

Public praise was generous. Bill's story was called a "noble epic" and "in every sense of the word an amazing performance" unsurpassed "in merit and interest" by any other correspondence of the war.[18] At the Savoy Bar, hardened newspapermen congratulated him with tears in their eyes. Arthur Balfour, whom Bill had never met, sent a personal message calling it "the greatest battle story in our language," an overstatement that lowered the great Liberal leader a notch in Bill's esteem.[19] Within three days after the original publication, Northcliffe yielded to popular demand and reprinted the story in a penny pamphlet, running off a first edition of a half-million copies. The story was published elsewhere in several other languages.

Bill suddenly was a celebrity. People followed him on the streets like a new heavyweight champion. When he purchased clothes in a haberdashery and gave his name for their delivery, the proprietor insisted on shaking his hand and introducing him to all his shop assistants. Invitations came from people he had met at Lancaster Gate and from strangers high in London society. He had two or three luncheons at 10 Downing Street with the new coalition prime minister, Herbert Asquith, and his wife, and he finally met the Liberal opposition leader, Balfour, who pumped him on the chances of getting American support in the war. He was the guest of Lord and Lady Astor at Cliveden. Britons were impressed by his western simplicity and energy and his strong, hearty handclasp; sincere and direct, he made friends easily. The last thing he sought was social success, but when it came, like a windfall, he enjoyed it. He had read about English lords and ladies ever since he could spell two-syllable words, and hobnobbing with aristocrats and political leaders on palatial estates and in exclusive clubs made him feel like "Willie in Wonderland."[20]

Even as society lionized him, however, his profession ostracized him. Jealousies arose among the American correspondents in London, who could write only "dope" and British politics instead of hard news of the war. If they broke censorship they might be recalled by special request, jeopardizing their job. A free-lance writer like Bill could afford to risk ejection.

Instead of improving his chances of getting to the front, his beat, which failed to change the policy of the War Office, hurt them. From across the channel he heard that the French resented his story. They thought he had given them insufficient credit for coming to the rescue of the small British force at Ypres. He admitted that he had written his story from the British angle.

The very popularity of his story gave pause to Northcliffe and others who wanted to send him to the front to report how the army was opposing machinery with bodies. They had intended to send him over quietly as a guest of an officer at headquarters, from where he could casually find his way to the lines. Now, publication of any story he gathered there would make him, an alien, look like Field Marshal French's fair-haired boy, and the reaction would do him more harm than good. He was frequently about to get his trip to the front, but it was always delayed.

Though a pariah, he wrote to Inez, he felt he had accomplished something significant. Even if the story forced him back to the United States, no one could beat it.[21] Yet, as he wrote, a challenge to the veracity of that notable achievement arose back home.

Robert Herrick, the American novelist, publicly accused him, among several war correspondents, of faking reports. Why, Herrick charged, Irwin had obtained the whole story of Ypres in the Savoy Bar and then had written it as if he had witnessed the entire battle. Indignantly, Bill admitted getting some information at the Savoy Bar, but certainly not the whole story, and he pointed out that not a word hinted that he had witnessed the events. He had based his story on evidence, a standard journalistic practice. A reporter did not have to witness an event, be it murder or the sinking of the *Titanic*, to report it accurately. Interviews, documents, and that "sixth sense of truth and falsehood which a good reporter develops" sufficed. Pointing out the similarities between the journalist's method and the historian's method, Bill said he was as much a faker as Edward Gibbon, who had never seen the Roman army in action.[22]

In London Bill went daily to Lancaster Gate and witnessed preparations for a shakeup in the government. Apparently Moore was serving as spokesman for Field Marshal French and the line faction in their opposition to the outdated methods of warfare dictated by Field Marshal Horatio Kitchener and his staff in the War Office. Cooperating with Moore, Bill had become virtually an unofficial publicist for the line faction. But tight censorship, strict British libel laws, and Northcliffe's opposition to both French and Kitchener prohibited him from publishing the big political stories he gathered at Lancaster Gate.

*****

With Moore's help, Bill finally received permission to enter the war zone in France with restrictions, and he was back in Boulogne on April 22, 1915. That night he learned that the Germans had violated The Hague Convention of 1907 and launched a poison gas attack in the Ypres sector. Moore, hurrying from headquarters to London through Boulogne, briefed him. The unexpected attack involved a narrow sector of the line. The gas had come first in a cloud on the east wind. Then the Germans had bombarded rear areas with shells that generated gas as they burst. German infantry had charged wearing gas masks. Moore said the wind was changing, and he believed the Canadians had plugged the hole in the line. Bill telegraphed this information to the *Daily Mail* and *Tribune*, then caught an empty hospital train going forward.

The sky was beginning to lighten when the train stopped at a station in a rear area, where the Royal Army Medical Corps (RAMC) had set up a first-aid dressing post after evacuating its regular post near the line. British soldiers lay in rows on the platform, choking. Ambulances added more wounded and dead, while from the distance Bill heard the frantic drum-drum-drum-drum of artillery. As he helped carry stretchers, he noticed a peculiar smell but tried to ignore it; the air seemed to burn, and he began coughing. It seemed like forever before the train, loaded with wounded and dead, backed out for Boulogne.

This was Bill's "second battle of Ypres." At first the gas from the "asphyxiating shells" which broke the French line near Bixschoote did not seem especially lethal but, he reported to the *Tribune*, "one that rather overpowers its victims and puts them hors de combat for a few days without killing many. Its effect at Bixschoote may have been due to panic caused by the novelty of the device." The effect of "the noxious trench gas" was deadlier than he had at first thought. "Some of the rescued have already died from the after effects," he reported two days later. "How many of the men left unconscious in the trenches when the French broke died from the fumes it is impossible to say, since those trenches were at once occupied by the Germans."[23] He did not report that he, too, had been gassed.

Suffering from the effects of the gas, Bill on May 8 went to the Boulogne harbor to board the morning boat from Folkestone. With it came the news that a German submarine on the day before had torpedoed and sunk the *Lusitania* off the Irish coast and that many Americans were among the casualties. He hoped that meant that the United States, which had been supplying arms and munitions to the British, would now actively enter the fighting.

Ever since witnessing the German guards kick their British prisoners, he had believed that the Entente Allies must win the war for civilization's survival, but he had clung to the rags and tatters of his neutrality in reporting and tolerated the Germans "as a fine and able but oversentimental people grossly tricked and miseducated."[24] When he had seen the victims of the gas attack cough out their lives, he had lost that tolerance. After the sinking of the *Lusitania*, whose death toll of over a thousand included eight acquaintances, he hated the Germans.

In London he immediately went to work for Northcliffe, writing the lead on the running story of the *Lusitania* sent by legmen. By day's end he felt too sick to care whether or not the United States declared war. The next morning he awoke with a severe case of quinsy complicated, he thought, by abscesses caused by whiffing the chlorine gas at the first-aid post or by bacilli picked up in the military hospitals.

While he rested in bed for several days, under the care of the Savoy's physician, Northcliffe wrote for his *Daily Mail* a scathing editorial exposing the munitions shortage and the confusion in the War Office and attacking the highly respected Kitchener, who was running the British show. "This will raise hell!" Bill said to himself. He dressed, then caught a taxi for the *Times* building; on the street, people were burning the *Daily Mail*. Over dinner, he encouraged Northcliffe, who was unusually subdued, by drawing on his own experience. After recounting his exposé of "nigger gin," he said, "But it hurt neither *Collier's* nor me."[25] Bill returned to his room suspecting that Northcliffe's increasingly controversial position would adversely affect his already precarious status.

When he returned from a vacation in Edinburg, land of his forefathers, he discovered that he had been correct. Opposition newspapers were alluding to a conspiracy between the press lord and nameless journalists from overseas. Although Bill had not written a line about the munitions shortage, he had defied the censor with his first story of Ypres, and the War Office was waiting for an opportunity for revenge. Northcliffe was bulwarked behind five million circulation, but a mere alien reporter was a vulnerable target.

Blocked from access to the British front, Bill accompanied Northcliffe to Paris, via Boulogne, hoping to gain admission to the French front. The high-ranking, exquisitely polite French officers said they felt obliged to cooperate with their allies, and the British army had ordered that Monsieur Irwin be arrested whenever he tried to embark at a port. Northcliffe extracted the real reason for the "freeze-out": the British had misinformed the French that Irwin's splendid story of Ypres contained matter offensive to France. The officers had not read the story themselves.

To save Northcliffe any possible embarrassment, Bill planned to return alone to England via Dieppe, the regular port for civilians. On the pier, a

British captain inspected Bill's passport, called a sergeant, and remarked, "You are under arrest."[26] The darling of London society in March, Bill was a prisoner of the British army in May.

As the cockney sergeant marched Bill off to jail, his manner changed from formal to respectful to genial. Wasn't Irwin the author of the "Splendid Story of Wipers"? The sergeant had pasted that story up in his quarters and marked a paragraph about an unnamed force that had performed with great valor in the big attack on November 11. It was his battalion of Coldstreamers.

In the morning, Bill was allowed to continue to England, only because of a special order apparently from Ambassador Page, whom he had cabled. As he left, one of his captors said, "I shan't conceal from you that you're in a very bad odor with my superiors."

A few weeks later, Bill was back in Paris, risking arrest again. The French had interrogated correspondents taking a Maison de la Presse tour about a "Veel Ihr-r-vang," and ordered his arrest if he ever appeared at the front. He was a German agent![27]

Writing fiction to reinforce his dwindling bank account, Bill lingered in Paris. He improved his French with a tutor and visited the homes of new French friends. At the Café du Dôme, he wined and dined some of the hungry ex-mistresses of artists, while across the street at the Café Rotonde, waiters told him, Trotsky, Zinovieff, and Lenin conspired to overthrow the Russian monarchy. For once, Bill's nose for news failed him.

Late in July, a friend tipped him off that the authorities had issued a new order for his arrest and if he remained in Paris he would probably go to jail. Feeling like a fugitive, he took a train to Madrid. After several days there and in Lisbon, he sailed on a French freighter across the submarine zone to the United States.

When he landed in New York and discovered that Inez, to whom he was secretly engaged, was still in San Francisco, he was very disappointed. It was frustrating enough trying to cover battles he could not witness; now Inez was a continent away. Adding to his gloom was the feeling that he was broke.

It was possible, even probable. In 1915 he had no foresight in his personal affairs; he had always lived from hand to mouth financially. Blocked from the battle fronts, he could write only so much home-front dope for magazines and newspapers, and the latter paid low rates. He would have to produce magazine pieces on other topics, even if it meant writing trivia like "How Clothes Really Came To Be" for the *Ladies Home Journal*.[28]

In September 1915 his financial condition improved with the publication in New York and London of his first collection of war correspondence.[29] *Men, Women and War* contained articles from *Collier's* and the *American* and, for a climax, "The Splendid Story of Ypres." The book was widely praised. "Few of the correspondents who have followed the armies have given so sharp a picture of the squalor of modern war," the *Nation's* reviewer wrote, and praised Irwin's uncommon "genuineness." Reviewers especially liked his "terse, rapid detail" and his crisp, narrative style.[30]

While in Washington researching articles on business and finance, Bill waged a personal campaign at the British and French embassies to erase the suspicion that prevented him from returning to the war zone without being arrested as a spy. With the help of the secretary of interior, Franklin K. Lane, a friend from his San Francisco days, he mended his differences with the French; but he was unsuccessful with the British. The best he could do now was ignore the War Office.

About this time, Lorimer called Bill to Philadelphia and proposed that he become the *Saturday Evening Post's* man in Europe. Under this arrangement, he would report for no other magazines in the United States without Lorimer's permission, give the *Post* first choice on his fiction, submit ideas for articles, and consider himself on call for assignments. In turn, Lorimer would raise his rates and, if the arrangement worked out, add further raises. The financial security especially appealed to Bill, and he accepted.

He would now receive higher rates than his fiancée received from the *Saturday Evening Post*. Was she jealous? On the contrary, she responded upon hearing the good news, she was happy for him; he deserved more money than he would ever get.[31]

With the door open to French sectors in the war zone and with an exclusive arrangement to write for the most prestigious and best paying magazine in America, it looked like Bill's next move was to book passage to Europe. But personal matters kept him home.

For one thing, Hoover appeared unexpectedly in New York to deal with a crisis in the Commission for Relief in Belgium (CRB). Someone had filed charges with the State Department accusing him of usurping power and endangering the foreign relations of the United States. With Quaker modesty and almost fanatical self-sacrifice, Hoover was directing the CRB without salary, paying his own expenses, and keeping his name out of publicity. Bill thought it was admirable, but a mistake. Hoover was virtually unknown in Washington. At Bill's request, Secretary of Interior Lane arranged for Hoover to talk to President Wilson at the White House, the matter was straightened out, and Hoover retained his leadership in the commission.

Early in January 1916, "Dearest Billiam-William, Bridegroom Elect," as Inez addressed him, went to Louisville to be best man for Wallace who, after being a widower for more than a year, was marrying Laetitia McDonald, an author of vaudeville sketches.[32] Later that month, Bill took out a marriage license, confirming public rumors that Inez Haynes Gillmore, whose "Phoebe and Ernest" stories and *Angel Island* novel were at the height of their popularity, had divorced Rufus Gillmore, the mystery-story writer, to marry Will Irwin, the war correspondent. Divorce involving a public figure rated a few scandalous lines in the newspapers, though to Inez's and Bill's friends there was nothing at all scandalous about it. Nor was it a surprise to them.

The couple seemed well matched. Inez looked very feminine, with small hands and feet, Spanish combs in her black hair, and loose, flowing dresses; but her interests were unusually masculine for that post-Victorian day. In her view, a single or married woman of 1916 needed to be athletic, open-minded, and absolutely self-reliant. Also, she needed a highly developed social consciousness. Inez epitomized the liberated woman of 1916.

She seemed like the ideal mate for a man who had grown up with two brothers among cowboys, pioneers, and prospectors, who had enjoyed the rollicking banter of unpolished frontiersmen before he enjoyed the delicate Victorian intimacy of refined women. He admired the dozens of capable, intelligent women among her friends, and she admired his talk and his writings. And they shared similar interests in art, history, movies, museums, plays, prizefights, Shakespeare, and women's and labor's rights. Yet how could two writers possibly live together happily?

When Bill told Lorimer of his matrimonial plans, the editor joked, "Don't quarrel over who gets the plot!"[33]

Bill and Inez were married on the evening of Tuesday, February 1, 1916, before an open fire in her younger sister's studio home in Greenwich Village. Among the guests were her brothers, Walter and Harry; her older sister, the widowed Mrs. Stephen I. Dugan, and her niece, Phyllis Dugan, a fledgling writer. The Sam Adamses, the Jack Cosgraves, and the Al Thomases also were guests. Two of Bill's oldest friends, Billy Erb and Jimmie Hopper, were witnesses. Wallace was in the West Indies on his honeymoon, and there was no best man. Neither was there a bridal attendant. The minister of the Morningside Presbyterian Church married the nominal Episcopalian and the confirmed agnostic in a special ceremony. Bill's wedding present to his bride was the two lots next to her Scituate home.

Their departure for a honeymoon in Europe was delayed when the Department of State refused to issue Inez a passport because she belonged to the National Woman's Party. Lane finally cleared the way, and on February 8, 1916, the newlyweds sailed on the decrepit *Chicago*. Both writers held credentials from American magazines.

After a week of honeymooning in Bordeaux, the Irwins boarded the Grande Vitesse for Paris. The faces of the travelers on the train were white, stony. The German spring drive had begun two months early. Departing from the usual official, bald communiqué, the newspaper reported an intense bombardment before Verdun. It looked like the greatest German movement on the western front since the twin battles of Ypres and Flanders had locked the line in 1914.

Within a month after the Irwins' arrival in snowy, wet Paris, the Maison de la Presse gave Bill "every reasonable facility" as a correspondent for the *Saturday Evening Post*. While Inez and a friend, Helen Gleason, took a safe trip to Château-Thierry, he ranged the rear of the armies, occasionally visiting the trenches in a quiet sector and getting telescopic glimpses of the ruins of Verdun. But front line atmosphere interested Lorimer less than life behind the lines and business conditions. "Send copy on the front line only when you can get some new angle," he ordered.[34] In the Café du Dôme, Bill heard of an opportunity to visit the Italian front and find the fresh front-line angles Lorimer wanted. Only one American journalist had been allowed forward previously.

Bill left Inez in Rome early in April and accompanied by Walter Hiatt of the AP, Bill got his first extended close-up look at the battle front. Their guide, an Alpini lieutenant, took them to a ship fortress in the sand on the eastern end of the Allied line at Monfalcone, where Bill heard Austrian shrapnel boom and rattle against the steel hull, and to dugouts in the rocky desert of Carso, where they were fired upon. At Zagora, they visited a strategic house held for five months by both the Austrians and the Italians, who were camped in different rooms; shelled on their way back, they took cover in a regimental dugout until a mountain mist covered their departure.

Bill was at his guide's regimental headquarters picking up papers of permission to visit the highest theater of operations in the Alps, when an officer clutching a sheaf of dispatches excitedly popped out of an inner office. "This will interest you!" he told Bill, and translated: President Wilson had called a joint session of Congress to consider the submarine crisis that had grown out of the torpedoing of a French steamer, the *Sussex*, with several Americans among the injured. An ultimatum seemed imminent.[35] The news made Bill homesick.

On Easter the correspondents, guided by the lieutenant, began their ascent to what Bill would call "The Roof of Armageddon."[36] Although the Alps shot up in gigantic hogbacks, walls, and pinnacles, without wide, high plateaus, they reminded him of the Rockies. Via foot, mule, and teleferica—a large shallow carriage on a high double cable strung between mountains—they ascended beyond the timberline. On the last day of the upward journey, the effects of Bill's heavy smoking bothered him more than the effects of his long-dormant tuberculosis. At last they reached the summit of the pass, and resting on a sled, Bill looked out upon the grey rock pinnacles jutting through the swirling snow.

ᵗination, he looked down upon three-hundred Alpini,
ᵈding cake, hauling a large gun by hand. As the
settled, he glimpsed through binoculars the
ᵑ looked near but were hours away. Bill
ᵗt his guide would take the correspon-
ᵴ of their hearts and lungs.
ᵗt, Bill had heard some things
officers had referred to a
ᵻs "our sea," as though it
not realize it until later,
fascism. Having nothing
ᵑgs.

Iowa State University Press

is pleased to present you with

a REVIEW COPY of

The Writing Game

Publication Date: June 28, 1982

Price: $14.75

We request that you send two copies
of your published review to:

Publicity Department
Iowa State University Press
2121 South State Avenue
Ames, Iowa 50010

a brief, unsanctioned visit
ᵃd been heroically holding
ᵼ Field Service ambulance
ᵴon and Bill to visit sensi-
ᵼw wanted the publicity to

tees, and gas mask kit, Bill
first ambulance run before
helping load wounded, he
ᵼed on the ruins; banks of
ᵼisted iron lined the streets.
ᵼwns, but never one as badly

ᵧ arose to go forward on an
ᵉr to an old, shell-perforated
ᵈ Fort de Dugny. The scene

ᵼe lines of stretcher bearers,
ᵈ dust, to put down their
wounded on the earthen floor in disorderly rows and plod back into the black
mouth of the tunnel toward the shell holes and trenches in which the French
that morning were holding Fleury. From that direction the rattle of machine
guns punctuated the steady boom of artillery. Some of the stretcher bearers
would come back on their own stretchers or not at all.

In the barn the surgeons, as filthy and matted as the wounded, toiled
in a silent, concentrated fury. When they glanced at Bill's strange uniform,
he saw that their eyes were bloodshot and that the lines of their faces had
fallen. They worked down the rows methodically. Their hands clumsy with
fatigue, they bandaged an infantryman newly snatched from the rain of

steel; the trail of blood staining the path of his stretcher was still wet. They gave another man first aid, inspected his bandages, and rolled him aside to await the ambulances. They took one swift look at others, rose up, nodded to each other or shrugged, and filled a hypodermic needle. One of them, standing beyond the condemned man's vision, would make an almost imperceptible gesture, and from a corner would appear the chaplain, only the stole about his neck distinguishing him from other officers. If the dying man could speak, the priest would kneel beside him, and there would be a whispered interchange and the hand raised in absolution. Usually the man was beyond whispering, and the chaplain would stand over him, with all the authority and dignity of his church in his pose, and administer the last rites.

In one row was a young, blond German private in a buttonless tunic and heavy boots. Only his eyes and one side of his face were visible between the bandages and congealed blood. The surgeons came down the row and, too weary to hate, stripped open the tunic at the chest. Against the German's deathly white skin lay the black cross of a crucifix, the nailed feet bathed in a rivulet of blood. The eyes of the surgeons showed no resentment, only wonder. The priest, approaching to administer last rites, started slightly as he recognized the uniform, and then raised his hand in absolution.

Outside the aid station, the air was tainted with the sharp odor of burning explosives and the stink of old, exploded gas shells. But compared with the horrible stench of blood and death in the dressing station, it seemed clear and fresh, and Bill sucked it into his lungs "like the ozone of the Rockies."[38] In the gaps among the booming of heavy cannon he heard a strange, solemn, reedlike sound—the chord of an organ. Crouching, he crossed the road.

Behind a buttress he discovered a long dugout, crowded with uniformed men silhouetted in a dim light. The men kneeled, revealing the back of a priest and a small altar with candles, and Bill saw two Germans, one with a bandaged forehead, nearest him. Apparently they were new prisoners. Beside them knelt their guards, the butts of their bayonetted rifles resting on the floor.

Bill recalled a dinner in a restaurant far behind the lines only two days before. Hearing of the death of a favorite violinist, who had turned out to be "Boche," his dinner companions had laughed, their lips drawn back from their teeth in a snarl. But here, in this sacred spot behind the sandbags, a mysterious holy spirit seemed to absorb the poisons of hate.

For Bill, the trip forward to the aid station was a religious experience. From it he carried away a deep, lasting feeling of the unity of the human spirit. It gave him hope.

After his tour of northern France, Bill and Inez went to England and visited the Hoovers and Shakespeare country, while he hoped for permission to visit the British front. By late 1916 the Allies recognized the value of modern propaganda, and were taking correspondents on official tours of the war zone; but Bill was barred. Though Lord Kitchener was dead, the "old taboo lingered in the files of the War Office like mustard gas."[39] Hoping to get off the blacklist, Bill wangled an appointment with the new secretary of state for war, David Lloyd George, and rehearsed an indignant speech.

At their interview, Bill was made to feel that he was the one man Lloyd George had been waiting his whole life to meet, and he had to brace himself to deliver his speech with proper emphasis. For ten minutes he boldly confronted Lloyd George with straightforward Yankee talk. "Except for one honest overestimate of the casualties, that story has proved true in spirit and detail," he said, defending his splendid story of Ypres. "I've never met Field Marshal French in my life. But he commanded in that battle, didn't he? And the British Army won it!"

Lloyd George interrupted with an emphatic gesture toward the window overlooking the Horse Guards, where French now commanded the Home Forces. "You were right, Mr. Irwin. The little man over there saved England that day."

At last, Bill's name was wiped off the War Office blacklist.

After three months in England, Bill returned to France. At the Folkestone military control he presented his passport to an English Red Cross man. "An American!" the man sneered. "We don't like Americans. And neither do the French."

"Probably," Bill replied. "But the French are more polite about it."[40]

Bill's association with any of the Allies was strained. Although he supported the Allies, he could not wholly believe that the European slaughterhouse was the business of the United States. Yet suppose the Allies could win only with the support of the United States. Even with Russia fighting, the war began to look like a stalemate. At times he hoped his country would enter the war, but usually he sided with Wilson. He was disturbed, irritated, and irrascible.

He was visiting the muddy Canadian sector with William Philip Simms of the United Press when he heard that Wilson had won another term in the White House. Wilson's victory on the he-kept-us-out-of-war platform ended the good feelings with the Canadians, who had seemed like people from back home. The Canadians interpreted public support of Wilson's hesitation to enter the war as weakness and cowardice, an impression bolstered by German propaganda. Bill longed for friendlier New York.

After witnessing the British capture of Courcelette, he crossed the channel again and booked homeward passage for Inez and himself on the *Philadelphia*. He felt that he had experienced enough war. It was, he decided, over for him.

Before sailing, he had a long talk with Ambassador Page, who predicted that the Germans would declare unlimited submarine warfare and that the United States would enter the war before spring. Once the country was in the war, Page told Bill, Hoover would be just the man to head war production. Yet unknown in Washington, Hoover needed somebody to speak up for him. Page explained that he would talk to Wilson but for his strained relations with the president. "Won't you—as a patriotic service—see the President and pass all this up to him?" he asked Bill. "And for the Lord's sake, don't even mention my name!"[41]

Bill agreed to do what he could for Hoover.

Within a week after the Irwins landed in New York on November 26, 1916, Lane had arranged an audience with the president, and Bill met him in the Green Room of the White House. When Wilson entered, looking more youthful than in his photographs, and said, "Have a seat," Bill started toward the chair with its back to the windows. "Not that chair, please, the other one," Wilson said.[42] The President took that chair, and when they were seated his face was in shadow and Bill's in full light, where every expression would be apparent.

Bill had hardly begun explaining his man's qualifications to direct war production when Wilson interrupted to say that he was well aware of Mr. Hoover's merits. He certainly intended to make use of him, "in case we're unhappily forced into the war," although perhaps in another capacity. The president was more interested in the strength of peace sentiment in the Allied countries than in Herbert Hoover.

For the remainder of the hour he kept Bill answering questions about the situation in Europe. Bill correctly conjectured that Wilson was about to offer mediation. Clearly, he wanted to keep the United States out of the war if it could be done with honor.

Bill told him about dining in London with Lord Courtney, an outspoken pacifist who had said peace by negotiation " 'could be brought off now. But the trouble is that there isn't a man in the world big enough for the job.' " When Bill delivered the last phrase, Wilson exploded indignantly:

"What!"

"Lord Courtney was thinking only in European terms, of course, Mr. President," Bill hastened to explain. When he left the White House, he wondered uneasily whether he had hurt Hoover more than helped him.

The Irwins settled into an apartment in the early nineteenth century Rutherford mansion, four stories of brick and iron work on the corner of East Eleventh Street and Second Avenue in New York. It was a pleasant retreat from the politics, blood, and stench of war. Although he was usually at his genial best among friends, his wartime experience had muted his exuberance, left him more earnest, grave. At times he even declined invitations, preferring to feed the English sparrows of St. Mark's churchyard from the wrought-iron balconies.

But in the winter of 1916–1917 the United States was drifting toward the European whirlpool, and Bill had invested too much time, interest, and emotion in the war to drop the subject America wanted to hear and read about. So he continued to write articles related to the war, filling in with an occasional amusing short story in a peacetime setting. He also spoke publicly about Belgian relief and German atrocities.

American audiences were indignant over the reports, verified or not. The planned, cold-blooded atrocities seemed to Bill "more starkly horrible and inhuman than the impulsive crimes of faulty men impelled by lust or rage" because the former were part of the Germans' mechanization of man.[43] His own sense of fairness made him reject rumors that the Boche had cut off children's hands in Belgium; he had been unable to verify even one case. His saying so drew accusations that he was pro-German, which hurt him deeply.

His democratic ideas found a favorable audience in readers of the *Saturday Evening Post.* He received many letters of praise for a political essay, "The New Aristocracy," in January 1917.[44] Bill feared that once Germany was defeated, the aristocratic minorities in England, France, and Italy, encouraged by the success of the aristocracy in Germany, would try to take over their governments. The same thing could happen in the United States, he warned in his essay; since the beginning of the war he claimed he had observed a rising financial oligarchy fascinated by the idea of arming a nation.

He was preparing his second collection of war correspondence, this one containing many of his personal experiences under fire in 1916, when Washington broke off diplomatic relations with Berlin. After the exposure of the Zimmerman note proposing an alliance between Germany and Mexico against the United States, the country seemed inexorably headed into the war. How could he sit home and feed the sparrows now?

On March 13, 1917, Bill and Inez—both representing American publications—sailed aboard the *Antonio Lopez,* a safely neutral if slow combination of sailing ship and steamboat, for Spain. Also aboard were Hoover, who was returning to Europe to put Belgium relief in neutral hands, and Edgar Rickard, a member of the commission. One morning they heard, via the ship's wireless, that German submarines had sunk three United States merchant ships without warning; America's entrance into the war seemed certain. In mid-voyage the wireless announced a revolution in Russia and abdication of the Czar. On March 25 the *Antonio Lopez* docked at Cádiz, and the Irwins, Hoover, and Rickard went to Madrid.

In Madrid they learned that the French had commenced a general attack in the Champagne region and the border was closed. Hoover and

Rickard had diplomatic status, however, and were permitted to cross. While Inez wrote, Bill worked on articles for the *Saturday Evening Post*, studying the confusion of Spanish politics and the nest of espionage and international intrigue. German propaganda aimed at commercial exploitation of Spain made it difficult to winnow truth from falsehood. Daily the front pages of Madrid newspapers carried appalling figures of submarine sinkings that Bill thought were German exaggerations; but they were true. It was the darkest hour of the submarine campaign.

As expected, the United States soon entered the war. "I ought to be divided between sorrow for what we must face and solemn joy that we have taken the right path," Bill wrote. "But the only feeling in me, here in a land remote both from home and from the war, is simply a great wave of homesickness."[45]

When the border opened after the Champagne fiasco, the Irwins took a train to Paris and Bill, relieved to be back among the French, set up his headquarters. Occasionally he wrote articles on single topics, such as the new food controller for the United States, Herbert Hoover; but usually he set down his impressions, experiences, and reactions in diarylike "Letters" for the *Saturday Evening Post*.[46] With the blessings of the Maison de la Press and the British War Office, he traveled frequently to the French and British battle fronts. He found his countrymen everywhere among the French army, although the Yanks had not yet arrived en masse. He accompanied American drivers of French motor transports on their first assignment to the front and an American ammunition train with the first armed Yanks to enter French lines. He gathered material about the new aviation warfare, and witnessed the preliminaries to the siege battle of Messines Ridge on the British front. After seeing the devastation in the Noyon sector, he returned to Paris "in a mood of hatred for all things German."[47]

French morale was extremely low. Although the United States had declared war on Germany, the French believed that the soft, luxury-loving Americans wouldn't fight if they could and couldn't fight if they would. Bill spoke up for his country, but his voice was drowned by German propaganda. The strikes of Parisian models, sewing girls, and clerical workers were symptoms he could write about, but no correspondent was allowed to write about the French troops refusing to march or actually mutinying. In the summer of 1917, French morale began to rise.

The Yanks were really coming!

On July 4, Bill and Inez watched from the window of their hotel room on the rue de Rivoli as a squad of mounted policemen cleared a passage ahead of the first American troops to arrive in Paris. Up the street the seasoned regulars and raw recruits of the Sixteenth Infantry marched, led by tall, stalwart Gen. John J. Pershing, majestically mounted on horseback. When the ranks, struggling through the cheering crowd, began to pass the hotel, the Irwins saw old men, elderly ladies, Parisian girls, and French soldiers marching arm in arm with the Americans. Bill and Inez rushed downstairs and through the crowd and linked arms with a soldier who happened to be an American Indian. On they marched to Picpus Cemetery where Lafayette was interred. No longer would Bill have to defend the courage of his country.

After a tour of recovered Alsace with an official party of American correspondents, Bill went to Switzerland, accompanied by Inez, to gather material for Lorimer on the spy center in Bern, the capital of the one neutral country that formed a direct link between the belligerents. In Geneva the Irwins witnessed riots protesting the high price of bread and had to push their way out of a yelling, surging mob. From Switzerland, they went to Italy.

It had changed since their last visit in the spring of 1916. In Milan the dining room of their hotel was closed for the war. In Rome beggars haunted the Forum, crowds were somber, food scarce. In Florence the people were even hungrier. From Naples, the Irwins went down to Sorrento to interview David Lubin, the American delegate to the International Institute of Agriculture, about the world's food supply. Bill was seeing Italy but not the front. Who was blocking his way?

It was the Italian Foreign Office, Bill discovered through Ambassador Page. Someone there considered Irwin's latest collection of war correspondence, *The Latin at War*, released that summer, "unfriendly to Italy."[48] Although Bill had dedicated his collection of *Saturday Evening Post* articles about his experiences in France and Italy "To/The Alpini/Good Hosts, Perfect Comrades/Valiant Fighters," an Italian officer objected to the association with the French under the Latin label. Page got the bar lifted by blaming the publisher for the title.

Bill left Inez in Udine while he toured the Carso front, from the Trentino to the Adriatic. He had just returned when the opportunity arose to join a party of correspondents, including representatives of the London *Express, Daily Mail*, and Associated Press, to view the action at Gorizia. That was one of the few places Bill had not seen.

The rocky, bleak Carso desert was noisy with battle. On the horizon fighting planes twisted and dived. A shrapnel shell burst in the air only fifty yards from the correspondents' auto, and the chauffeur accelerated before another shell broke a hundred yards to the rear. To the right and left large shells burst in open fields.

The party rounded the heel of Monte San Michele, green with trees and grass again after receiving a terrible blasting in the previous year's attacks, and the town merged white against the red hills of the Carso. Nile green mists hung over the valley. Allied guns were banging and booming on every hill.

While the correspondents waited by the door of a headquarters for permission to enter the sector, Bill thought he could hear the continual noises of arrivals, which were slighter but more dangerous than the departures. He had forgotten his nerves. Now he remembered them all too consciously.

He felt ashamed of his nervousness when the correspondents drove into the main streets of a pretty Venetian town where civilian life was proceeding calmly under whistling shells and pouring rain. All around were shattered windows, peppered walls, and destroyed buildings. The Austrian lines on San Marco were scarcely two miles from the center of town.

A battery of field guns camouflaged in a garden was firing away and the hills were echoing and reechoing the reverberations of heavy artillery when the correspondents pulled into a dugout. Leaving the auto there, they climbed to the half-ruined citadel.

When they reached the plaza before the church of the battered citadel, they could hear the rat-a-tat-tat-tat-tat of a machine gun commence. "It sounds like a little attack," said Captain Pirelli, their guide, and they pressed on upward to a dirt parapet. It was raining heavily. "I think it is misty enough so that we may look over," the captain said. "I don't believe we can be spotted on a day like this."[49]

In the rain the correspondents lined up about twenty yards to the left of a vacant artillery observation post. Bill stood nearest to it, to the right of the group, with Captain Pirelli close beside him and Charles Thompson of the Associated Press on the other side of the captain. The other two correspondents stood together a short distance away.

Through the mists rose San Gabriele, and below the observers lay tawny San Marco, spitting fire. Captain Pirelli did not need to point out the Austrian line, scarcely a mile away, where puffs of white were breaking along a trench line with mathematical alignment and rhythm. Bill adjusted his field glasses to see whether he could catch a glimpse of the gray line when it broke from the trenches.

Suddenly, among the shells whistling overhead, he heard one whistling ten times louder than the rest. He had an impulse to duck. No, he thought instantly, that is passing overhead.

Then something with all the overwhelming, monstrous force of an ocean wave breaking over a beach struck him on his shoulder and back. It rolled up, up, over his head. Then the world went black.

The next thing he knew he was standing in the mud of a trench below the parapet, unable to explain how he got there, but apparently not hurt. Beside him stood Captain Pirelli, his green gray uniform stained and splashed with mud. Bill could see that the captain was talking but could not hear him at first, for the ringing in his ears. He dug a mess out of his right ear and it began to hurt terribly. In a daze, he scrambled out of the mud and walked the length of the parapet, gaining an undeserved reputation for coolness.

"Was it a three-inch shell?" he asked, trying to be professionally calm. Just possibly, he was thinking, that shell might be followed by another.

"Oh, no," Captain Pirelli said. "A hundred and fifty-nine—six inch, English measurement. We shouldn't have heard the whistle of a three-inch shell. They don't announce themselves."

Bill looked back. To his near right what had been the smooth line of the parapet was a trash heap of tangled iron, splintered boards, and tossed earth. Looking again, he realized that Thompson had lost his spectacles and a trickle of blood was running down his temple to his right cheek. They recovered Thompson's spectacles and, over his protests, took him to a first-aid post. His wound was superficial.

Not until the correspondents had taken refuge under a hill shelter with half a dozen Italian soldiers did Bill know he had been knocked down. A soldier who had seen it said Bill had been picked up and thrown against the captain, who knocked down Thompson, like three dominoes. Bill felt his upper lip swelling and figured he must have hit Captain Pirelli with his face. The six-inch shell had struck the observation post dead center, obliterating it. Bill and his companions probably owed their survival to the slush of mud that caused the explosion to fountain.

They wiped off the worst of the mud and after the bombardment, motored through the shell zone back to Udine, unaware of what was happening on the rest of the front but jubilant over their narrow escape from death. Afterwards came word of a local attack in the Tolmino sector. Gorizia must have been a holding action.

In the morning Bill, shaky from the shell blast, and Inez, suffering from occasional stomach pains, arose early and took the train to Venice. As the train pulled out of town, he saw a cloud of smoke against the distant Alps and wondered if the Austrians had shelled an ammunition dump. Exhausted, he settled back in his chair.

Their train turned out to be the last Italian passenger train out of Udine. In Venice that afternoon they learned that the Italian line at Caporetto had broken; less than six hours after they had left Udine, the Austrians had marched into town, led by a troop of Turkish cavalry. The cloud of smoke had been from the supply base at Civedale, burned by the Italians to keep the stores out of enemy hands. By accident the Irwins had missed the retreat from Caporetto.

On a bleak November morning the Irwins arrived in Paris, feeling like the weather. December and January brought the severest cold spell in years, and January 1918 was dismal. The Irwins' morale sank as low as that of the Allies. The inside of Bill's head hurt and he had trouble hearing in his right ear; then he became delirious with the "Spanish flu," which left him weak, languid. Inez had difficulty digesting food, an ailment that defied diagnosis, and she lost weight. Finally, weary and depressed, they sailed home across the submarine zone in February.

CHAPTER SIX

Propagandist

REFRESHED after a relaxing voyage, Bill was in Washington when George Creel, a former magazine and newspaper journalist who directed the Committee on Public Information (CPI), happened to be looking for a man to develop a government bureau for foreign propaganda. The subject had interested Bill for some time. His observations abroad had led him to believe that "thorough, extensive and well-managed propaganda was one of the most important tasks ahead of us in Europe." So on March 11, 1918, he officially became chairman of the Division of Foreign Service, apparently planning to stay for six months, and went to work in CPI headquarters on Lafayette Square, diagonally across from the White House.[1]

Before he could hang up his fedora, he was besieged by a line of senators and congressmen seeking positions for constituents who had none of the qualifications for the specialized work that foreign propaganda entailed. A senator influential in the Wilson administration virtually ordered him to appoint as director of the Latin American office a wealthy constituent who knew nothing about journalism. Bill refused, and the senator did his best to have him replaced with his constituent, but the president stood by the new chairman. Such intriguers wasted a lot of Bill's valuable time.

So much needed to be done. Being considered a Republican by a Democratic Congress, which suspected the CPI of serving as a presidential mouthpiece, compounded the pressure. The first week on the job was, in his words, "terrifically trying."[2]

He wrote to Ernest Poole, who ran the foreign press bureau in New York, that "I have got to settle the question of a man for a hundred places in a few days." The CPI foreign operation was "sadly lacking in team work" and funds. "At this moment," he told Poole, "I find myself screeching for money to do a thousand things."[3]

Before the end of March he was already yearning to return to France and cover the war again. But, he thought, that would not be until May or June, when he expected to have his organization "perfected."[4] He was overly optimistic.

While he opened new offices abroad and staffed them, his division crowded the wires and mails with accounts of America's military preparations to convince the skeptical peoples of Germany and the Allied nations that the United States was able, willing, and almost ready to provide full combat support. Part of the problem was getting news reports and Wilson's speeches into hostile territory. To do this, the CPI experimented with their dissemination by aircraft, artillery, and balloons, and used the subterfuges of espionage.

CPI propagandists at home and abroad spread the word that, contrary to rumors, the United States was preparing to send over an army fresher, larger, and more potent than any belligerent had begun the war with. That much was true. "But we never told the whole truth—not by any manner of means," Bill would admit after the war. "We told that part which served our national purpose."[5]

At home Bill's division worked closely with the more extensive domestic divisions, which had been operating for almost a year when he joined the CPI. The foreign division often disseminated abroad propaganda materials prepared by domestic divisions. On several occasions the foreign division and the Division of Work among the Foreign Born, headed by Josephine Roche, successfully cooperated to take advantage of the large population of aliens and foreign-born citizens. Their most successful joint project was Loyalty Day.

The plan was to turn over celebrations of the Fourth of July to foreign-born Americans for demonstrations of their patriotism. Public demonstrations of their loyalty to the United States and to free institutions would stir up enthusiasm at home and influence public opinion abroad. When the Central Powers heard that Austrians, Germans, and Turks were marching to repudiate publicly the autocratic governments of their origin, and when the peoples of neutral nations saw men and women of their blood declaring faith in American ideals, the Allied cause would be strengthened. Thirty-three foreign national groups agreed to cooperate, probably in some cases rather than suffer further persecution for their ancestral affiliation with Central Powers nations. Bill persuaded Wilson to proclaim the Fourth of July as their Loyalty Day.

Preparing for Loyalty Day, expanding the international operation, working on a collection of war correspondence, and making speeches kept Bill busy throughout the hectic spring of 1918. Once he addressed an audience of suffragettes. Another time he made one of his several addresses over the years to the Council on Foreign Relations, on this occasion explaining problems of disseminating government propaganda abroad. As a member of the Authors League of America, he accepted an invitation to represent authors at a congressional inquiry on the weak copyright laws that failed to provide safeguards against international piracy.

In June, Lorimer wanted to know whether he would be ready to resume reporting for the *Saturday Evening Post* by late summer or early autumn. "Never in my life was I so uncertain of my future," Bill replied. "I have taken hold of a job here which is hard to let go, just because experts on European propaganda in this war are very rare birds." He had intended to return to Europe and take general charge of American propaganda operations there and resume writing, but he was too enmeshed in the politics of his job to leave the country. Perhaps after the Fourth of July celebration, he told Lorimer, he would know his plans.[6]

They depended some on how well he got along with his boss. In May a disagreement with Creel over appointments of CPI commissioners in Europe had flared into a hot-tempered dispute and he had almost resigned. Bill and Creel were bound to clash. Each man was strong willed and wanted to do things his way.

If Bill had not "perfected" his organization by late spring, he had at least filled the major posts and built a going operation. Informally, it consisted of two subdivisions. One consisted of fourteen semiautonomous foreign offices. The other consisted of the home offices, with the small directing staff in Washington and the news operations in New York. He needed more funds to expand the cable and foreign feature services and to open more offices abroad.

On the Fourth of July, the extensive planning for Loyalty Day came to fruition. Demonstrations from coast to coast provided thousands of words and pictures for Bill's propaganda mill. In every large city (except Chicago, where Mayor Thompson's administration was uncooperative), organizations of foreign-born citizens—among them German-Americans displaying the service stars of their sons—marched in long parades with banners, streamers, native costumes, and national emblems to display their patriotism. The New York parade, which included a memorable company of Spanish-American girls in mantillas and brocaded shawls, lasted from nine o'clock in the morning until twilight. From Bill's point of view, the parades were for the benefit of foreign newspapermen and motion-picture cameramen. Loyalty Day, with its parades, pageants, mass meetings, resolutions, declarations, banners and speeches—the keynoter a stirring oration by President Wilson at Mount Vernon—was a big success, according to Bill. Creel agreed. He considered Loyalty Day "one of the great ideas of the war."[7]

As head of foreign propaganda, Bill worked closely with several arms of the federal government. One of the smoothest working arrangements was with the War Trade Board. The foreign division censored and licensed virtually every film exported, and required commercial distributors to include propaganda films in export shipments of entertainment films. The Department of State was an even more important partner in foreign propaganda. The diplomatic corps supported and received support from the CPI, although embassies were not always as cooperative as Bill desired. The Department of War was a constant headache. The propaganda effort against enemy forces was continually bedeviled by conflicts of authority between military intelligence and the CPI, and Secretary Newton D. Baker seemed blind to the value of propaganda. Other officials made Bill's battle of Washington frustrating, too.

Not the least was President Wilson himself. The irritations of Bill's job were aggravated particularly by the president's failure to comprehend the importance of manipulating the news flow from the executive branch and by his distrustful attitude toward journalism. One instance involved Lord Northcliffe, who had opened to the CPI his own propaganda pipeline into Germany. Bill estimated that it would take the United States two years to open a similar pipeline; but Wilson, who disliked Northcliffe, ordered him to cease using Northcliffe's system. In some ways, Wilson seemed small-minded.

During those busy months in Washington, Bill lived alone at 16 Jackson Place and occasionally saw Hoover but rarely saw Inez. On a strict diet, she had improved in health, but no physician could diagnose her pains; Bill worried about her. He also had health problems of his own. His humorous, blue eyes, now tired, deepened in their firm pouches. The failure of hearing in his right ear, whose drum had been split by the shell blast at Gorizia, and his attempt to compensate by paying extra attention with his own good ear, added to the strain of his job.

In July Lorimer wrote to him that George Pattullo, a special correspondent for the *Saturday Evening Post*, was returning from Europe, "so if you feel the call of the wild, France is yourn." The offer was extremely tempting. In times of crisis abroad Bill ran over daily to the War Department to pick up the "raw, uncensored news" from Europe, and that July the news was as hot as the Washington weather.[8] The Germans had aimed a drive toward the Marne River and ultimately Paris, evidently a supreme effort to end the war before the Americans, already eighty-five thousand strong in the Marne Valley, reached full strength. He was itching to get back to the front and weary of bucking uncooperative politicians and government executives. Another dispute with Creel and interference in foreign propaganda by Edgar G. Sisson, an associate of Creel's, further stirred his discontent with Washington. "From present indications," he replied to Lorimer, "I'll be ready to go back at the end of August."[9]

After expanding propaganda operations into thirty-three countries, Bill resigned his $5,200-a-year job effective July 31 to resume foreign correspondence for the *Saturday Evening Post*. Neither Creel nor Bill was unhappy over his departure.[10] Not surprisingly, Sisson succeeded him.

American counterpropaganda had not gathered force until late spring and much of Bill's work would never have time to reach fruition before the signing of the peace treaty dissolved the Committee on Public Information. Looking back in 1919 Bill thought that "in some respects it was a success and in some a dreadful mess." He admitted that he bore as much as anyone else "the responsibility for its messy spots," but he believed that its successes—notably the cable service—outweighed its failures.[11] Although United States foreign propaganda had been a late entry in the international war of words, he thought it had contributed to the Allied victory in the war of bullets.

While Bill prepared to return overseas, his collection of wartime "letters" from the *Saturday Evening Post* was published as *A Reporter at Armageddon*. Reviewers especially liked the human interest and the vivid description, as usual the distinctive attribute of his prose. The *American Review of Reviews* even recommended the book as "a model for all reporters in vividness of description." The Springfield *Republican*'s reviewer thought that the human interest gave the author "high rank among war correspondents."[12] Certainly these dispatches contained some of Bill's most crisp and lucid reportage.

In the middle of September Bill sailed for Europe, leaving Inez crying on the dock. Her health had improved, but physicians advised her against accompanying him during the hard European winter. Although Bill and Inez had enjoyed time together since his resignation from the CPI, they had seen each other too infrequently over the last six months—and now the Atlantic Ocean would separate them for perhaps six more months.

By the autumn of 1918 conditions had improved in France; the U.S. Army had contributed to this transformation. German morale was collapsing, and officers at the American front knew that Germany had lost the war. To avoid disappointment among the troops, the leaders at General Headquarters told them that Germany would hold out until about June; but Bill, recalling the sobbing German-Americans on the Bellevue Wharf after the *Slocum* disaster, believed that once the Germans started to crack, they would disintegrate quickly. He expected the end before Christmas.

On the morning of October 6 he heard at press headquarters that Austria had abandoned the war and asked for terms. That afternoon he set out for Rheims, evacuated two days before by the Germans, with an American major in the Red Cross, a French captain of noble ancestry, and a mayor returning to the ruins of his small town. Driving toward the front, they passed weary battalions streaming along the roads toward the slaughter to the north and east; for many of them the armistice would come too late.

Bill and his companions parked their automobile behind the camouflage of a broken wall and stood in what was left of the mayor's town. The mayor had been born in a cottage on the main street and had known every stone, but it took him half an hour to figure out exactly where he stood. The hillocks were strewn with ruin.

The mayor and the Red Cross major went exploring, leaving Bill and the French captain on the highest mound, overlooking the rubble. The buildings were slivers of walls, the streets mounds of debris. To the right, Bill spotted a set of human rib bones, bleached white, and he realized that the spot had been a churchyard and those were bones of the old dead.

Around the knoll on which the village had stood ran a line of German dugouts, half of them blown open. After making certain there was no booby trap, Bill picked up a souvenir German helmet; its hard enamel paint was burned and blistered. The conquerors had cleaned out the dugout with liquid flame.

Before him lay an insane landscape. Where the fertile checkerboard fields had once yielded grain, sugar beets, and potatoes, only the clay subsoil remained. Where big, plump draft horses had plodded down tree-shaded roads, not a tree, road, or steeple could be seen, but only a grotesque network of fallen, broken military works. Here and there trenches deepened into gullies where you could have hidden a mansion. Strewn over it all lay artillery wheels, junked ambulances, broken cannon, old clothes and shoes, and broken, rusty bayonets and rifles.

Through field glasses Bill could discern skulls and thighbones, the gruesome remains of old battles blasted out of trench graves by intensive shell fire. Near the horizon he saw metallic flashes and then heard a distant reverberation, the Allied heavy cannons spreading more desolation fifteen miles beyond. An airplane droned overhead. A sheet of tattered corrugated iron, still attached to a shattered wall, clanged dismally in the autumn wind.

He turned toward the tall French captain, who was looking at him.

"Isn't it all foolish?" the captain said in French, breaking their silence.[13]

"It is," Bill replied in the captain's language. "It must be stopped."

The captain shrugged his shoulders. "How can it be stopped? Look, my hobby is the ancient Greek philosophers. Their words and commentaries upon them fill half of my library. I read them constantly. And I cannot see that the moral nature of man has improved in these two thousand years. No. This is folly, folly, but man cannot make it cease. It can't be done."

Bill did not care to dispute the issue in French at that moment, but under his breath he responded in English for himself: "It can be done!" The idea seemed to burst upon him, as if he had been searching for it throughout the war. Those four words—it can be done—symbolized America's great-

The "Irwin Boys," Willy (left) and Wally (right) in the 1870s (Courtesy of Wallace Irwin, Jr.)

Will Irwin probably about the time he attended Stanford University in the 1890s. (Courtesy of William Hyde Irwin)

Encina Hall, Stanford University, where Will lived as a student in the 1890s. (Photo by Robert V. Hudson)

Harriet Hyde, who became Will Irwin's first wife, in the 1890s about the time they were married. (Courtesy of William Hyde Irwin)

Party at the Bohemian Club, San Francisco, around 1900, for visiting writer Samuel Hopkins Adams (tuxedo). Will Irwin is at the far left. (Courtesy of Donald Irwin)

Will Irwin probably about the time he was a star reporter for the New York Sun, *1904–1906. (Courtesy of William Hyde Irwin)*

San Francisco earthquake story written by Will Irwin, published in 1906 on the front page of the New York Sun.

Inez Haynes Irwin, Will's second wife. (Photo by Robert V. Hudson)

The summer home at Scituate, Mass., that Inez Haynes Irwin built with earnings from her early writings. (Photo taken in 1970s by Robert V. Hudson)

Will Irwin's landmark criticism of "The American Newspaper" began in this January 21, 1911, issue. It ran fifteen instead of fourteen installments, another article having been added later.

Collier's
THE NATIONAL WEEKLY

Containing the first of a series of Fourteen Articles on

The American Newspaper

By Will Irwin

VOL. XLVI NO 18   NEWS-STAND EDITION   JANUARY 21 1911

Announcement for Will Irwin's landmark criticism of "The American Newspaper," which ran for fifteen installments in Collier's *beginning January 21, 1911.*

The "Irwin Boys" as famous writers, Wallace (left) and Will (right), in a "Photograph by Hollinger" in the American Magazine *of March 1912.*

WITH CANADA AT THE SOMME

By WILL IRWIN

SOME of the Canadian divisions were resting in the peace trenches when we saw them in November, and some were still in the fiery muck of the Somme. "Resting," as they use the word, is only a comparative term. In November last there were two great areas of blazing action along the great line—the Somme and Verdun. Elsewhere proceeded the same old winter trench warfare. The very intensity of the Somme and Verdun actions had drawn much of the vim from this fighting; it proceeded perfunctorily, especially in the sectors defended by the Saxons, whose motto is "Live and let live." A Canadian captain, just back from his turn in these front trenches, came one night into a headquarters where we were visiting. He had been through the mill with Canada since the first—the gas attack of Second Ypres, the long five months of passive endurance under concentrated fire on the Ypres Salient, and finally the indescribable battling at the Somme. "Well, thank God for peace!" he exclaimed as he threw off his pack.

And one afternoon, when a glimpse of sun gave a chance for observation, we climbed to a ridge from which we could view the bloodiest sector of the old line—Notre Dame de Lorette Ridge, all one great graveyard, where skeletons lie unburied in the shell holes; the curve—like a light surf on the beaches—of Loos, where Britain got at cost her education in trench warfare; the battered, deserted mining villages that fringe Lens.

While we watched the British were bombarding desultorily; and presently seven great, wide-spreading British aëroplanes, back from a raid, came coursing out of the clouds and crossed the line. The Germans, of course, fired on them fired high-explosive shell, which bursts sharply, trails black smoke instead of white, and seems more sinister than the puffy shrapnel burst. They sent exactly five shots at this squadrilla. You could imagine the gunners remarking as they loaded and let go: "Well, it has to be done." The casualty clearing stations reported as many cases of ordinary small accidents as injuries by enemy fire. War's incidental harms lose pleasant and comfortable, as war goes, but for the mud. I have heard of tropical rains. If they can pour any more violently than those of Northern France, take me to the Arctic. When we crossed the Channel the rain was coming down in sheets that seemed to beat flat even the Channel chop.

A Land of Mud and Muddy Men

THE road from the coast base is one of those perfect highways first laid by the Romans and improved by centuries of intelligent care. It seemed the only dry thing in the landscape; but even then our wheels were always stirring up dirty spray. The brooks were rivers; the hollows in the pastures, ponds.

Up by the front, engineer companies were mucking and growing profane in sharp, crackling North American speech over communication trenches which slid now and then like the Culebra Cut. The men waded to position in hip-high gum boots. And an apocryphal legend grew up and passed on from brigade to brigade, so that we heard it at every headquarters where we stopped for dinner or tea or a bed. When—so the tale goes—the Canadians took over a certain section of trench they found an English lieutenant stuck in the mud. And the English commissary sergeant, an imperturbable soldier of the old army, turned him over to the Canadians in the list of "trench stores." The men relieved from the trenches staggered back to the rest stations with gunny-sack coverings over the locks of their muskets, and as they marched the caking crust over their uniforms crackled like thorns in a fire.

The very mules, sometimes, looked as though they had been painted for protective coloration.

"We'll have to get a bath," panted a chatty sergeant from Saskatchewan as he got his breath against a pile of sandbags, "before we can tell whether a Fritz has mired himself among us!"

There were three days of these wanderings among a comparatively resting army before we began to see that field of action which has made all the other battles of the world appear insignificant, and they were interesting days enough. Whisked from brigade to brigade, we heard more tales of old action, consorted with more interesting characters, than the human memory can carry. Even the places which serve as division, brigade and corps headquarters have become confused in my mind, picturesque though they be in their present condition.

One morning we drove up to a very pretentious structure grown ripe with age. The entrance ran through a conservatory built on to a kind of morning room where the family had their noon breakfast, I judge. The palms and tropic orchids, though drooping from lack of care, stood to the family left them. Up against their fronds was a solid burlap screen pinned and repinned with military maps. The floor was tracked deep with mud left by soldiers too much in a hurry to clean their feet. Tables knocked together from plain boards filled all the floor space; they were littered with the papers and paraphernalia of an army at work. The family had taken away the paintings, and the wall space so cleared was covered with reports, notices, blank forms pinned by thumbtacks into the wall paper; but above the wainscot ran a very good collection of old Dutch china, which the owner had doubtless preferred to leave with the soldiers rather than trust to the transport of those days.

Again, keeping our car to a route which hid us from enemy observation, we dropped into a brigade headquarters one afternoon to find a rather over-prettified modern French château, furnished with much heavy carved wood. The family had taken away the lighter objects, but the great dressers, sideboards and wardrobes stood in place, storerooms for military papers. The owner had evidently been a huntsman. His trophies, such as wild-boars' heads, stuffed foxes and stag horns, rimmed all the walls. He had left behind, too, a big stereoscopic apparatus, with many pictures, and as we entered a Canadian Highlander officer, his kilts all mudsoaked, sat looking at pictures with the delight of a boy. Finally, there was a beautiful building with a still more beautiful park. This the owner still uses, along with his military guests. A fine set of family paintings, dating back into the Middle Ages, and a collection of Renaissance Art of great merit, still held the walls, though all the elegant furnishings have given place to objects of military use. These are the remote shaking the window glasses and rattling the thatch, headquarters are more primitive—only things of military necessity.

Also, we have met forceful and engaging characters too numerous for mention or memory. Officers of all nations are likable fellows, and yet, after reconciling one's native ways to Frenchmen, to Italians and to Little Englanders, it is like homecoming to fall among men who speak your native tongue with all its dialectic peculiarities, who joke as you do, who know Broadway. The professional officers among them might have been our own West Pointers, the others might have been trained from our militia. The major general, for example, is all of the Western "Continent." He it was who commanded the Canadians at the immortal affair of Second Ypres, where, when the line broke before the new peril of poisoned gas, these men of the West plugged the gap and saved Calais. He commanded, too, during those trying months on the Ypres Salient, a dreary memory to Canada. He is tall, with a stalwart figure growing a little portly. He has a fine forehead, a face all intelligence and determination, and a direct eye. He talks entertainingly, without undue amount either of optimism or of pessimism, concerning the present condition and future prospects of the operations up there—a mind which keeps its balance and observes, whatever the personal interests in the game.

Some Fine Canadian Types

MAJOR GENERAL TURNER is different physically as may be. Little, dark, quiet, spectacled, he looks somewhat like the modern type of American college professor. He talked little, while we were about, and listened much. Possessed of nerve in the absolute—he is with his men at the fighting front almost every day—he gives in time the impression of vast reserve power. A grave man, he has the kind of solid popularity in all ranks which goes with merit. Major General Dave Watson, who came to us from a newspaper desk, represents a type different from either of these others. They might have been born on either side of the Great Lakes, so purely do they represent the universal English-speaking breed of North America; but Watson is from Quebec. In a keen face, deeply lined, he has a steady gray-blue eye; and he, too, possesses nerve in the absolute.

We had a long smoke talk one evening with Brigadier General Elmsley. Quite common among the Canadians, both officers and men, is that type of Colonial who has kept his roots in the Motherland. Elmsley speaks with an English accent; it is impossible to tell it from the maple-leaf insignia on his collar—from lish officer of the Imperial Force; quiet-spoken, always performing more than amanders. Among the officers of the line again types so much like the men I States all my life that I grew homesickness. A certain major walked down through a twilight heightened by gun one of those stock-exchange privates, as he passed some comments on the fight and indeed, he might, except for the close of Wall Street, though he had been fifteen weary, perilous months, and has One night, too, we waded kneedeep to advanced headquarters in a board shack

(Continued on Page 42)

One of Will Irwin's many pieces of World War I correspondence for the Saturday Evening Post.

Will Irwin in his World War I correspondent's uniform. (Courtesy of William Hyde Irwin)

OUR NEW CIVIL WAR

How Uncle Sam's Mysterious "G-Men" Destroy Public Enemies—The Inside Story of America's Most Sensational and Successful Attack on Organized Crime

by WILL IRWIN

One of Will Irwin's articles for Liberty *magazine, which he wrote* for frequently in the 1930s.

READING TIME • 1 HOUR 3 MINUTES

PART ONE—EXTERMINATING THE KIDNAPERS

WE are a criminal people. Let us begin with that confession. Our murder rate is six to forty times that in the European countries from which we derive our blood. Our burglary, robbery, and arson rates run even higher. During the past few years we have seen gangsters virtually ruling some of our greater cities. We have seen other cities offering refuge to hunted murderers and highway robbers on condition that they behave themselves while in town. In the year 1928 we saw the people of Chicago bled for $300,000,000 by commercial racketeers. Attorney-General Cummings said once that for every man in the national army, navy, and marine corps we have an armed criminal. Called to account for this statement, he looked up the statistics and discovered that he had spoken inaccurately—for every guardian of the Republic we have not one but two armed criminals.

In orderly nations like Great Britain the average citizen has no patience whatever with crime or criminals. The accused gets a quick trial and, if convicted, a short shrift; and every one in the upper world applauds. We have developed a fascinated interest in the criminal; and interest grows unconsciously into sympathy. Bruno Hauptmann is arrested, charged with kidnaping and murdering the Lindbergh baby. Three days later the newsreels show him handcuffed and trapped—in itself a kind of plea for sympathy—show his wife dandling the baby which the law will orphan in case New Jersey finds him guilty of murder.

As soon as a criminal is arrested for an atrocious crime, the tabloid newspapers give him a familiar nickname, photograph his home, make fiction characters of his associates. And every journalist understands that to know a man is to like him. For three or four years the motion pictures flooded the country with gangster-idealizing films. Do not blame the cinema unduly. We, the public, were clamorous for such films.

Now the American people are passing into a healthier mood. Just when it seemed about to overwhelm us, we declared war on organized crime. It amounts to a civil war. We are not entering this war entirely unprepared. Happily, we have a trained expert general staff. It has laid out a plan of campaign and has won its initial battles. The Department of Justice has maintained from time immemorial its Bureau of Criminal Investigation—a force of about 400 skilled detectives who worked on all offenses against federal law except those involving the Treasury and the Post Office. After the blight of Harry M. Daugherty was lifted from the department, direction of this force fell into the hands of J. Edgar Hoover, a superpoliceman with wide and original ideas. Against much political pressure Presidents Hoover and Roosevelt kept him on, gave him room to expand his program.

Director Hoover believed that police work in the United States was bound to become, in the end, a kind of learned profession—as it has already become in Austria and several other European countries. He built up a staff of men with superior education. Most of his operatives are law-school graduates. He did not forget that the ideal policeman, like the ideal army officer, must combine a

The second installment of a series Will Irwin wrote for Liberty *in t* 1930s.

PART TWO—CRACKING DOWN ON THE BANK ROBBERS

THE Lindbergh kidnaping case drew the federal government and its little force of superdetectives into the war on national crime. Hitherto kidnaping had been no business of the authorities at Washington. Congress, moved by the popular clamor which followed the Lindbergh affair, passed a law making kidnaping a major felony; and the average citizen began to hear for the first time of the "G-men." In two years they rendered

When the law caught up with Buck Barrow and his wife. He is the screaming, in the clutches of members of the posse that captured

wounded man kneeling with his back to the camera as she struggles, them. The Barrows were pioneer roving desperadoes in their line.

their souls. I need cite only one instance. Getting from a robbery, they needed a car. They found possession of a farmer's wife. Even when she gun, she objected to handing over the keys. When they knocked her out with a chain and assailing criminally before they went their way.

From small holdups at filling stations they passed to bank robberies. Rather early in their game shot at Buck. He died miserably a few weeks later infection in his wounds. Clyde and Bonnie Parker ried on. She was a blonde with a hard mouth who smoked black cigars, had herself photographed guns in and shot as well as her man. When hiding out with wilds they practiced their shooting constantly photographed each other standing beside their car. Except for a sentimental streak in Bonnie which prompted her to write atrocious poetry, vanity was the only human trait they possessed.

Gradually the posses hunting them grew larger larger. Once Governor Murray of Oklahoma called four companies of militia and all the deputies in or five counties. Sometimes they sneaked through cordons; just as often, they got away by accurate shooting with machine guns or automatic. Before they had as leader a down murderer on their Most of the victims were police officers doing these One murder reveals again what kind of people these rows were. They had held up a grocer in the pre

At right: Bonnie Parker, Clyde Barrow's moll, who smoked black cigars and shot as well as her man."

OUR NEW CIVIL WAR

kidnaping for ransom more dangerous than throwing a torch into an ammunition dump.

But meanwhile the forces of disorder in this country were handing them a new job. With the repeal of prohibition approaching, gang murders in our great cities grew a little less common; and yet the crime rate did not decline. In place of the rat-faced, expensively tailored thug who served in the pretorian guards of the illicit liquor business, there arose the roving footpad and bank robber who harassed the broad spaces of the Middle West. And the country began dimly to realize that here, too, was a situation which Uncle Sam alone could handle.

Clyde and Buck Barrow, together with Bonnie Parker, Clyde's lurid light-of-love, were the first of this species to shoot their way into national notoriety. Let us look at them as they were—we have of late hung too many romantic trimmings upon thugs and morons of this sort. The Barrows were mental, moral, and physical scrubs. Buck measured five feet five inches in height; Clyde, the worse of the pair, five feet three. Neither weighed much more than 100 pounds.

Parenthetically, most of the really dangerous characters whose Bertillon measurements decorate the criminal archives at Washington rate in the flyweight class. Any modern psychologist will tell you that this is no accident. The scrubby little boy with criminal tendencies has in his childhood stood for bullying and persecution by other little boys. When he grows up and goes on the loose, he has a complex of physical inferiority; and he compensates for it by brutality with those instruments which made dwarfs stand equal to giants—guns. The bodies of the Barrows were colossal compared to

of his wife. He hoisted his hands and made no resi while they stripped his till. Then, as they turned one of them shot him dead—" just for luck."

Both Clyde Barrow and Bonnie Parker took s wounds in their brushes with the law. They sneak last into the remote bayou country of Louisiana Henderson Jordon of Bienville Parish, learning o presence from federal agents, formed a posse clever trap, annihilated them with automatic rifl machine guns. He said afterward that he hadn' thought of killing a woman; but what else could sponsible officer of the law do with a Bonnie Park

The Barrows were probably the first to show futility of our pale protection against the roving perate criminal. This scourge grew to an epidemic Barrows lacked imagination. When robbing country banks, they did picayune business fellows and successors—men like Albert Bates. Ha Bailey, Wilbur Underhill, Harry Pierpont, Charle ley, John Hamilton, Tommy Carroll, Homer Van finally John Dillinger—played for big money and robbery to an art.

One of the little jackals who fringe the unde would spot a small-town bank as a prospect. Learn thing of its habits with money, and sell the inform to a more eminent criminal. The big shot w take, by the way, to assume that a gang in this of the crime business, is a hard-and-fast organ like a lodge. The big criminals and even their t combine and recombine according to their needs a vey Bailey, now spending the rest of his natural prison at Alcatraz Island, teamed at different t

At left: Marvin "Buck" Barrow and (inset Both were "mental, moral, and physical scrub

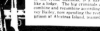

continued on page 83

To I.E.T.

Portrait of your Uncle Bill calling you a disagreeable child and trying to keep his face straight.

Will Irwin 1930

Will Irwin in 1930. "I.E.T." refers to "Ebie" Thompson, daughter of Irwin's younger sister-in-law. (Courtesy of Mrs. Roscoe (Ebie) Sturges, Jr.)

*William Hyde Irwin,
Will's son, by his
first wife. (Courtesy
of Donald Irwin)*

*Scene from the Broadway production
of* Lute Song, *starring Mary Martin
and Yul Brynner, in 1946. Photo
courtesy of Michael Myerberg.*

est quality. It could be done. War could be stopped. And Americans could stop it.

Bill would carry that message with him throughout the rest of the Great War and its aftermath, bursting to spread his gospel.

Two days after his visit to Rheims, Bill arrived at Bar-le-Duc. At the press headquarters for the battle of the Argonne Forest he saw Grantland Rice, Damon Runyon, Frank Taylor, and other newspapermen he knew. One cold, rainy afternoon Gerald Morgan, now a captain, emerged from the telegraph room and, in a voice trembling with excitement, read Germany's proposal to discuss peace on the basis of Wilson's fourteen points. Shortly afterwards, Lorimer cabled: "Drop military affairs and rush copy on reconstruction."[14]

Bill was back in Paris in time to celebrate the false armistice on November 8, 1918. Like many of the Allies, he was misled by an unintentionally false report, apparently based on valid information, by Roy Howard, president of United Press. Howard had thought he had a worldwide beat. Afterwards, he was widely criticized for being overly eager, but Bill believed that any newspaperman worth a job as a copy boy would have done the same thing.[15]

Three days later Bill was submitting an article to the censor at the Bourse building when a friend told him that the armistice had really been signed. Paris went wild, and Bill joined the celebration. Parisian girls flocked around Americans, pecking kisses on their faces. By dusk American flags outnumbered the British or Belgian or Italian flag four or five to one, and the tricolor flew everywhere. At dawn a group of soldiers and young women gathered up Bill and rushed him along to the Tuilleries Gardens. Twenty-two hours after joining the hysterically happy throngs, he headed for bed, exhausted but elated.

Bill thought that the cosmopolitan crowds had caught what he regarded as the old American virtue of hope. For the moment it seemed that humanity had triumphed over politics, statesmanship, and diplomacy, that the world had indeed been made safe for democracy, that there would never be another war to cover. "The greatest day since the crucifixion," he wrote — apparently meaning the Resurrection; years later he would blush when he recalled those words.[16]

With the signing of the armistice, he vowed that he had covered his last war. He had seen the Great War from start to finish on the home fronts and on the battle fronts. He had witnessed some aspect of almost a dozen major battles, including the final actions at the Argonne and on the Hindenburg drive. He had talked to thousands of soldiers, in small cafes behind the lines, in hospitals, in mess halls, in observation posts, in dugouts, in trenches. "When it was all over," he later wrote, "they said of me that I had seen more of the World War, in all its various aspects, than any other American."[17]

After the armistice, Bill toured Northern France and wrote articles about reconstruction. Few Americans knew more about postwar conditions in France than Will Irwin. His friend Lincoln Steffens regarded him as "one of the most informing among the writers."[18]

While the Allies prepared for the peace conference at Versailles, Bill accompanied the victors on an early December expedition into disputed Alsace-Lorraine to take official possession of Metz and Strasbourg. Poincaré, Clemenceau, Haig, Pershing, Foch, and other Allied celebrities were received enthusiastically, convincing Bill that most Alsatians wanted to return to France, which is just what the French hosts wanted the American correspondents to believe. A tour of Alsace after leaving the official party confirmed his assessment.[19]

Although Bill wished that Inez could have accompanied him on the tour, her precarious health made him realize that she never could have withstood the inconveniences and discomforts of winter motoring and sleeping in the aisles of trains. He missed her, but there was too much work to do in postwar Europe to return home.

"Myself, barring the unforeseen, I anticipate that there will be at least a year of profitable work for me over here," he wrote to her in mid December. "There may be even more; and in case one is here and doesn't want to come home, he can write fiction and generalities here as well as in New York. . . . I want you here with me." He suggested that she come over in March. He asked her to cable her decision because letters took about a month and "because uncertainty plays Hell with one's plans in times like these." "If you don't want to come here or if you are not well enough to come, I shall come back to you as soon as I honorably can," he wrote, and concluded: "I wouldn't pass a year away from you for all Mr. Curtis' gold!"[20]

By mid January 1919, Bill had received a favorable report on Inez's health. Her stomach was much better, and she could even drink a cocktail and a little wine without the "slightest bad result." He was in Brussels finishing an article about the widespread desire of the Germans for a republic when he heard that she planned to join him in March. Then came a disturbing letter in which she said she had suffered a digestive attack, with sharp pain, the worst since she had arrived in San Francisco.[21] Judging by her symptoms, Bill believed she might have gallstones.

Back in Paris, which was crowded with writers covering the peace negotiations, he made plans for Inez to join him. He hoped that she would arrive in time for the settling of the peace terms, which would be "one of the great, picturesque events in history."[22] Paris was decked out in international dress.

Within a few days came two month-old letters from Inez that made him fear her illness would block their reunion. The first letter described a slight attack, her second in two weeks, and the second, dictated a week later, indicated that she had been in bed with neuralgia and stomach trouble. He would have called off their reunion but for his strong yearning. "Oh, how I hope you do arrive," he wrote. "You can be contented in California without me; I can be contented nowhere without you."[23]

He was planning to tour the Balkans when he heard that she had undergone major surgery. He received cables from a mutual friend, Albert M. Bender, a wealthy San Francisco patron of writers and artists, that she was all right.[24] Though relieved, Bill walked the boulevards distracted, fearing the worst. Physicians and friends in Paris assured him that a gall bladder operation was not critical, and he suppressed an impulse to cable Lorimer and start for California.

Writing to her from the American Press Headquarters for the peace conference, he rationalized his decision. Now was the time for him to make money in Europe; they would need it to pay her medical bills. He told her that he would never leave her again—"as I shouldn't have left you this time except for a feeling that the war was a supreme duty."[25]

He had glimpses in his mind's eye of Inez dead. "I have never fully visualized that before, and it was terrible—terrible," he wrote to her. "I shouldn't be saying this to you, of course, did I not know that you can't receive this letter until nearly a month after the operation, when you should be out of the hospital and of danger. And still I don't know exactly what to do."[26]

A week after her operation, he was still pulled between covering the peace conference and returning to Inez. He declined an invitation from his friend Herbert Adams Gibbons of the New York *Herald* to attend the conference at Versailles together and cancelled his trip to the Balkans because he did not want to venture any farther from San Francisco. He wrote to Inez's sister Daisy that he would start for the United States immediately if it were not that the CPI job broke him financially and he was hustling to make money while it was harvest time.[27] As if to expiate his guilt, he sent Inez a check for five hundred dollars.

He was having bad dreams and terrible nights. One night he had a strange psychic experience, "a state of body, being and nerves which I had never experienced before in my life." In the morning he analyzed his feelings as those of one recovering from an operation. The next night was full of dreams in which his wife was "alternately glad and rosy with me, and mad at me."[28]

"God send spring," he wrote to Inez on Valentine's Day. "I've packed a Hell of a cold for a month, but I'm pretty sure that awful attack of flu I had in Paris last winter gives me immunity."[29] Many of his friends were suffering in the widespread, deadly influenza epidemic; several got pneumonia, which was often fatal. He found a hard-to-get hotel room for one sick friend and cared for another at the leased house in the Etiole quarter where he was staying with Hoover and his assistants in the Food Administration. During an emergency, George Barr Baker, who was handling publicity for the Food Administration, came down with the flu, and Bill stepped in and did his job.

He was at the guarded Hotel de Crillion, headquarters for Americans at the peace conference, when President Wilson, who had been secretive and hostile toward the press, called a press conference. It was the first time Bill had seen the president since leaving the CPI six months before, and he was shocked by how haggard and exhausted Wilson looked. The idealism of armistice week, which Wilson was trying to uphold, had been lost among the intrigues of European politicians grasping for the plunder of war. Wilson told the reporters that France was the principal opponent of the League of Nations plan. Her leaders were demanding that league members not only supply forces to guard against German aggression on French soil but also bind themselves for fifty years to defend France against Germany. These terms were unacceptable to other nations.

While diplomats intrigued, Bill waited for more reassuring news of his wife's recovery. He was hesitant about everything. He was hesitant about leaving Paris, fearing he would miss a letter or cable or could not leave for the United States quickly in an emergency. He was hesitant about writing. "The trouble is that anything you write now will look so stale in two month's hence," he wrote to her. "However, I'm doing a piece called Soldiers of Peace appealing to the country to stand by the League of Nations plan."[30] Eventually, he would expand this appeal into the most fervent crusade of his career.

On February 17 he received a distressing letter, dated January 24, in which Inez told of her diagnoses, pain, and suffering. Now he wondered if her operation had been more serious than Bender had made it seem in his original cable. It was frustrating not knowing all the details about her condition.

Still, ambition continued to take precedence over love. "In two months more I shall be full of dope to write at home—I'm not now," he again apologized to her for staying in Europe. "And I need that money—not for me but for you in your recovery."[31]

One morning Vernon Kellogg dropped in at press headquarters. He was just back from Germany, including Berlin, where there had been minor riots by left-wing extremists almost daily. The socialists were ready to break loose whenever the heavy hand of the government was removed, Kellogg said. As far as the peace treaty was concerned, the Germans complacently believed they would get their way and would not have to pay damages or indemnities. Kellogg's report to the correspondents seemed ominous to Bill.

Trouble seemed imminent in England, too. Ramsay McDonald told Bill that labor had reacted to the government's refusal for a six-hour day and national ownership of the mines by setting March 15 for a general strike that would tie up all transportation. It sounded like an event worth covering.

Before leaving for England, he bought his wife some gloves and wrote to her that "there hasn't been a moment when I haven't wanted you. I get almost sore on myself to think that I could be so hipped on one little, small-footed, neat-handed, soft-eyed feminine and damned strong female! Whenever I think of what you must have suffered before an emergency operation, I get giddy and sick."[32]

A frustrating search for a room, his loneliness, and the dreary weather in London put him in "a state of suicidal depression." One night he got drunk with friends and wrote to his wife: "Inez, my Inez, *I am soused*. I am pickled." And he added: "Anyhow, drunk or sober I love you."[33]

At last he received two letters, including a "brave, sweet pathetic one" she wrote on the eve of her operation. "I sat and sniveled over it in the American Express," he replied. "I then swore, if oath were needed, that once I kiss your pretty hand again I'll never leave you until death gets one or the other of us."[34] If she believed his oath, she would be disappointed.

In London he attended a dinner party with George Gordon Moore, H. G. Wells, and George Creel. Some bitterness lingered from his disputes in the CPI. "George Creel has made George Moore believe that the foreign propaganda was a great success. . . . There's only one talent worth anything in this world—window dressing," he complained to Inez. "Because I lack it utterly, I have failed with the goods right on me. George has it. He has been leaping from court to court as the great American propagandist." Creel was writing his CPI memoirs, and Bill supposed that he would receive no credit in them, though he expected that his successor to the chairmanship of the foreign division, "the rat Sisson," would receive praise.[35] As it would turn out, however, Creel would acknowledge Irwin's contribution, too.

Although Bill was now comfortably, if temporarily, situated at the Royal Automobile Club in Pall Mall, he was miserable. There was a coal shortage and the weather was cold, damp. More letters came from Inez, written before her cable announcing her operation, and he learned that she had suffered repeated severe attacks, with intense pain that necessitated morphine. He wrote back from London: "I don't know whether, money or no money, I'm going to be able to stick it out here."[36] His resolve to reap the harvest was weakening.

The next day he received letters from Bender and from Inez's secretary, both written after the operation, and he felt intense remorse for failing to have headed homeward the instant he had received the first wire announcing her operation. Everyone had assured him that a gall bladder operation was as simple in quiescent periods as an appendicitis operation, and he had wanted to avoid his relatives in California and the five hundred dollars cost of a double crossing. Now he learned that her gall bladder had been "packed with rocks" and inflamed and there had been adhesions, which had made her operation serious. When he read her secretary's line saying that Inez had never been in such pain before, he decided to return to the United States as soon as possible.[37]

On March 20 he boarded the *Aquitania*. Settled in his cabin, he began writing about efforts to accelerate production in England and about the relations between Americans and the French in France.[38] In the harbor at Brest, he gazed out a porthole and reflected that he had lived on familiar terms, now, with soldiers of five nations, and very few of them liked war. Where would it all end? Sailing into the Atlantic, he was leaving behind the petty national hatreds and greedy jockeying for advantage in a Europe torn almost as much in peace as it had been in war. There would be a peace treaty, although the democracy haters were busily confusing the issues and trying to sabotage the League of Nations, but he would not witness the signing. The culmination of four and a half years of covering the Great War and perhaps the greatest news story of his twenty years in journalism! And he would miss it.

On the last Sunday of March 1919, he landed in New York. The United States, which had quickly demobilized, was utterly different from the war-geared nation he had left six months ago. The dry trend he had reported eleven years before had climaxed in the Eighteenth Amendment, and labor was pressing for socialistic goals. Americans were more concerned with the threat of a radical conspiracy than with the peace conference.

Their pessimism and doubt about the League of Nations surprised Bill. Europeans realized that immense obstacles stood in the way of an agreement between twenty-three contending nations, but they had faith in the ultimate settlement of many differences. To Europeans the League of Nations was almost a foregone conclusion. He feared that isolationist forces were undermining public opinion in the United States.

On the first Saturday of April, after completing some work in New York, he took a train to California, sending telegrams to Inez along the way. The closer he got to San Francisco, the more anxious he became about her health. He expected to find her on her sick bed, weak and suffering.

Instead, she met him at the ferry station. Although just out of her sick bed, she was on her way to perfect recovery. Weary from the trip, he joined her at the Clift Hotel.

Bill had been in town a few days when President Jordan asked if he would address a student assembly at Stanford on the peace and the League of Nations. It was an opportunity not only to boost the league, but also to make a triumphant return to the college that had once expelled him. And he could hardly decline an invitation from the man who had been his champion and mentor. After the assembly, the Irwins had lunch with the Jordans at the president's house. When they had finished the main course, Mrs. Jordan said, "I'm postponing the dessert. We'll go out on the piazza and have our ice cream there."[39]

They were sitting on the piazza eating their dessert and talking about the new Europe when Bill noticed a procession coming up the walk from the gate. As they came closer he began to recognize faces. They were older professors who had taught there in his time and younger professors who had been his fellow students. A big, deep chuckle rumbled in Jordan's throat.

"Bill," he said, for the first time addressing Irwin by his first name, "this isn't ice cream we're eating. It's the fatted calf!"

Later, Bill's father came over from Brookdale, and the three Irwins returned to the city together. For seventy-five, David Irwin was in good health. A stout man, he had large hands and heavy white eyebrows, a thick white mustache, and a bald head fringed with white hair. His sense of humor was drier than Wallace's or Bill's but, Inez thought, "sunny," and she liked him.[40]

Bill and Inez were soon drawn into a whirlpool of luncheons, dinners, speeches, and other activities. One Saturday morning they sold Victory Bonds at a booth of the National League for Women's Service at the foot of Victory Tower, exchanging their autographs for first payments. They were house guests of the Stewart Edward Whites in Hillsborough and of Charlie Field in Los Altos. Also, Bill saw his son, now sixteen. Bill was so busy "doing everything except laying corner stones," as he wrote to Wallace, that by May 8 he felt like "an utter moral, mental and physical wreck."[41] He had expected to return East in April, but he was too busy.

On several occasions in April and May he argued publicly for acceptance of the League of Nations. At an assembly sponsored by the League of Free Nations' Association, he warned that "The next war, which the militarists are already planning, would make the last one look like a game of tiddledy winks." The only hope to prevent another war was the peace treaty with the League of Nations covenant, he said, and he alerted his audience to a propaganda war against the treaty and the league. Oppose the propaganda of hate with the propaganda of love, he advocated, adding: "We need to be a nation of understanders of other people!"[42]

Bill had a good press. A speech before a large audience in Eagles' Hall one night moved columnist John D. Barry to write: "To hear Will Irwin lecture is to enjoy a clear, incisive mind working easily and rapidly."[43]

Soon after the peace treaty went to the Germans, Bill granted a long, stenographically recorded interview to the *Bulletin*, which touted him as "America's most brilliant war reporter and a diligent student of international politics." He predicted "a great social transition" in Europe and, eventually, in the United States. Although he believed that the extreme changes proposed by Lenin would be unsuccessful in the Western World, he did think that "within the next ten years we may accept in our social structure many principles which at present would be called Bolshevism." He expected that labor unions would be instrumental in the change. "Anyone who shuts his eyes to the vitality and the strength of the working class movement which has followed the war merely emulates the silly ostrich."[44] Such comments, made in interviews and speeches, were earning Bill a national reputation as a radical.

It was more than a week after Bender threw a farewell party for "the famous Irwins" before they could escape the hospitality of San Francisco for the tranquility of New England.[45] But Scituate wasn't the quiet, serene summer retreat it used to be. The automobile had turned it into a bustling year-round community. Peggoty Beach was crowded with bathing parties and unfamiliar faces, and most of the New York artistic crowd that had congregated around the Haynes tennis court had vanished. The marshes retained their emerald spring color, and off shore the unimpeded sky and vast stretches of water still maintained their lonely, mysterious immensity.

Bill settled down next door to his niece, who as Phyllis Duganne had become a successful writer, and her husband, Austin Parker. Around Inez's house, now the Irwin place, the scarlet tanagers and humming birds flew, and in the Fairy Pond the goldfish swam around the water lilies. Butterflies flitted over Inez's garden. Second Cliff seemed a long way from the unrepentant, resentful Germany signing the Treaty of Versailles, the revolution spreading through Europe, and even the labor strikes spreading fear of Bolshevism across the United States. Insulated from these postwar imbroglios, Bill played tennis and wrote articles and stories.

Because American readers were tired of war he concentrated on escape fiction for the *Saturday Evening Post*. Two yarns were set in a Rocky Mountain mining district reminiscent of his childhood home. In one story a supposedly exhausted mine, "salted" with stolen ore, was traded for a saloon only to pay off eventually and unexpectedly in silver-bearing lead carbonates for the new owner. In the other story a tenderfoot mining expert outwitted crooked mining camp officials and saved evidence that would convict them.[46] In both stories, Bill exploited the irony of the situations and effectively created a wild west atmosphere. He tended to write his best fiction when he drew on the happiest period of his childhood for action, atmosphere, and characters.

While the Senate debated the Treaty of Versailles, he drew on his experiences as a war correspondent and a government propagandist to wage

a journalistic crusade against war. He regarded himself as a muckraker for
peace, and his articles glowed with moral indignation characteristic of the
prewar Progressives. For the first time in four years, Lorimer, who was
unsympathetic toward the League of Nations, focus of the crusade, did not
instantly accept anything Bill wrote, and Bill had to seek other outlets.

Two markets he found were the weekly *Independent*, a crusading
proleague periodical of opinion, and the monthly *Sunset*, a magazine
for readers in the West. In them he expressed his belief that national and
racial hatreds ran so deep that the league alone could not prevent war. A
supplementary moral law was necessary. He placed the responsibility
for the formulation of that law on the moralists—the peace societies and the
churches. He also warned his readers to guard against the propaganda of
hate; if they did, he believed, truth would prevail.[47] Despite the Hell he had
witnessed in Europe, he steadfastly retained his western optimism.

With the advent of autumn at Second Cliff, masses of migrating birds
swarmed across the sky and alighted on branches. Exploring Plymouth
County by Ford, Bill and Inez rode through the richly colored landscapes
that smelled of cider and gazed at the old houses with building dates on
their chimneys, the old white wooden churches with steeples like carved
ivory, the serene old graveyards, the historic markers and monuments.
After their ordeals of the previous winter, it was a pleasantly normal and
tranquil life.

For awhile.

Bill grew restless again. He was missing too much. President Wilson
had collapsed from the exhaustion of his relentless, uncompromising crusade for American participation in the League of Nations, and political
observers considered Hoover, now nationally known, a likely prospect for
the Democratic or Republican nomination. Violence during a police strike
in Boston had kindled the Red scare in the United States. In Europe, France
was struggling to stand on her own mending legs and the new German
Republic, shaken by internal dissension, was struggling merely to exist. The
forecast by Bill and others that democracy would undergo its severest trial
after the Great War seemed to be coming true, and he wanted to reap the
new harvest of material on the continent. Inez had been playing tennis and
was well again, so they decided to return to Europe.

Expecting the cost of living in postwar Paris to be even higher than
during the war, Bill and Inez arrived loaded with sugar, condensed milk, and
cigarettes. However, they found two rooms with a fireplace and bath in a
good hotel for sixty francs a day (six dollars) and restaurants where they
could dine on soup, meat, salad, fruit, and a demitasse for about seventy
cents. Both food and accommodations were cheaper and better in Paris than

in New York, Bill reported in an analysis of French economic conditions for the *Saturday Evening Post.*[48]

Except for the two-week tour to look over the progress of recovery in the remote towns of devastated northern France, Bill spent most of his time in Paris writing and keeping up with news of the Communist threat in Germany. The extreme left wing Spartacists were threatening to upset the new republican government. Although he hated all things German, except the wine, he could not resist the lure of crucial events.

As he was starting alone for Germany, he received a cable from Lorimer, a Hoover booster, saying that presidential sentiment for Bill's old friend was growing in the United States and ordering an article reflecting the prospective candidate's business and executive acumen. Bill explained the assignment in an apologetic letter to Hoover. "Forgive much if I have to write you up and be thankful it is done by a friendly hand!" he concluded. In his article, he emphasized Hoover's leadership in the Commission for Relief in Belgium and stressed his "supreme talent—the organizing faculty."[49]

In Berlin, capital of the Weimar democratic republic, Bill attended dozens of political meetings, with an interpreter whispering into his good left ear a rapid translation of the speeches. He preferred that method to the awkward and inefficient ear trumpet, the only hearing aid available. He reported wide, if vague, approval of the republic and some harsh dissent, mainly from diehard royalists. Travelers he interviewed indicated that among the masses there was a smoldering sentiment for a monarchy. In the Hotel Adlon he lived on the same floor as General Erich von Ludendorff, the leading reactionary; in the dining room the orchestra played the reactionary battle song, "Deutschland Über Alles." He wrote down his observations and sent his manuscripts to Paris for typing.

In March 1920 he was in and out of Berlin. He was in Cologne when he heard that a band of conterrevolutionary royalists led by Wolfgang Kapp had forced the republican government to withdraw from Berlin to Stuttgart. Inspired by Ludendorff, Kapp was trying to restore the monarchy, and his putsch seemed to change everything Bill had just written about Germany. He rushed to Paris, where his typist was preparing a manuscript, to try to salvage the article for publication.

At first it seemed as dead as if he had written it in 1913. Like many observers, he was stupefied. Then the next day's news indicated that the German people were not joining the putsch, even though the army had defected. He repaired the article and, planning to interview officials of the republican government, boarded a train for Stuttgart.[50]

In Stuttgart, John Evans of the Associated Press briefed him. When the Junkers struck in Berlin the lawful government fled by automobile to Dresden, and when the rumbles of communism began to agitate Saxony, to

Stuttgart. The government called a general strike against the usurpers, and the German people ended Kapp's hundred hours rule. The Spartacists took advantage of the confusion. Shooting broke out in Leipzig, Nuremberg, Halle, and other industrial cities, and persons hazily described as Reds occupied Düsseldorf and probably Essen. The government rushed back to Berlin to avert anarchy, leaving Stuttgart in peace.

After the government's departure, Evans was assigned to the Ruhr. The newspapers reported that in the industrial Ruhr basin, near the Netherlands, working men were attacking the Reichswehr, the small military force granted the republican government under the peace treaty. The British reportedly had interned fifteen hundred Reichswehr troops who had been forced across the occupied border. Bill decided to accompany Evans.

Düsseldorf was bustling as usual. The only unusual aspect was pairs of armed guards wearing the red left armband of the revolutionaries or the green and white armband of the state police. After attempting to interview the government soldiers held prisoner, who were so exhausted they could not talk coherently, Bill and Evans learned where the shooting was. Accompanied by an interpreter, they made their way by train to Büderick, on the Rhine, where they obtained passes to cross to Wesel. The Reds were near the bridgehead.

As they approached the bridge, shrapnel burst overhead, "as black as the cinders of hell," Bill reported.[51] He found life in Wesel going on much as usual, except for the workers and others involved in the insurrection against the government troops. Returning, Bill and his two companions dodged shrapnel again, and when they were back in Büderick, the town was shelled. When the armistice had come, Bill never expected that within two years he would be under fire again, much less with the German army.

It happened again, the next morning. Bill, Evans, and their interpreter were at a Belgian area along the Lippe near a battle when a sniper opened fire. They were walking along a road about fifty yards from a small hill grove when Bill heard a buzzing and almost simultaneously the whip of a rifle shot.[52]

"Drop flat!" he yelled, and instinctively flattened out on the ground.

Buzz-crack, again.

His knees had just hit the ground when he realized how foolish and undignified he looked. There was not even the cover of a three-inch blade of grass. They were making themselves perfect stationary targets.

"Run for it!" he yelled, and scrambled up. Out of the corner of an eye he noticed the others were following.

A rapid burst of shots indicated two or three men were firing. More bullets sang past, then two leisurely shots. The snipers were taking better aim. A bullet hit the trunk of a tree just ahead.

Reaching the woods, Bill heard a pair of running feet beside him, and for a terrified instant remembered there should be two pairs. He whirled, afraid of what he might see, but the interpreter was coming along behind, running strong for an old man, holding the collar of his fur coat up around his ears as if against rain.

The three were settling in the cover of a bank when a little gray rabbit leaped out almost from under their feet and streaked down the road. For the first time, Bill understood how a rabbit in the sights of a hunter's gun must feel. Those snipers had been shooting at him with more personal intent than anyone had ever shot at him during the Great War.

When shortly before Easter the Associated Press ordered Evans to insurgent headquarters at Essen, industrial heart of the Ruhr basin, Bill and the interpreter went along. On the train they saw in the Cologne *Zeitung* an amazing report that the insurgents had reached agreements with the besieged to take over the industries. In Essen they expected to witness the end of the rebellion, but the gray city of massive, solid buildings was swarming with tough, swaggering young men with rifles, red ribbons in their caps, and red brassards around their arms. Except for the guards pacing the streets, searching parties seeking arms, and curfew regulations, life in Essen proceeded much as usual.

When Bill and his companions showed their credentials at the People's Palace, where the Red legislature was meeting in secret session, they were surprised to be admitted. The Reds wanted America to understand their cause. The meeting reminded Bill of a session of the San Francisco Labor Council he had attended the previous spring.

After listening to the speeches for a while, he realized that, as he put it, "the jig was up" for the Ruhr government.[53] Independent Socialists and labor unions in the rest of Germany had refused to declare a general strike in sympathy with the Ruhr insurgents. The insurgents played their last card and ordered a general strike of their own.

It paralyzed Essen. The Reichswehr ordered the Reds to surrender by noon. Everyone thought that the Red army at the front would not quit. Bill felt the tension mount in Essen.

On the Kettwiger Strasse he noticed that the crowd was congealing into groups. He had seen it happen before in moments of impending danger, as though people were looking for close human comfort. He had seen it in Louvain when the Germans entered, in Venice when news came that the Carso line had broken, in Cologne when the first news of the Kapp putsch appeared on the bulletin boards. The square before the Kaiserhof Hotel, usually occupied by passersby and sentries, was bare.

At the hotel, which was Red headquarters, Bill heard rumors that in an hour, precisely at twelve, Reichswehr artillery would open fire on the city, particularly on the Kaiserhof. He knew it was impossible; the lines were forty kilometers away. He also heard that at noon the Reds would massacre the bourgeoisie, which he thought equally improbable. Yet during the next long hour he could not suppress an occasional catch of breath.

He went for a look at the Kettwiger Strasse, two blocks from the hotel, at 11:15 A.M. and 11:30 A.M. and each time the crowd had diminished. The second time the women were gone and from all sides he heard banging shutters. At 11:45 A.M. Red soldiers, moving stolidly about army business, were the only ones visible.

At the Kaiserhof, Bill subsequently reported, "the manager had ordered the steel-latticed gate closed all but a crack. Before it he took his station, chewing a strand of his upturned Kaiserish mustache which had drooped away from its neighboring strands. Beside him stood his two clerks. At intervals they took a deep breath. Half a dozen American and British journalists waited with them. As the minutes wore on we found it impossible to talk. We just stood smoking cigarettes end to end, glancing every few seconds at our watches.

"Out of such silence as I have never heard at noon in a great city came the deep clang of a bell," he reported. "It was the clock in the old Münster on the first stroke of twelve. It finished. A minute or two more we waited. No scream of a shell, no roar of a mob, no rifle shots. Suddenly the proprietor gave a short, hard Prussian laugh; he turned and threw back with a bang the sliding steel gates. The noise seemed to waken us as from an enchantment. We laughed with him. . . ."[54]

By one o'clock the Kettwiger Strasse was again crowded and for the first time since early morning the people were talking. Some bold tobacconists even opened their doors for customers.

The rebellion evaporated. There was no surrender, no truce, no final act. The Ruhr insurgents merely put away their guns and returned to the factories and mines.

To Bill, it had been less a social revolution than a protest against militarism in its old Prussian form. The Ruhr miner or laborer had taken down his old army rifle and, led by the Communists, had gone gunning for government troops to satisfy his grudge. "The men who must make the rank and file of German armies seeking a place in the sun are sick to the heart of the goose step and the sharp edge of the sword, of officers who push civilians off the streets, of drill sergeants who enforce discipline with a belt buckle or a heavy boot," he concluded a two-part series on "The Ruhr Aflame" for the *Saturday Evening Post*.[55] He believed he had witnessed the birth pains of German democracy.

After the rebellion fizzled out, Bill left Evans and their interpreter and picked up Inez in Paris, where she had been writing, and took her to Belgium to find out why that little country, the first victim trampled under the German boot, was recovering so rapidly. The key, he reported, was the Belgians' national sense of cooperation in resuming normal production.[56] That May, Whitlock introduced the Irwins to the queen at Laeken; it turned out to be one of their last memorable experiences in Europe for 1920.

Returning home, Bill ended what he had thought in August 1914 would be six months of covering a brief war in Europe. He was forty-six years old, his reddish-blond hair was receding from his forehead, his girth was thickening, and his hearing was gone in his right ear. Sobered by the war, he now felt like settling down, once and for all.

CHAPTER SEVEN

Crusader

WITH Inez, Bill sailed home in mid 1920 burning to spread the message of peace and international cooperation that he had occasionally expounded in articles and speeches during the last few years. "Now," he thought as he alighted from the ocean liner, "I can turn loose."[1] But times were changing. His countrymen were more interested in the bright present and future at home than in the fading past or remote problems abroad.

The Senate had rejected the League of Nations and Americans were tired of crusades and causes. Weary, the older generation wanted to forget its idealism and look at the cheerier, materialistic side of life. Disenchanted, the younger generation, reacting with truculent cynicism, tried to drown out the world's troubles with the wail of saxophones and bathtubs of gin. Youth was replacing old mores and morals with a fresh, impudent set of new ones.

The changing times affected Bill's markets, too. He continued to contribute to the *Saturday Evening Post*, but mostly stories. Lorimer was not interested in the kind of articles Bill wanted to write, particularly pieces boosting the League of Nations, and fiction bridged the widening gap between their political views. He looked around for other markets for his articles.

One day in October as he was deep-sea fishing off the Atlantic Coast with Sam Adams, he received a telegram announcing the serious illness of Sara Graham. He hurriedly packed and caught the first train for New York and, from there, for Denver. At cities along the way, he sent wires of encouragement and brief messages expressing his love. Shortly before he arrived, Miss Graham, who was sixty-eight, died of pneumonia. Bill had more than repaid his financial debt to her. He had entertained her royally in New York and had sent her on a trip to Europe. When he had paid back her college loan, he had insisted on paying 6 percent interest, and in the long list of personal belongings she willed him were bonds valued at exactly that amount.

After the Irwins moved from Scituate to an apartment on East Fifty-sixth Street in Manhattan for the winter, Bill anonymously wrote Democratic campaign literature about the League of Nations, supporting James M. Cox for president because Cox supported America's entry into the League; finished some stories for Lorimer; and purchased a permanent winter residence. The house was a narrow, four-floor red brick, built almost a hundred years before and squeezed wall to wall between brownstones on West Eleventh Street between the Avenue of the Americas and Seventh Avenue in Greenwich Village, a haven for writers and artists. The house was rundown, but it had potential, given heat, electricity, new plaster, and wallpaper. Bill paid forty thousand dollars and had the place put in Inez's name.

Payments from the *Saturday Evening Post* for short stories and a serial, "Columbine Time," helped pay the bills in the early months of 1921 while he wrote his first major polemic against war.[2] A group of citizens interested in the disarmament conference and aware of his endorsement of at least part of President Harding's policies had suggested that he show that humanity must eliminate the institution of war before it eliminated humanity. Like most American partisans of the League of Nations, which had been rejected for a second time by the Senate, he hoped that the decision of Congress was revocable. Perhaps, he thought, he could arouse public sentiment to force Congress to reconsider American participation in the league. Every morning after breakfast he wrote "at white heat."[3]

Although he was summing up his philosophy against war, he wrote more as a journalist than as a philosopher. He hoped that by arraying facts and figures to expose the fantastically lethal nature of future wars, in which civilians as well as soldiers would be slaughtered in wholesale lots, he would help discourage all war. As he saw it, the struggle was between militarism and reasonable pacifism, between the aristocratic ideal of society and the democratic.

He acknowledged his intellectual debts to the English peace advocate, Norman Angell, and to his college mentor, David Starr Jordan. Angell believed that the victor as well as the vanquished lost in war. Jordan believed that in modern war, fought by conscript armies, the best young soldiers would serve on the front lines and die first, setting back the quality of "races" for centuries. Jordan's book, *War and the Breed*, which included an article by Irwin in its appendix, especially influenced Bill.

"War by machinery" would compound the slaughter in the next war, Bill asserted, and made some predictions based on his own observations and on conversations with military experts.[4] He expected no great improvement in guns and high-explosive projectiles because other methods of destroying life and property were more promising. He predicted—with a mixture of accuracy and error, it would turn out—that gas-bomb-carrying "aeroplanes," some possibly unpiloted, would probably become a standard weapon. He accurately envisioned the importance of tanks, but inaccurately expected massive mechanized warfare to displace vast infantry and result in small professional armies.

Warring nations would employ "every force of nature" they could, Bill argued. He foresaw the development of x-rays, light rays, or heat rays into some sort of lethal ray that would "shrivel up or paralyze or poison human beings." He only hinted at nuclear warfare, but he came close to prophesying use of the laser. He regarded germ war as the final form of warfare. He predicted that World War II would not be declared but would begin without declaration of hostilities, "following the precedent established by the Japanese in their war against Russia."

"Two great tasks lie before humanity in the rest of the twentieth century," he wrote. "One is to put under control of true morals and of democracy the great power of human production which came in the nineteenth century. The other is to check, to limit and finally to eliminate the institution of war. The last is more important."

He called for "a real law, not a mere set of gentlemen's agreements between nation and nation," to eliminate war. "We shall not strike at the root of wars until we organize fifty or sixty sovereign nations and self-governing colonies of the world somewhat as we organize individuals in a tribe or state or nation." He had in mind something like the League of Nations, organized by his own country. He pleaded with his fellow Americans to avoid isolationism.

His publisher, E. P. Dutton, wanted *The Next War* ready in time to influence the debates on disarmament in the new Congress, and the book came out in April. It was widely and favorably reviewed in newspapers, magazines, and scholarly journals. Most reviewers agreed that it was authoritative, concise, readable, and that everyone should heed its message. Robert Herrick, who had once criticized the author for his second-hand news sources, wrote in the *Nation*: "To the lethargic minded citizen who thinks 'Men have always fought and always will fight, but the world has survived many wars and will outlast my time,' Mr. Irwin addresses himself with an array of big figures and startling facts that may whip his jaded imagination to fresh conclusions."[5]

San Francisco editor Fremont Older sent Bill a copy of his own flattering review. Bill replied that if any one of the books would ever sell well, *The Next War* should, "because I wrote it con amore, having been made very tired by hearing a lot of blatant, ignorant, 'next war' stuff. The professional patriots don't know what war means now; and I went out to tell them. I have more than a selfish interest in getting it circulated and read."[6]

On June 6 Dutton announced the eighth edition. Americans might be turning isolationist, but the book was sensational, controversial, and in the increasingly popular nonfiction genre. It did not outsell H. G. Well's phenomenally successful *Outline of History* (which Bill read), but it did become one of the best selling spring books and Bill's own best seller yet. Unfortunately, for him, he had sold it for a flat sum of a few hundred dollars.

With no regular periodical outlet for political commentary because Lorimer still held exclusive rights to most of his copy under their 1915 agreement, Bill concentrated on writing short stories in the summer of 1921. Typically, his short stories were saccharine, lightly humorous, or slightly muckraking in tone, with twisty plots. His best stories were set in the old West, salted with humor, and spared the boy-gets-girl cliché. Some of his best and much of his worst fiction of this period was reflected in his serial, "Columbine Time," published as a short novel between hardcovers in September 1921.

In *Columbine Time* there was light humor and vivid action but no depth to the characters or setting, a fictional Leadville of the 1880s. In a belated springtime, the story goes, a widowed mother tried to marry her daughter to a rich older man, but the girl resists in favor of a shy, virile young man she met among nature's "great virginal white columbines," symbol of innocence and youth.[7] After a fire, a dance, two holdups, and a chase, the mother finally agrees to let her daughter marry the blond, blue-eyed, broad-shouldered hero; then she takes the older man for herself. The suspense Bill tried to build up was marred by his bromidic, predictable plot.

In October 1921 the Irwins settled down in their remodeled home at 240 West Eleventh Street. To pay for the unexpected high costs of restoring the house and of installing modern conveniences, Bill accepted an offer by the Coit and Alber lecture agency to make a tour capitalizing on the vogue of *The Next War*, which had entered its twenty-third printing. Rising prosperity, the yearning of a bewildered public for guidance, and an increasing interest in personalities generated a wide demand for lecturers. The lyceum course touched most towns of more than five thousand inhabitants between the Alleghenies and the Rockies and beyond. In November he headed west.

In Dayton, New Orleans, Vicksburg . . . he peered through round lenses in black wire frames at the audiences come to see and hear the famous war correspondent. He stood before them in dark ankle-high shoes and a rumpled suit with vest to deliver with the eloquence of a Shakespearean actor his plea for disarmament, peace, and international understanding. Drawing freely on personal experiences, he lectured with the vividness and conviction that characterized his best writing, spicing his earnestness with wit and humor. His audiences loved it.

Traveling the lyceum circuit was fatiguing. Often there were long jumps with several changes of trains to points far between lectures, such as from Indiana to Colorado, and sometimes downpours threw the railroads off schedule, making it difficult for him to keep his commitments. Half the time he reached his destination between five and seven o'clock in the evening, bathed, dressed, gave an interview to the local newspapers, perhaps ate, rushed to the hall for his eight o'clock lecture, delivered it with an eye on his wristwatch, and rushed to a waiting taxi to catch a ten-thirty or eleven o'clock train. In Idaho he climbed out of a sleeper at three o'clock in the morning and changed cars twice to arrive in Lewiston by eight o'clock, and at dawn a sick headache began. By noon it was fierce, but an osteopath eliminated it, and despite the dopiness left by his headache, he managed to deliver his lecture. It took all his nerve not to quit in the midst of it.

Where he arrived before noon he seldom got away with only one speech. To advertise the lecture the local manager usually had booked him for an impromptu address on any other topic to a Rotary, Kiwanis, or Lions Club luncheon, to a women's club, or to a seminar at the local university. In Portland, Oregon, he talked to high school students from eight-thirty to noon, addressed a luncheon of the League of Women Voters, caught a nap, drank a cocktail at his host's house, spoke at a dinner given by Portland newspapermen, and delivered an eight o'clock lecture—altogether six speeches in one day. He wearily wrote to Inez, "I might as well be a candidate."[8]

Returning home from a lecture trip, he would unlock the front door, enter, and call, "*I-knees!*"

"Yes, Bill, dear, I'm still here," she would call down from her desk upstairs. "Nobody has abducted me or kidnapped me."[9]

Then she would rush downstairs to greet him and to hear about the bishops, publishers, mayors, lieutenant governors, and other interesting people he had met and about the funny things that had happened to him. While he was shaking hands with members of one audience, a sweet young thing had come down the reception line and complimented him. "I enjoyed your 'Seed of the Sun' so much," she said.[10]

"Very nice of you," he replied, "but my brother Wallace wrote that." Bill frequently was confused with his writing brother.

"Oh, I know," she said, "I was mixed up! You're the Japanese schoolboy."

"Brother Wallace again."

She gulped, persisted. "Didn't you do those delicious studies of adolescence—"

"Phoebe and Ernest," he said, a bit grimly. "Written by my wife, Inez Haynes Irwin."

"But you *did* do the Judge Priest stories?"

"No. Irvin Cobb."

Finally, the sweet young thing retreated. Here was the most discouraged looking back he had ever seen. This was one of his favorite anecdotes.

Between lecture tours, Bill lived a normal, stable life: entertaining guests; attending luncheons, teas, and dinners; and, in the mornings, writing. Whether in New York or Scituate, he was surrounded by six females, whom he jocularly called his "harem." Inez's two sisters, the younger Daisy and older Maude, lived with the Irwins at long stretches. Daisy had left her husband and brought along Inez Elizabeth Thompson, her little blonde charmer, whom Bill informally adopted. One or two maids and, of course, Inez rounded out the household.

Besides driving west on a working vacation with Inez in their Model T, Bill traveled to thirty-seven states to lecture in 1922. About 300,000 Americans heard him warn of the horrors of the next war and of the insidious influence of isolationist propaganda. He always closed with an appeal for international cooperation, the cornerstone of his crusade.

In February 1923, Bill ended his exclusive relationship with the *Saturday Evening Post* so that he could continue his crusade for the League of Nations in print. He told Lorimer that another periodical—unidentified but undoubtedly *Collier's*—would allow him to express exactly what he thought on national and international affairs and pay as much in a year as he had ever made writing for the *Post*. Also, he could write for whatever other markets he pleased. He hoped, "perhaps vainly," that Lorimer would continue to buy his fiction and an occasional article unrelated to politics. His relations with the *Post* had been very satisfying, he told Lorimer: "I have never had more agreeable business relations with any man."[11]

Lorimer immediately replied that he did not expect Bill to make a financial sacrifice for the *Post*'s sake or stick with the magazine if he would be happier with another. And, he said, he certainly did not expect Bill to change his political views on the *Post*'s account. He would consider any suggestions for articles or stories at any time and at any price, he said; then added, discordantly, that he could not pay very high prices.[12] Favored contributors, however, were getting several thousands of dollars for a short story and several tens of thousands of dollars for a serial.

Collier's would pay Bill up to a thousand dollars for brief pieces, but the really important thing was that he could write on issues he was burning to publicize. He had to make up for lost time. He allowed his friend Mary Austin to use his name in support of the American Indian Defense Society but declined her invitation to serve on the publicity committee. He would be too busy crusading for international cooperation.

He wrote ten major articles for *Collier's* in the next several months. Although the magazine, which had been sold to the Crowell Publishing Company after Rob Collier's death, lacked the wide influence it had boasted before the war and had about half the circulation of the *Saturday Evening Post*, it was a popular national forum. In the first article calling for international cooperation, published in the March 31, 1923, issue, Bill appealed to his fellow Americans' self-interest rather than their conscience (he had an explicitly moral appeal in mind for a book); "America! Go forth to Peace!" resounded with the Puritan zeal of an evangelist.

In another piece he depicted a composite "unknown soldier," not the one who lay beneath the stately tomb at Arlington, but the unknown genius who had died before his work had begun. "He it was whose vision would have found the formula by which men of different tribes, tongues, and creeds may get along together in this world, and whose force of character would have infused that formula with life. Had war granted him forty more years, we should have raised his sepulcher above those of kings." This unknown soldier's death, Bill believed, was the supreme tragedy of the war.[13]

For two pieces that appeared in August he drew on his lectures, articles written years before, and experiences with the Committee on Public Information to warn his readers how the menace of organized lying threatened them through the American press. Most newspapermen might have a mania for truth, "but what are they to do with a trained liar or a subtle exponent of half truths guarding the gates of information?" An editor could not ignore publicity when it was newsworthy. The modern propagandist's tricks had suddenly ceased to pay dividends, he thought. "It seems nature has endowed the human mind with a curious sixth sense for truth," he wrote, reaffirming his faith in the ultimate victory of truth over falsehood. He hoped that the mystical "sixth sense" he had himself often relied on would divert Americans from the pitfall-laden path to isolationism.[14]

By the time those two articles appeared he had been abroad several weeks. *Collier's* had sent him to Europe to report on the activities of the League of Nations. The first close-ups of the league given to Americans constituted his most significant body of magazine work since his series on the American newspaper for the same magazine. They were mostly the "Flemish paintings on a thumbnail canvas" that had been his specialty, and they reflected a deep, abiding commitment characteristic of his best journalism.

In these articles he concentrated on refuting American isolationists who said the league did nothing or who feared it would trample on the natural rights of member states. In Geneva he covered an agreement toward the regulation of international opium traffic and marveled at the cooperation among "men so widely different in background and character, meeting under circumstances calculated to raise all possible suspicion, dislike, mutual distrust." In Vienna he gathered evidence to show how the league rescued impoverished Austria by helping its government economize and build its assets. To further refute the isolationists, he told how the league had been gathering reliable commercial, health, and military statistics on member states to help them understand one another better. With information from "reliable inside sources," he revealed how the league had helped settle the recent dispute between Italy and Greece over Corfu. The pressure of publicity that forced Mussolini to evacuate Corfu may have averted another Sarajevo, Bill wrote. Indeed, he speculated, if the league had existed in 1914, there might have been no Great War.[15]

The conclusion of his final article from Europe climaxed them all. Americans, he warned *Collier's* readers, must change their image of the League of Nations.

> Call the League, as did its opponents in 1919, a dangerous super-state, aimed at the blood-bought independence of these United States, and you are talking passé nonsense. It has so far failed to perform any super-functions. It has not been able to hamper French liberty of action in the Ruhr, French and British liberty of action in Syria. Attack it because it has failed to do these things, or because it links itself too intimately with the Treaty of Versailles, and you have some logic on your side.
>
> The fact remains, however, that the League is now the one bright spot in a mad and tortured Europe—the single political nucleus of sanity and good will. Weak it may be; yet every year since its foundation has seen it stronger. After four years of existence, it is so firmly fixed in the international structure that if it did not exist, Europe would be obliged to create it.[16]

He believed that an imperfect league was better than none.

The positive work of the league was in marked contrast to the hatred Bill witnessed in France and Germany. The Germans believed that the French were committing incredible atrocities in the Rhineland, and the French believed that the Germans were preparing for an uprising. Both were fed a steady diet of lies. Greatly disturbed, he embarked for home on the Cunarder *Mauretania*.

Back home, he was spurred by the hatred he had witnessed in Europe to complete a sequel to *The Next War*. In this appeal for peace, he invoked the spirit of Christ, although he was no church-going Christian himself. He responded to ritualism and mysticism rather than to the clear, cold spirituality of Protestantism. How tragically unfortunate, he thought, that those sects whose practices most appealed to his temperament held tenets most often at variance with his knowledge of fact and his conception of social justice. As an agnostic, he could still believe in Jesus' command "that ye love one another." As an evolutionist, he could not swallow the concept of a fallen people redeemed by the sacrifice of God's own son, though he could have believed that God had sent His son to help lift a rising people. He could accept Jesus as historical fact. Man or god, He remade the world.[17]

That the churches had failed to apply His kind of love to ending war was the theme of Bill's new book, *Christ or Mars?* The United States had turned isolationist, and without its participation, the league might not be able to prevent the next war. In desperation, Bill put his dwindling hopes in organized religion, the very institution that he thought had proved "a complete, final failure" in mitigating war.[18]

Christ or Mars? which was dedicated to Inez, condemned the "righteous hatred" and "conceited nationalism" of war and chastized the churches for invoking God on their side, for bidding Christians to slay their enemies in God's name, for making what was in peace the supreme sin in war "a consecrated and glorious act." Yet it was organized Christianity, with Judaism, that "must determine the causes of war, and having found them set about to eliminate them from the human heart and from human society." The only common instrument in the world large enough and powerful enough to make men cease to want war was the church in league with the temple.

In the last chapter, he recalled looking over the ravaged fields of Pas-de-Calais in 1918 and believing that Americans could "lift mankind to a new plane of progress" by abandoning war. Five years later he found them hesitant, afraid. America was a stranger to him. "Has our soul suddenly gone flabby? Or are we only blind? And," he concluded, "what can toughen our soul, open our eyes, save that power which has wrought conversion and borne light these twenty centuries?" That power was Christ's love.

It was also Bill's last, feeble hope for lasting peace.

Reviewers commended the author for the conviction and power behind his challenging message in *Christ or Mars?* but some thought he was overly zealous. Neither the reception in the newspapers and magazines nor in the bookstores equaled that of *The Next War.* The public was more interested in Emily Post's *Etiquette* than in Will Irwin's jeremiad.

Bill continued his crusade for international cooperation in articles and lectures with diminishing fervor, frequency, and hope in 1924. Having nearly exhausted the commercial value of his war experience, he looked for new topics to meet the changing magazine market. *Collier's* purchased "Youth

Rides West," a long serial he had researched in Colorado; a tribute to his old friend Arthur Gleason, who had died of spinal meningitis; an article about the Foreign Language Information Service, which he had helped originate; and an essay about the two "Irwin Boys," written in the spirit of a josh. *McCall's*, the *Ladies Home Journal*, and the North American Newspaper Alliance (NANA) also published his pieces. In a NANA feature on authors' favorite literary characters, he included Isabel Archer, David Copperfield, D'Artagnan, Lorna Doone, Alan Quartermain, the Virginian, Sir John Falstaff, and, from his wife's *Phoebe and Ernest*, Phoebe Martin.[19] Feeling like a muckraker again, he investigated the Veterans Bureau scandal in the Harding administration for the newspaper syndicate. These and other writing jobs kept him busy most of the year.

Although he continued his friendship with Hoover, he voted for John W. Davis in 1924 because the Democrats supported the League of Nations. Refusing to abandon his ideals, if not his optimism, he served the National Council for Prevention of War as vice-chairman, a position that helped rate him blacklisting with such other well-known radicals as Inez Haynes Irwin. The big Red Scare was fading slowly, and the Irwins were regarded by the Daughters of the American Revolution and other old-line groups as parlor pink, if not fire-engine red. For requesting a fair trial for some members of the International Workers of the World (IWW) in 1918, Inez was now rated by the Tory blacklist as "an active and dangerous Red Radical." Contrary to accusations, she had not been a member of the IWW Defense Committee, but, as charged, she was a member (though an inactive one in 1924) of the International League for Peace and Freedom. In 1920 Bill may have called Lenin "the most extraordinary brain in Europe," but Bill had never been a member of the Socialist Party, although he sympathized with some of its civil rights goals.[20] He and Inez believed in social progress through peaceful evolution rather than violent revolution. The Red reputation of the Irwins was an indicator of the prevailing hysteria and conservatism.

Bill tried to refute the accusations, but his explanations probably confirmed any suspicions. Like many Americans who had no idea what was really going on in Russia, he thought that the country was "settling back from her Bolshevik jag to a more or less orderly socialized republic." Soon, he dared to predict in the liberal *Nation*, Americans would have to trade commercially with the Soviets. In his own defense, he accused some people of calling anybody they disliked a Bolshevik, which was how many conservatives regarded him.[21]

He would rather have been regarded as a playwright. The opportunity to return to the theater, his first love, arose in 1924 when he met a Chinese scholar who told him that A. E. Zucker of the University of Maryland had a copy of a literal French translation of *Pi-Pa-Ki* by an eminent nineteenth-century sinologist, Antoine Pierre Louis Bazin. Bill had known the Bazin family in Paris during the war, but they had never discussed the play. Borrowing the rare translation from Zucker, Bill had a typewritten copy made.

But how to adapt the play? It had to be rendered in more or less Chinese fashion, Bill decided, but he was uncertain how to turn Oriental symbolism into Occidental action. Also, over the years American audiences had changed, and he feared that his dramaturgic knowledge was outmoded. He was pondering these problems when he ran into Sidney Howard, whom he had last seen in Europe flying with the Lafayette Escadrille. Howard was a professional playwright and a fellow Californian who liked Chinese theater and had just the kind of expertise Bill needed. In January 1925 they agreed to collaborate on an adaptation of the play and to split all rights and royalties equally. At last, it looked as if Bill's dream of almost a quarter century might really come true.

Before rewriting *Pi-Pa-Ki*, Bill and Howard decided to adopt the fiction that the audience was the guest of a Chinese mandarin who had brought in a company of players to entertain them and that the players were using a dais pavillion at one end of the great hall for a stage. Then came the formidable tasks of translating the French interpretation of the Chinese original into a faithful English version, of condensing the day-long Chinese version into an evening's performance, and of digging out nuggets of dramatic significance from the thin symbolic action. Bill and Howard decided to omit the ballet and incidental songs of the stylized Ming dynasty rendition in favor of preserving some of the realism of a popular fifteenth-century rendition. They also omitted scenery. Bill suggested they rename the play "The Voice of Jade," the term for an imperial edict, or "The Story of the Lute," *Pi-Pa-Ki*'s subtitle.[22]

In February 1925 he temporarily dropped *Pi-Pa-Ki* to write a thirteen-part series about the furious controversy over air power then under congressional investigation. NANA assigned him to the story because his coverage of the Great War had given him first-hand knowledge of the issues and because editors regarded him as "the foremost reporter and news-writer in the United States." Although he professed impartiality, he obviously supported the campaign of Brig. Gen. William Mitchell for a united and independent air force. In his last installment, Bill injected a personal plea for limitations on aerial armament by international agreement.[23]

While working on the air-power series, he received telegrams from Brookdale saying that his father, who was eighty-one, had died of a cerebral hemorrhage. Bill could not attend the funeral unless it was delayed five or six days, for getting to Brookdale would take almost a week by train; but he did not want to go, anyway, because he believed the rumors about Hallie and Herman. He wrote to Wallace that "the situation would have been too scandalous to lend dignity to a funeral."[24] Brookdale symbolized a part of Bill's past he would prefer to forget.

*****

In February 1925, Alfred A. Knopf published the *Collier's* Wild West serial, and Bill hoped that sales of the book would take up his financial slack. *Youth Rides West*, which he dedicated to his mother, had more depth of setting and character and more complexity of plot than *Columbine Time,* his shorter novel-length excursion into the retrospectively pleasant Rockies of his childhood. This time he buried his bromidic boy-gets-girl plot under violent subplots and thickly textured atmosphere. Although *Youth Rides West* contained no character so engaging as Rosalie Le Grange (who in short stories, two novels, and a play had caught many fancies), it was his best novel, partly because he had refreshed his memory with on-site research, but especially because he had put more of his childhood past into it than into any other work.

In the story the raw, raucous civilization of Cottonwood lures Robert Gilson, a recent Harvard graduate whose ancestry dates back to "Second Cliff, Scituate, in 1633," from gold digging among the placers.[25] Gilson takes up newspaper work and falls in love with a young, though experienced woman of mysterious background who politely tries to discourage his attentions. After stagecoach robberies, saloon gunfights, lynchings, and other violent events involving a crusading newspaper editor, vigilantes, good guys, and bad guys, the virtuous (if not virginal) heroine saves the innocent tenderfoot from hanging. As it turns out, the woman is married, but by the end of the novel that is all over and boys gets girl. The story was packed with ingredients of the wild western genre.

The outstanding attribute of *Youth Rides West* was its vigor. In an exemplary scene, the narrator describes the interruption of a lynching in a saloon:

> "Drop that rope!" came a voice, a voice with a ring and carry, which seemed to dominate all the noise. . . . It seemed that everyone froze in the midst of whatever he was doing—all except the new-comer. He was a tall man with a heavy brown mustache and imperial. He wore a black slouch hat of the G.A.R. pattern; and for all his height he moved with quick, flowing certainty. He did not wait for that mood of frozen hesitation to break; in two strides he had crossed to one of the empty chairs pushed against the wall when the players dropped their game. He stepped into it, stepped just as lightly to the table, his feet crunching on chips and the spilled stacks of twenty-dollar gold pieces. As the silence began to break into sinister mutterings, he spoke again:
> "Bring that rope here—and that prisoner too!"
> Momentary silence again. He stood, his feet planted apart, a drawn revolver in his left hand—which I thought odd. It rested so, close to his body, its muzzle a little lowered. His eyes seemed to take us all in.
> The leader of the mob stood alone in the middle of the floor. He spoke suddenly:

"We'll hang a city marshal as quick as a pickpocket," he said. "Boys, bring on your rope. It's long enough for two."

"Drop that rope!" came from the man on the table, shifting his eyes, shifting slightly the muzzle of his gun.

There the leader made his mistake. The muzzle was turned away from him; he had an instant to act. His hand went to his hip. In the same instant I had a glimpse of a dozen forms beginning a prudent drop toward the floor.

I never saw the man on the table change the direction of his muzzle from the back door to the centre of the floor. The motion was too quick. I was only aware that his right hand, held flat, had brushed across his gun. The "bang" sent the crowd to the floor as a strike in howling drops the tenpins. The leader had his gun out, and no more. It dropped clattering to the floor. His left hand went to his right biceps; and he sank slowly on to one knee.[26]

The roughness of his prose was probably due less to his own inherent limitations as a writer than to his newspaper reporter's haste in composition and his aversion to rewriting. But few reviewers denied that his prose had power.

Reviewers did, however, have mixed reactions to the novel. Most of them disliked the hackneyed plot, with its trite love story, but liked the authentic flavor of life in the western mining town. One of the few who took exception to that view was a New York *Tribune* critic who thought that Irwin had not distilled the raw, researched material artistically. More typically, a New York *Times* critic thought that the frontier history raised the novel "somewhat above the ruck of merchantable Western fiction," and concluded that Irwin was a "deft and practiced writer" who in this novel did not disappoint his followers.[27] Bill was too much the reporter to ever challenge such contemporary writers as Sinclair Lewis and F. Scott Fitzgerald, but he could write entertainingly.

Youth Rides West capped his attempts to retrieve his youth in his imagination. Whatever he would publish about his childhood Leadville again, it would never be with the same intensity.

After completing the air-power series, Bill participated in a radio program, rewrote a short story about a woman driver marooned in the Rockies, began an article about the oil-rich Osage Indians, and completed his half of *Pi-Pa-Ki*.[28] The entire adaptation was turned over to Brandt and Brandt, a literary agency in New York, on the same day that Howard won the Pulitzer Prize in drama for *They Knew What They Wanted*. Bill hoped the timing was a good omen.

While *Pi-Pa-Ki* circulated among producers, he sold an anecdotal article based on his experiences covering American baseball and wartime England to a new national magazine called *Liberty*.[29] But his magazine articles and stories were producing what he considered insufficient income, he had made only two lectures for money, and his novel was selling slowly. He was worried about maintaining his comfortable standard of living. At fifty-one he sensed that he was rapidly exhausting his potential in the unpredictable game of free-lance writing. So he was especially gratified to hear from Carl Brandt, his literary agent, that Lorimer wanted to end their estrangement and do business again.

Intending to gather material for the *Saturday Evening Post*, he left Scituate in May with Inez for another motor tour of the Southwest. They drove through Pennsylvania and on through Dayton, Indianapolis, St. Louis, Kansas City, and Tulsa, pausing frequently to repair their flivver. Once he threw a rock at the Ford when it refused to respond to his cranking. He still "possessed the temper that inevitably accompanies so swift and radiant a personality," as his wife described it, though he had learned since his youth to direct it toward inanimate objects. "I try never to permit myself to lose my temper with people," he told her when she protested against a torrent of profanity. "I take it out on things."[30] Although he occasionally lost his temper with rude people in a subway or on the street, he controlled himself better than he had a quarter of a century before.

In Santa Fe the Irwins met Herbert J. Hagerman, former territorial governor of New Mexico and now federal commissioner to the Navajo tribe. Hagerman invited them to accompany him on a six-week tour of Navajo country. Both Bill and Inez were horrified by the living conditions they saw.

From Leadville, Bill sent an article to Brandt about widespread trachoma among Indian children, asking him to submit it to the *Saturday Evening Post*. He also wrote a rambling account of his tour for the *Post*, "in case the Peace Protocol is signed between me and George Horace Lorimer."[31] After that, he began an article about Indian dances for the *American Mercury*.

In an interview given to Leadville's newspaper, the *Weekly Carbonate Chronicle*, he impressed the reporter with his unaffected personality and vibrant sense of humor. The reporter noted the quiet humor in Irwin's eyes when he talked about his boyhood, and his picturesque and expressive language, often spiced with slang and colloquialisms. Several times Bill burst into hearty laughter when recalling humorous incidents. He frequently laughed at his own jokes, sometimes so hard he could hardly deliver the punch line, but people laughed with him. His wife once described his infectious laugh as an "accelerating, deepening peal, coming in bubbles, each split with a breathless gasp." The reporter for the Leadville paper had gone into the interview expecting the great Will Irwin, the hometown boy who had made good, to be an arrogant aesthete, but there was nothing "upstage" about him. "He is absolutely free from affectation," the reporter wrote, "and has none of the mannerisms popularly associated with a writer."[32]

After a visit to the South Park, where the Irwin boys had punched cattle, Bill and Inez went to Denver, sold their flivver for $335, and took trains back to Scituate, via New York City and Boston. After their trips through the Southwest, their summer home charmingly displayed their own interests in the cultures of both East and West. Their house combined American Indian, Early American, Victorian, Chinese, and modern styles in an unconventional, comfortable blend reflecting their cosmopolitan tastes.

At Second Cliff Bill's tennis outfit consisted of a white polo shirt with long sleeves rolled up to his elbows, long baggy white trousers with cuffs, and sneakers. Tennis helped to control his weight and provided a setting for a short story now and then, though he wrote about it more authoritatively than he played it.

Lorimer bought a story with a tennis motif but rejected the Indian articles because they resembled too closely other pieces he had recently published and had already accepted for publication. The articles invariably came back from magazines with—as Bill explained to Hagerman—the "parrot-like answer: 'No one is interested in the Indian.'" Some editors said the trachoma article was too controversial, and the *American Mercury*'s Mencken changed his mind about the Indian dance article. Bill considered the rejections a disaster. "I haven't had such things happen to my copy in twenty-five years," he told Hagerman. He was thankful that he had fiction "for a second string in my bow."[33]

Through the summer and autumn of 1925, however, he sold only a trickle of fiction. His consolation that year came through basking in his wife's successes. Inez won the O. Henry Memorial Prize for the best short story of 1924 for "The Spring Flight" and was elected president of the Author's Guild of the Authors League of America. (Bill served on the council.) Bill's brightest news that autumn was a letter from Hallie saying she soon would no longer require alimony.

Was he slipping behind the times? The Jazz Age, those hectic years of shallow values and short-skirted flappers, bootleg liquor and bathtub gin, fantastic paper profits and equally fantastic spending, raged around him but hardly touched him. Youth had gone wild, shattering the dainty, prissy inhibitions of his Victorian Age. He could no more embrace the new morality than he could avoid the disillusionment that had swept away the residue of optimistic indignation left by the Great War, which was, after all, more than half a decade past now. He tried to make allowances for "the natural tendencies of a middle-aged man to deplore new things" and to understand youth's gleeful assault on the old values, including some of "the mealy-mouthed hypocrisies" of the Victorian Age, but he still felt there was more "old-fashioned sin" in the younger generation than in the older.[34] It was difficult to swim against the swift current of change.

The current swept him out to sea professionally, as well as personally.

New channels of freedom in the Roaring Twenties opened new outlets for creative energy. Serious writers dealt with large sectors of life that had been taboo to their predecessors, while hacks wallowed in smut for money's sake. Slick-paper periodicals adopted the sexy personal confession piece from the wood-pulp magazines and published confessions unrelated to sex that were more indecent spiritually than those exploiting the pleasures of the flesh. At least that was Bill's view. He would have none of it.

As 1925 drew to a close he confided to his diary that he felt "up against a tide."[35] Sales of *Youth Rides West* had been under eight thousand copies during its first six months, too slow to provide a satisfactory income. He had sold only two short stories. He would receive only a consolation payment from the Baltimore *Sun* for some copy it had ordered but declined. Neither his Indian articles nor his play had sold. Lectures had added insignificantly to his income. His weight had gone up to 180½ pounds, uncomfortably heavy for his five feet eleven inches. He was sleeping later mornings and his energies were fading. It was a disappointing year and, in his estimation, his worst year professionally since 1914.

Nineteen-twenty-six began on a brighter note. In January Hallie terminated her alimony, saving him several hundred dollars a year, and NANA paid him $1,700, probably for the air-power series.[36] But he continued to have difficulty selling his copy. He lamented to his wife that all of the short story ideas she gave him sold, while his own were rejected. So he kept on writing fact as well as fiction.

In April he went to Washington to represent the Authors League of America in a hearing on a new copyright bill before the House Patents Committee. The bill, introduced by committee chairman Albert H. Vestal of Indiana, provided for automatic copyright and for worldwide protection. Bill testified that the circulation of American literature abroad was hampered by the lack of recognition given to United States copyrights, which led to misunderstandings that jeopardized the country's foreign relations. Allied propagandists, he stated, had learned that literature presenting a true picture of a nation best promoted international understanding.[37]

Occasional speeches, work for the Authors League, and frequent parties took time away from his writing, but they were welcome respites. The rejections accumulated, his income dropped, and he feared that he would have to dip deeply into his bank account of about two thousand dollars. In May he quit New York, as he told Wallace, "rather out of sorts—nothing the matter, but hog fat and corrupted by my own juices." At Scituate he winked enough stones from his yard to build a wall around the garden. "For the last month," he wrote in early June, "I have been engaged mostly in clearing an acre of land. I have worked off ten pounds and restored my sylph-like figure. But I haven't written enough copy to make a respectable High School essay."[38]

His son came and they played golf at Scituate and went sight-seeing in New York City. Billy, now twenty-one, resembled his mother more than his father, but he had untamable locks and his father's voice. Like his parents, he had an artistic bent, but favored his mother in his greater interest in illustration and painting than in writing.

Writing was a habit Bill could not easily abandon, and after his son's visit he resumed a regular schedule of writing fiction, but without enthusiasm or ambition. He often arose around five o'clock, made his breakfast of coffee and toast, and about six o'clock went upstairs to his work room, wearing a sweater against the early morning coastal chill. Late in the morning he would walk about a mile to pick up his mail. He frequently played nine holes of golf, shooting in the high forties, ate a late lunch, and played more golf or drove along the coast. When he was fired-up on a story or against a deadline, he would resume writing in the afternoon, but that seldom occurred in the summer of 1926. Severe headaches occasionally interrupted his routine, and when they struck he was too sick to work or play.

In August he began to pull out of his slump. The first sign was the sale of an often rejected manuscript to the Shrine magazine for $1,500. The second was an arrangement with Marie Meloney, new editor of the *Herald Tribune Sunday Magazine*, to write a weekly series about New York for the magazine at a guarantee of $150 per week for nine months. He knew enough about Manhattan through his walks, alone, to write a book. "I catalogued my own acquaintances in the four blocks surrounding my own house, and enumerated sixteen people whom critics would call first-raters in the arts," he wrote. "In five years, two Pulitzer prizes and one O. Henry prize for literature had rewarded inhabitants of this little acre or so, besides I know not what guerdons for music and painting." Greenwich Village, once a haven for struggling artists, had grown "clean, smart, sanitated, a trifle sophisticated" since he had first lived there, but many residents still gossiped over the back fence. The third sign of his financial recovery was the sale of a short story to *Liberty* for $1,750.[39] A few lectures in the Midwest also added to his bank account.

When he saw his name over articles and stories and especially on checks, some of his old enthusiasm returned, and he began writing a book based on articles he had written about radicals in the United States. As fear of a Communist revolution financed from the Soviet Union abated, socialistic ideas gained wider acceptance, particularly among the ranks of labor and liberal intellectuals. But he had always believed that the Red menace had been overplayed in the press and used statistical data to show that Communists and anarchists actually constituted a minute minority of the radical movement in the United States. In December he delivered his manuscript to J. H. Sears and Company. By year's end he was writing with much of his former zest.

But it was too late to prevent 1926 from becoming, in his opinion, "another rotten year." While he had earned about fifteen thousand dollars, his lowest income since 1914, Inez had made almost twenty thousand dollars, her best year yet. Her investments in securities and savings totaled $47,000, his $3,750.[40] They were still living off his earnings and saving hers; he insisted upon it.

From the beginning, 1927 promised to be a busier year than either 1925 or 1926. He agreed to write a house biography of Adolph Zukor, the pioneer movie tycoon and head of the Famous Lasky Corporation and Paramount chain, for a large payment, a royalty on bookstore sales, and the freedom to say what he pleased. And he arranged with E. H. Suydam, illustrator of his *Herald Tribune* articles, to publish the series as a book. By spring he was working on both books.

At the same time, his "cold-blooded survey of the so-called 'red' element in the United States—their numbers, their power and their methods" entitled *How Red Is America?* was published.[41] His answer was not very. With the rise in unprecedented prosperity, which he did not expect to last, he estimated that revolutionary radicalism had dwindled to no more than 1 percent of the population. Most reviewers considered his red-covered book a fair, factual, comprehensive account. A *Nation* reviewer was one of the few to note the "slipshod" analysis, but he did not challenge the conclusions.[42] The book was valuable principally as an early popular study of the radical threat in the United States.

In May, Bill was diverted from his Zukor biography to accompany Hoover south into the area in which the Mississippi River had overflowed its banks. President Coolidge had appointed his secretary of commerce to direct the relief work, and Bill went along in the official railroad car as a correspondent for *The World's Work*, a quality monthly that stressed current events. In his articles he reported Hoover's efficient and effective handling of the political and engineering problems of relief. To Bill, he seemed to work miracles.[43]

Hoover had emerged as the man who might bridge the gap between the ideals and realities of the new era. More than anyone else he exemplified the hopeful individualism of a progressive, cooperative future. He was recognized as a brilliant, efficient, and socially oriented engineer, economist, and master organizer. Many politicians were mentioning him as a possible successor to President Coolidge.

Bill first realized this on the flood relief project, but not from Hoover, who was too busy working along the levees to campaign. Although Bill admired Hoover's character and abilities, he had never considered his friend presidential material. One afternoon while they hunkered in the shade of a railroad car waiting for a report on a bridge in jeopardy up the line, Bill casually mentioned the subject. If Coolidge, who had everyone guessing about his plans, should decline to run for a third term . . . , Hoover said, then paused, and Bill asked: "You will be a candidate for the nomination?"

"I shall be the nominee, probably," Hoover said. "It is nearly inevitable."

"But if Coolidge decides to run?"

"I won't get in the way. Naturally."[44]

That night, as the official train splashed axle deep over submerged tracks, Bill lay awake in his berth comparing his political views with Hoover's. Should he support his friend? Although he had written for Roosevelt's Bull Moose campaign in 1912 and had worked for Cox in 1920 and supported Davis in 1924, political parties had not been significant in his choices. He had voted Democratic because the party's platform favored United States participation in the League of Nations, a stale issue now. Hoover had supported the league with reservations, but he had by far the closest acquaintance with foreign affairs of any American statesman. The domestic platforms of the Democratic and Republican parties were similar, and no politician would do anything to disturb the unprecedented prosperity. And Hoover had proved his skill as an administrator.

One thing bothered Bill, though. Before Hoover had accepted federal office he had occasionally taken a drink, such as a glass of wine at dinner; but he had turned dry, believing that humanity would be better off without alcoholic beverages, which disturbed efficiency, domestic relations, and morals. To Hoover, Prohibition was an experiment worth trying; but Bill had never believed Prohibition was the solution to the liquor problem. If Gov. Alfred E. Smith of New York became the Democratic nominee, Bill assumed, that party would advocate repeal. Bill weighed Al Smith against Herb Hoover, and decided that even with repeal an issue, he preferred his old friend. He did not agree 100 percent with either Smith or Hoover, but he had known Hoover for more than thirty years and had tremendous respect for him.

A couple days later he said casually to Hoover, "My hat's in the ring for you, on one condition."

Hoover's round face set, his hazel eyes hardened. Now that he was in practical politics, a condition meant a request for office. "What is that?"

"That you never offer me a political job!"

Hoover laughed.[45]

After covering the flood relief project, Bill joined his family at Scituate. He continued to work on the Zukor biography, among other things, occasionally visiting the movie mogul's estate to conduct interviews. Zukor was shy and reserved, a man who did little to create anecdote, either by pleasant folly or by flash of wit, and it was difficult to get the dramatic, illustrative anecdotes and fine, representative details a Boswell needs to recreate a Johnson. At the end of August, Bill extended his research to Hollywood.

He spent most of September interviewing people in the movie industry. One day he toured the Famous Players lot and had lunch with Kathleen Norris, Rupert Hughes, Marion Davies (with Hearst lurking in the background), and other movie notables. On other days he had lunch with Sam Goldwyn, his wife, and their small son and with C. B. De Mille. On September 14 he saw the filming of *The Main Chance* and was feted at a birthday party thrown by his Hollywood friends. He was fifty-four.

In October, *Highlights of Manhattan*, containing thirty-five of hs articles and thirty-three of Suydam's pencil drawings from the *Herald Tribune*, was published by Century. Bill's descriptions of the Battery, the Black Belt, Broadway, Chinatown, Gramercy Park, Greenwich Village, the Metropolitan Museum, the Public Library, Stuyvesant Square, Trinity churchyard, Wall Street, and other local scenes were crisply written, vivid. Writing about Irwin in the *Herald Tribune*, Elmer Davis said, "If he sees more than you have seen here and there, remember that Mr. Irwin has attained renown precisely by his ability to see it all and to give it the proper glamour in the telling."[46] Bill's affection for Manhattan was apparent. Many New Yorkers bought the book, but more readers bought William Durant's *The Story of Philosophy*, the top nonfiction seller of 1927.

Shortly before Bill's Zukor manuscript was completed, the publisher of *Highlights of Manhattan* asked him to write another biography. Now that Coolidge had ostensibly chosen not to seek reelection, Hoover was hot copy. Bill agreed to write a biography of his friend for a $2,500 advance consisting of $1,000 on signing the contract, $500 on delivery of the manuscript, and another $1,000 on the date of publication. With a deadline of February 15 of election year, he would have to rush the manuscript through in three months.

Hoover promised that it would be the only authorized biography, and early in December Bill signed the contract with Century, momentarily boosting his bank account to $12,500, his highest balance yet. After squabbling with Roy Howard over price, he accepted $4,500 from Scripps-Howard's United Feature Syndicate for the newspaper serial rights. With characteristic pecuniary pessimism, he noted in his diary, "I shan't get rich with it."[47]

Throughout December he worked hard on the book. Like Zukor, Hoover was taciturn and modest; appealing attributes, perhaps, but frustrating for a biographer. One day Bill was scrapping with him over something greatly to his credit that should go into the book. "Oh, you can write all that after I'm dead," Hoover said.

"I'm exactly your age, and you're disgustingly robust," Bill retorted. "What do you expect me to do—assassinate you? I could at this moment."[48]

The year 1927 had been an especially busy one of writing and lecturing, not to mention entertaining friends. On New Year's Eve, Bill could not recall having a single day off, including Sundays and holidays. It was his hardest working year since he had been young.

Financially, it was Bill's best year ever from writing. He earned about $28,000 and felt secure enough to send $100 a month to Billy, who was studying art in Europe. Inez's income dropped way down to around $7,000, but together they still earned a substantial $35,000. The worth of their savings and securities totalled about $60,000. Before investing more money, Bill decided he would await the outcome of Hoover's campaign for the presidency.[49]

While Bill wrote furiously against the increasing pressure of the deadline for the Hoover manuscript, his story of the rise of Adolph Zukor was published. *The House That Shadows Built* was praised for its smooth, concise prose, some of his best.[50] As he had anticipated, the book was criticized for its lack of fine detail and illustrative anecdotes. Reviewers also chided him for his uncritical portrait of Zukor. The principal value of the book lay not in the story of its hero's victories over defeat as much as in the story of the growth of the embryonic motion picture industry.

Aiming for publication of Hoover's biography in time to boost him for the nomination, Bill sent the chapters in manuscript to Washington for Hoover to scrutinize. The closer he wrote toward the present, the more crucial the effect on Hoover's political career, and the more sensitively the Chief edited the manuscript. Bill did not always incorporate Hoover's suggestions verbatim, but he usually retained their meaning. The book finally was published on March 23, 1928, in time to distribute to each delegate and alternate to the impending Republican National Convention and to other influential people.

Herbert Hoover: A Reminiscent Biography was effective campaign literature. Whatever disagreement readers might have had with Hoover's politics, they were usually impressed with his engineering. Like many reviewers, Silas Bent had his doubts "about the use of a standardizing, engineering mind in the White House," but had to admit that "Mr. Irwin's book made me feel mostly kindly toward his hero." "The effect of this volume of reminiscences is to make the personal doubts seem ludicrous," the *Herald Tribune*'s chief editorial writer wrote in a review. "By all the past here is a great public servant, peculiarly fitted to handle the problems of the present day. Unless there is a hopeless incompatibility between democracy and the engineering tradition—which is to say, between the art of public leadership and the modern breed of silent organizing doers—Mr. Irwin has written the life of a great President."[51] Other reviewers also acknowledged the author's persuasiveness.

The political build-up began with the very first sentence, a terse, thematic Irwin lead: "Herbert Hoover derives from Colonial stock." Obviously, Bill intended to paint his subject red, white, and blue. Describing Hoover's birthplace, he made an analogy between Hoover and Lincoln, not coincidentally a Republican president:

> Cedar county lies little more than a hundred miles from the country where Abraham Lincoln kept store, rode circuit, and ran for Congress. Though thirty years had passed, though crude machinery was replacing tools, though more and more the rural population was clothing itself from the country stores instead of from its own looms, the life had not changed its essentials from that which Lincoln's people lived and with which his biographers have made us so familiar. "Then," said Hoover in afteryears, "the farm produced eighty percent of what the farmer consumed—and now only twenty percent."...[52]

Bill then listed products that the farmers provided for themselves. He seemed to be trying to impress the delegates and voters with Hoover's self-sufficiency and self-reliance, two traditional American values associated with the Lincolnian image. However strained in time, place, circumstances, the analogy undoubtedly appealed to believers in the cooperative individualism of that day—although Bill was blatantly partisan in his portrayal of Hoover. As Oswald Garrison Villard of the *Nation* remarked somewhat harshly, the book was "neither critical nor discriminating."[53]

Bill's biography of Hoover also suffered weaknesses similar to those in his biography of Zukor. In later chapters especially, *Herbert Hoover* lacked characteristic details and illuminating anecdotes. In both biographies Bill had written about living and taciturn personages who had vested interests in their life stories.

The rush job on the campaign biography compounded the deficiencies; by necessity as well as desire, Bill had put a great deal of his first-hand knowledge of Hoover into the book. That technique was both a liability and an asset. More than anything else, his observations and feelings concerning Hoover brought the man to life. A later biographer of Hoover would remark that it was precisely this intimate, personal information that made the book valuable.[54]

A well-written book by a prominent a writer about a prominent public figure engaged in such a topical event as the presidential campaign was bound to sell, and *Herbert Hoover* did. By arrangement with Century, Grosset and Dunlap published a cheaper edition in March, and about the time the big bull market collapsed in June, it went into its third printing. Hoover was outdistancing all rivals for the nomination, and the book soon headed for its fifth printing. *Herbert Hoover* was on its way to surpassing the previous better sellers among Bill's books: *The Latin at War, A Reporter at Armageddon*, and even *The Next War*.

After a week's vacation, Bill took a desk at Hoover headquarters in New York, where he could work on national publicity in the afternoons after writing at home in the mornings. In June he went to Kansas City as an unpaid assistant to press representative Henry Allen, who had more experience in political publicity. President Coolidge left the question of his renomination up to the convention until it was too late, and Hoover was easily, if unenthusiastically, nominated on the first ballot. Now, Bill thought, he could return to writing full time.

But as author of the Republican nominee's authorized biography and as an accomplished public speaker, he was in demand to make speeches in Hoover's behalf. He hesitated to accept. There was no quandary about where he stood on the overriding issue of government activism, personified by the Catholic, cigar-smoking Al Smith, versus laissez faire, personified by the Quaker, teetotaling Hoover; but the emotional side issues of Prohibition and religion bothered Bill. He finally yielded to pressures to take the platform on two conditions. One, he would not defend Prohibition. And two, if the religious issue arose, he would emphasize Hoover's own statement: "I don't want anyone to vote for me because of Al Smith's religion." That resolved, Bill traveled up and down the eastern seaboard from Maine to Virginia, usually delivering a biographical tribute to Hoover.[55]

On Tuesday, November 6, 1928, 58 percent of the popular vote and 444 of the 531 electoral votes swept Hoover to victory. With him came sizable majorities to the House of Representatives and the Senate. Investor optimism bloated the bull market and stocks soared, smashing all earlier 1928 records.

Hoover voted at Palo Alto, and without returning to Washington, he began a friendship cruise around Latin America. Bill covered the tour for NANA, living in officer's quarters aboard the battleships carrying the official party and a large press corps. For him, the highlight of the cruise was the visit to his wife's birthplace. After a pleasant nightmare of Portuguese-American hospitality, he left the famous Sugarloaf, buff-colored slate roofs, brilliant green vegetation, exquisite tropical parks, and mosaic-inlaid pavements of Rio de Janeiro convinced that it was the most beautiful city in the world. Even more beautiful than San Francisco.

Bill's return to the United States ended a chaotic year in which he had campaigned for Hoover, written for syndication and magazines, and seen three books published, including one that would turn out to be his last novel. Published by Brentano's of London, *Cecilie and the Oil King* was a frothy, suspenseful tale set in a fictional part of Europe. Bill's European reputation was further recognized by his fourth major award for championing freedom abroad, this one from Lithuania.[56] Early in 1929 Elkin Mathews and Marrot of London published his biography of Hoover.

Despite Bill's professional accomplishments in 1928, his earnings dropped to about $3,400 below those of 1927, partly because he had devoted so much time to politics. But $24,570 was still a good income, and he ended 1928 with $11,000 in savings. His wife's literary slump had continued and, together, they earned about $31,000 from writing and securities.[57] Despite the drop of about $4,000 in their total income, 1928 had been a productive, fulfilling year for Bill.

Early in 1929 Bill resumed his crusade for international cooperation and peace, lecturing in Massachusetts, New York, Ohio, Kansas, and Michigan. To his favorite topic of "The Next War" he added a rejuvenated version of a worn antipropaganda lecture and the new topic of Latin American social and economic development. In the late 1920s the growing popularity of broadcast radio was cutting into the lecture business, and his crowds were neither so large nor so enthusiastic as they had been earlier in the decade. Although the tour was wearing, he returned after two weeks with the old "glow of primitive patriotism" he always felt after seeing the country and making new friends.[58]

For Hoover's inauguration, the Irwins had a ticket to the platform outside the Capitol on the House of Representatives side. In December the stock market had broken sharply, challenging investors' optimism, but recovery had been reassuring, and Hoover tended to drown out the few discordant voices on the rainy Monday of March 4, 1929, when he declared that the economy of the nation was sound. "I have no fears for the future of our country," Bill heard him say confidently. "It is bright with hope."[59] Reassured, the Irwins, like many Americans, considered it safe to expand their investments in stocks and bonds.

On March 22 the Irwins made their first of many visits to the White House as guests of the Hoovers. Bill and Inez stayed in the Rose Room and attended their first formal dinner with President and Mrs. Hoover, Secretary of State Frank B. Kellogg and Mrs. Kellogg, and other high ranking officials. Other guests included Bill's collaborator on the *Stanford Stories*, Charles Field, who had become the popular radio personality "Cheerio."

Bill was making more money from lectures than from writing, and frequent rejections worried him; but concern over money did not inhibit his generosity. He donated a hundred dollars to the Foreign Language Information Service and to the Authors League memorial fund named for his friend, the late Harvey O'Higgins. He was first vice-president of the Authors League Fund, which assisted writers in times of temporary misfortune. His generosity was almost legendary. "People were as attracted to Bill as iron filings to a magnet," Inez would remember. "His kindness and gentleness streamed to everyone. He could not, for instance, possibly have enumerated the young, back-country newspaper men for whom he got jobs in New York."[60]

In the summer of 1929 Americans were more interested in soaring stock prices and paper profits than in European problems, national bogeymen, and Latin America, so Bill fell back on old themes with new slants or didn't write at all. He and Inez escaped the doldrums at home by motoring through Canada and the Midwest. Disturbed by his ebbing creative vitality, he went to Oklahoma and Texas to gather material for an article about the new oil-rich, urban Southwest. He was back in New York in time to meet his young artist son at the dock on his return from study in Europe. In October Bill, accompanied by Inez, left on a five-week lecture tour through eastern Ohio to western Kansas.

He was in Detroit when the market began to sink. On Thursday, October 24, investors scrambled to unload, and as prices plunged, he worried about their own investments; but he was too remote from Wall Street to judge the extent of the panic. Like most people, he had no way of knowing what the crash really signified.

By the time the Irwins were back home the bull market was dead, and a major economic depression had commenced, although few people yet understood its catastrophic dimensions. Bill began selling his bonds and buying stocks. He later noted in his diary, "What a bonehead play!"[61] When he went to his bank a few days later he found a balance of slightly more than $5,700, less than he had hoped. While the press finally admitted a business depression was at hand, he tried to put his finances in order.

The crash had come too late in the year to have a marked adverse effect on the Irwins' investments and earnings, and it had been a fairly good year for each of them financially, although their combined income slipped to $28,527. Bill alone had made almost that much in 1927, when their income was $35,000. Although he considered the $19,992 he earned in 1929 a substantial sum, he did not get so far ahead as he had expected, partly because of losses on the stock market, but mainly because of remodeling their townhouse and purchasing additional land at Scituate. On New Year's day, 1930, he estimated their assets at a substantial $155,000, about half in savings and securities.[62]

Although Bill had done more lecturing than writing in 1929, he had a substantial year-end record of sales of articles and stories to such magazines as the *American, Herald Tribune Sunday Magazine, Nation, Nation's Business, Popular Science, Scribner's,* and *Tower.* By year's end, he had contributed to every major magazine in the United States since becoming a writer.

Although Bill's income had dropped from his peak year of 1927, he had done notably better in 1928 and 1929 than in some years earlier in the decade. The recent downward trend in his income, particularly from writing, reflected his flagging energy as much or more than the difficulty with which he changed with the times. Riding closely alongside Hoover had kept him in the mainstream, or at least along the bank, and from his nearsighted vantage point the future did not look so bleak as it had in some years since the Great War. Like most of his countrymen, he was concerned but not gravely disturbed by the financial depression. Few people, including his friend Hoover, suspected that it would cut deep and run long.

CHAPTER EIGHT

Man of Letters

THE opening weeks of the first full year of the Depression were busy ones for Bill. They included lecturing in New Brunswick, trying to sell Billy's art work, lobbying for reform copyright legislation, attending (with Inez) a cabinet dinner at the White House, and preparing to represent the American PEN as its president at an international congress in Warsaw. He also sold articles or stories to the *Herald Tribune, American*, and *Liberty*.[1]

It became more difficult to sell to magazines, which were feeling the financial pinch. The contracting magazine market and the worldwide business depression worried Bill, even though Hoover said the worst was over and recovery was just around the corner. The Irwins' finances were dwindling at a rate that worried Inez, too; to economize, they dismissed their cook. The one bright spot was the possibility that Brandt and Brandt had a producer for *Pi-Pa-Ki*.

This was the situation when the Irwins, with Daisy, Ebie, and a friend, sailed aboard the *Bremen* on May 20, 1930, for Europe. Before going to Warsaw, the Irwins visited England, where Bill addressed the British PEN at a dinner presided over by the international president, John Galsworthy. In Poland's parliament building, Bill optimistically told the 150 delegates from twenty-three countries that the antiquated copyright law in his country, where publishing was the fourth largest business, would soon be modernized.[2] After the congress, the Irwins explored the country.

At the end of June they met the three other members of their shipboard entourage in Paris and went sightseeing and shopping while waiting for customs to release Inez's baggage, which was delayed because she had too much jewelry. At Bon Marche, Bill bought seven pairs of gloves and Inez bought twelve scarves. If they were worried about the Depression, they did not behave like it.

Their life in Paris was a constant round of parties. They dined with Gelett Burgess, and on the quais they ran into Dosch-Fleurot, Bill's fellow prisoner in Louvain. As a famous husband of a famous suffragette, Bill addressed the American Women's Club. When a production of *Pi-Pa-Ki* seemed imminent, they cut short their trip and returned home for rehearsals.

The play opened in the Stockbridge, Massachusetts, Playhouse. Jack Kirkland, Joanna Roos, and Dorothy Willard played the leading roles, with reviewers and Broadway scouts in the audience. When the audience wept after the death scene, Bill knew he had won their sympathy. Playgoers liked *Pi-Pa-Ki*, reviewers liked it, and scouts from New York producers thought it was fine—for Shakespearean audiences, the epitome of condemnation. Producers saw no commercial value in it, for it was neither sexy nor funny. After a brief run, *Pi-Pa-Ki* closed, leaving Bill bitterly disappointed that no one wanted to produce it on Broadway.

That autumn, however, he had little time to fret over what he hoped was a temporary setback. He met his new daughter-in-law, the former Edith Eleanor Liliencrantz; lectured in Wisconsin about propaganda; spoke on the radio about child welfare; lobbied for the Vestal copyright bill; supported United States participation in the World Court; persuaded Nobel Prize-winner Sinclair Lewis to speak at a PEN dinner; and contributed to *World's Work* and the *Saturday Evening Post*.[3] Two pieces purchased by Lorimer, a Hoover supporter since the early 1920s, polished Hoover's political image, badly tarnished by his inability to end the Depression. In the capital Bill wrote for *Washington*, a Republican newspaper designed to support the party's candidates for congressional seats and state offices in the November elections and to counterattack the vitriolic barrage of Democratic news releases and speeches against the Hoover administration. But national disillusionment with Hoover's diehard individualism brought striking victories for the Democrats in the mid-term elections.

Bill was still better off than millions of Americans although his earnings had fallen off sharply in the first full year of the Depression. His income dropped by almost $8,000 to $12,172, less than half that of three years before. But he was fortunate to have done even that well in 1930. "Saturday Evening Post connection has saved my bacon," he noted in his diary on New Year's Eve. "Hope it keeps on next year. Wrote nothing this year in which I can take pride."[4]

After the copyright bill died in the Senate, Bill resigned as president of PEN to concentrate on his income-producing work of writing and especially lecturing. In the spring of 1931 he and Inez went to Knox College in Galesburg, Illinois, where he offered a course on "Writing for a Living" and delivered public lectures on his favorite topics of propaganda, the next war, South America, and Shakespeare. With his unruly hair, rimless spectacles, and rumpled single-breasted suit, Bill could easily have fit the stereotype of a professor.

Enroute home, the Irwins stopped in Chicago, where Bill gathered material at Hull House, juvenile court, and the Institute of Juvenile Research for a series about juvenile delinquency that he sold to the *Pictorial Review*, a woman's magazine.[5] His first depth immersion into the subject of crime, it would lead to the development of a new, marketable specialty, especially when public indignation against all crime rose sharply after the kidnapping of the Lindbergh baby in March 1932. Few subjects were more vital in the Depression.

It was difficult for Bill to concentrate on writing because of the desperate condition of the nation and Hoover's precarious position. Bill was shocked by the failure of the archaic banking system to prevent banks all over the country from collapsing, but he retained his Hooverish blind faith in the nation's ultimate recovery. Early in December stocks tumbled to a new low, and it looked like the almost legendary "Hoover luck" had run out for both the president and the people.

Despite the hard times, the Irwins continued their indulgent, if not lavish, style of living, though at a slower pace. In 1931 Bill's income had increased by only about $300, but at least it had not decreased, although his savings had. Unanticipated expenditures of $2,000, some to help down-and-out newspapermen, but mostly to help Billy, had depleted his savings. With no end to the tight magazine market in sight, the future looked grim.

Bill spent a great deal of personal and professional time in 1932 defending his friend Hoover. An article about the president for *Liberty* and a long feature on him for NANA were frank attempts to counteract the insidious smear books that had appeared in the last two years.[6] Authors accused Hoover of cheating the Chinese government, of oppressing coolie labor, of engaging in slave trade, of making money from Belgian relief, and of causing the execution of Edith Cavell, the heroic nurse who had helped Allied soldiers escape from German-occupied Belgium. Reporting conjecture as truth and distorting facts at will, they drew a scathing portrait that was enlarged and perpetuated by the Democrats. The popular hatred of the president wounded Bill almost as much as it did Hoover.

In June, Bill and Inez listened to the broadcast of Hoover's nomination by a dull convention in Chicago Stadium and then wired the nominee congratulations. The one issue that pierced the lethargy of the convention was Prohibition. After a debate, the Republicans straddled the question unintelligibly, angering the drys without pleasing the wets. Several days later Bill listened to the Democrats nominate Gov. Franklin D. Roosevelt of New York and adopt a wet plank.

Public opinion was running against his friend. Hoover was blamed for the decline in production to less than half of the 1929 peak, for the rise in unemployment to near twelve million, and for the rapid drop in the standards of relief. The election year would be the cruelest year of the Depression for the jobless, for the homeless, and for Herbert Hoover and Will Irwin.

Even on remote Second Cliff, Bill felt the strain of the political campaign vicariously. When he got a sick headache it now had a double rhythm, a brief slight ache followed a day or two later by a severe pain. Nothing alleviated the headaches and only age seemed to diminish their frequency, which had been almost monthly. At the end of July he had two disturbing nightmares that kept him up the rest of the night. In one dream he was elected vice-president of the United States and in the other someone was announcing to him that Hoover had been shot. Early in August he suffered a violent ulcer attack, and he stopped drinking coffee and went on a strict diet.

Hoover, too, was showing the strain. As the campaign progressed, his underestimation of his opponent turned to fear that Roosevelt would expand federal powers and to greater determination to defeat him. Bill felt that an old silent Hoover film he was making into a campaign talkie might be crucial to Hoover's campaign, and he worried that it might fail. He also wrote radio and platform speeches to rebut the Democratic publicity machine of Charles Michelson and anti-Hoover writers of editorials and books that poured ridicule, unfairly Bill thought, on the Hoover administration. Late in October he ventured into the hustings.

On election day Hoover was defeated by about seven million popular votes, carrying only six states and about 11 percent of the electoral votes. Bill was relieved. The anticipated worst had occurred. It was all over. Repeal or no repeal of the Eighteenth Amendment, the administration in office when the Depression struck was bound to lose the election. But he had hardly anticipated such a landslide.

Between the election and the end of 1932 Bill had not earned "a bean." He finished the year with $2,000 in the bank, not bad for the times, but not enough to pay the bills indefinitely.[7] Fortunately, the National Council for Women had asked Inez to write the first comprehensive history of the feminist movement in the United States, and the Irwins could fall back on that income when she collected it.

In a way, Bill had gone down with Hoover's ship of state. Despite the rarity of a sale in the winter of 1932–1933, he refused to demean himself by accepting insultingly low payments for articles. When NANA offered him only five hundred dollars for a ten-part series, he declined even though he needed the money. "Bad precedent," he thought.[8]

Late in February it looked like he might get a job writing for motion pictures in Hollywood, but the banking moratorium prevented the movie industry from acting. "Fearful sense of apprehension underlying everything as bank moratoria in the states go on like creeping paralysis," he noted. "Maybe just the final low point. Am trying to hold to that."[9] Although he expected his New York bank to close, he left most of his money in his diminishing accounts because he thought it was the patriotic thing to do. The next day he heard that his bank had closed temporarily.

In April Inez received three thousand dollars for her feminist history, *Angels and Amazons*, and became the temporary breadwinner in the family. Regretfully, Bill declined an invitation to attend the Bohemian Club camp with Hoover, who had retired to Palo Alto. "I'm pleased and touched by your invitation to go to your camp in the Grove this summer but I am afraid I cannot make it," he replied. "The situation here is bad for us writers and I have a good many people first and last to carry, and so I'm just going to stick to my desk and turn out copy."[10] Creating became more and more difficult, and in May he wondered if he was finished as a writer.

Moving to Scituate helped to restore his spirits, and he wrote mornings and trimmed the house in verde green afternoons. His weight dropped from an uncomfortable 186 pounds to 178 pounds, and through the summer he wrote with some of his old vigor. An occasional sale boosted his morale.

Liberty was his most accessible market, especially for crime articles, going back to a series he wrote about extortionists in 1932.[11] He saw himself as a muckraker against crime, although he realized that "the public taste for muckraking has been for fifteen years as dead as Julius Caesar." Still, he told Hoover, he hoped the public would want it again.[12]

As payment for articles he had written for a Hearst syndicate lagged and his bank balance dropped below seven hundred dollars, he sold his last bond, Colorado Electric Power. Unfortunately, most of the recognition he received that autumn of 1933 was honorary rather than pecuniary. His fellow Republicans elected him one of 212 county committee members in the Tenth Assembly District; the Authors Guild elected him president; and PEN asked him to represent the American Center at a London meeting of the International Executive Committee to arbitrate a critical dispute between the Paris and Berlin centers. Having only three hundred dollars in the bank that October, he went reluctantly.

The international president of PEN, H. G. Wells, briefed him in London. The French wanted to expel the Germans from the organization because the German Center had been expelling all Jews, communists, and liberals—any writers who were unwilling to support the new Nazi state. At the executive committee meeting, the president of the German Center argued vehemently that Hitler would likely modify his policy and allow dissenters to belong to professional associations. Most delegates wished to avoid expulsion of the German Center, and Bill seconded a resolution that the Germans had violated a basic principle of PEN by "interference in the political views of its members."[13] Only the German delegate voted against the resolution. Defeated, the Germans resigned and their delegate left the meeting to circulate a report that PEN had turned Communist. It took Bill weeks to remove PENs pink taint in the United States.

Following the ups and downs of the new Roosevelt administration, Bill and Hoover gloated that the New Deal was drawing vociferous opposition, but they still feared a dictatorship in the United States. "My own impression is that the policies of this Administration are today driving more clearly to Fascism and Nazism than even toward socialism," Hoover wrote to Bill in December 1933. The idea prompted Bill to write for *Liberty*'s Washington birthday issue an article, "If Washington Had Been King," which concluded with a strong hint that Roosevelt would like to "occupy the venerable throne of King George Washington!"[14]

Hoover had a more ambitious attack on the Democrats in mind. "I have had in mind some days writing you a letter as to a possible great journalistic service you might consider for the American people," he told Bill. "Incidentally I have a certain personal interest." Fearing the demise of personal and economic individualism, he objected to what he considered government attempts to stifle free speech. The administration, he charged, was trying to stop criticism of federal programs by intimidating broadcasters and newspaper publishers. It was time "to attack the attitude of a government which is not now an umpire but that of an advocate of revolutionary ideas with an enormous propaganda organization. My thought therefore was that you might through some great medium write a series of three or four articles on the subject of modern methods of propaganda, and thus while you approach the thing somewhat indirectly give it the exposure which it needs." Hoover suggested that the first part describe the methods of organizing propaganda during the war and show how truth had been subverted and deliberate lies propagated by various governments, including that of the United States. The second part would describe postwar propaganda, including "the campaign of calumny" against his administration and himself. The third part would analyze the National Recovery Administration and New Deal propaganda. According to Hoover's proposal, Bill would not only respond to the villification of the past Republican administration but also attack the present Democratic administration.[15]

Bill expected that it would be difficult to find a publisher. The "power of the government as expressed through the codes" made it "virtually impossible to get anything critical of the present administration into any first class magazine," he replied.[16] But he thought the idea might be developed into a book.

He explained the book treatment this way: "First, I don't want to be too Republican—partisan—a matter of personal temperament, plus a feeling that a cool and reasonably detached tone will render it more effective. More importantly, it should be done in such a way as to avoid making you seem a persecuted man. . . . Such an attitude puts one immediately on the defensive. This," he continued, "can be avoided by making this book a *study in propaganda*. Offhand, I think it should be opened with a dissertation on that modern technique of propaganda which was worked out in the war. This consists largely not in outright lies but in slanting and tainting the news over a long period." This was of course a subject he had lectured and written about many times. "Then," he planned, "go on to show how when Michelson was put into Washington for the purpose of making your administration unpopular, he took advantage of the popular craze for personalities instead of principles and employed the modern technique. The story follows—cold-blooded, scientific, light enough to make it interesting, even humorous in spots. But when the job is finished, the plain inference to even the most stupid reader is that you were the most maligned President in American history. In spots," he concluded his plan, "there will have to be some heavy digging—mostly in order to see how far one can go without bumping into a libel suit."[17]

Hoover liked the idea, and on May 23, 1934, Bill began laboriously researching and writing the book. The early chapters comprised a philosophical history of news, somewhat like his 1911 series about "The American Newspaper" in *Collier's*, "because some understanding of fundamental principles is necessary before the reader can perceive just how this propagandist or that gets his best effects, and also because no one has done it before."[18] The rest of the book involved events in which he had been a participant or an observer. With breaks for other writing jobs and for lecture tours, he worked on the manuscript until it was ready for submission on July 18, 1935.

Responding to the request of McGraw-Hill, Bill toned down his treatment of the anti-Hoover smear campaign, which stood out as the most partisan section. He had let his bitterness override the "cool and reasonably detached tone" he had originally intended. He softened his criticism of Hoover's severest critics and accepted a modest $1,000 advance and a 15 percent royalty. He wondered if his finances could hold out until the publication of *Propaganda and the News* in January.[19]

Bill's earnings from writing in 1935 were $8,069.38, about the same as he had earned altogether in 1934; he netted only a few hundred dollars from lectures. Fortunately his wife's savings and investments provided substantial reserves. She had enough investments to put her total liquid assets at about $63,000, which Bill considered touchable only as a last resort.[20]

After two postponements, *Propaganda and the News: Or, What Makes You Think So?* finally went on sale on Monday, January 27, 1936. Five days before, he had seen an advance copy of a New York *Times* review for January 26 and gotten a bitter taste of the criticism he could expect. The reviewer commented: "Mr. Irwin's book makes interesting propaganda against propaganda. . . . At the same time his book embodies its own fair share of special pleading. His very sympathetic and extensive discussion of Herbert Hoover's disastrous encounters with various unappreciative elements arrayed against him can certainly be called that." Bill thought that the long review was unnecessarily "nasty."[21]

He was especially disturbed by the apparent assumption that he was a professional propagandist. To him propaganda connoted falsity, and he had dedicated his book implicitly to Truth (and explicitly to the memory of Arthur Gleason). He had meant not only to defend Hoover, but also to warn that the lies perpetrated by unfair politicans and irresponsible journalists had, like Truth, a chance of ultimate victory in the free marketplace of ideas and therefore endangered freedom of the press. He feared an irresponsible press would invite government repression. He still put his libertarian faith in the responsible, professional journalist, though his faith had thinned in the last twenty-five years.

Of his twenty-seven works to appear between hard covers to 1936, *Propaganda and the News* was the most controversial. It was extensively roasted and boosted over network radio and in leading newspapers and national magazines. Entire pages about it appeared in New York literary supplements. The controversy stimulated massive publicity, but some of the criticism was too vituperative to suit him. "Practically all the reviewers leaped upon my frame for being too partial to you," he wrote to Hoover the day after publication.[22]

Reviewers often dealt with the book according to their political opinions. Republicans and Democrats alike saw the climactic chapters about the smear-Hoover campaign as the only part of the book, although they constituted a minor fraction of the total volume. Republicans praised the analysis of Michelson's caluminous publicity campaign against Hoover, and Democrats cursed it—and Hoover. Although Bill had toned down his climactic chapters, they emerged in print with vitriolic force. He accused John J. Raskob, the multimillionaire turncoat Democrat, of engineering the smear that Michelson had carried out, and blamed the press for cooperating with Michelson, Raskob, and Chairman Jouett Shouse of the Democratic National Committee. "Gutter Journalism," he called it.[23]

Reviewers in popular magazines and scholarly journals thought that *Propaganda and the News* was readable but superficial. A writer in the *Saturday Review of Literature* recognized Irwin's "narrative gift" but thought the subject demanded a "critical faculty." Although the reviewer exaggerated the deficiency, he correctly perceived that Bill's talents were more reportorial than critical. A few critics could accept the book on its author's own terms. One wrote in *Social Education*: "The author, a veteran reporter with an unparalleled experience in wartime news hunting and censorship, has set down not merely some biographical reminiscences of extraordinary interest but a philosophy of freedom of expression that it would be difficult to match for authority or cogency."[24] Professors who adopted the book for their social science classes at Princeton University and the University of Minnesota seemed to agree.

By April 3, McGraw-Hill had sold 2,225 copies of *Propaganda and the News*, which ranked with *The Next War* and *Herbert Hoover* as one of Bill's most significant books. Bill expected sales to continue, but slowly. His book was no competition for Dale Carnegie's *How to Win Friends and Influence People* or Margaret Mitchell's *Gone With the Wind*, leading sellers of that period.

During the flurry of interest in *Propaganda and the News*, Bill kept busy lecturing on a similar topic, "Stranger Than Truth," and trying to write fiction. Suddenly his articles were in demand by Universal Service, *Forum and Century, Survey Graphic, Reader's Digest*, and other markets.[25] Fulton Oursler, editor of *Liberty*, asked him to go to Kansas to do a character sketch of Gov. Alfred M. Landon, a possible candidate for the Republican presidential nomination. Bill apologized to Hoover, a prospective candidate himself, explaining that his acceptance would remove any accusation that in writing about him for *Liberty* last December, following a long silence on the subject, he was serving as Hoover's personal press agent; besides, if he did not go, Oursler would send somebody who might give Landon a big build-up.

"Landon: First-Rate Second Rater?" was a typical concise, easy-to-read *Liberty* article. For the weekly's 2.5 million readers, the editors indicated the average reading time of each piece in minutes and seconds, and the Landon article ran fifteen minutes and twenty seconds. Since the war, Bill's style had become leaner, crisper, which fit *Liberty*'s editorial requirements perfectly; in 1936 the magazine published articles by him on Congress, gambling, J. Edgar Hoover, John L. Lewis, politics, and the veteran's bonus. As a frequent contributor he received an increase in rates to $850, his first since the Depression had begun. He noted in his diary, "Maybe we eat."[26]

In the spring his Scituate neighbor and brother-in-law, Walter Haynes, died after an emergency operation for cancer. At fifty-nine, he was the youngest of the Haynes brothers and sisters, and his death, just when he seemed to be recovering, was the first break in their ranks. It reminded Bill that he was approaching sixty-three, and it frightened him. Fearing that his football ankle, which had been hurting, might be cancerous, he went to a specialist and was relieved to learn that he had only broken tendons.

After addressing the Daughters of the American Revolution, which had once blacklisted Inez, Bill brought *Highlights of Manhattan* up to date for a revised edition and, upon the invitation of Scituate's Board of Select-men, wrote a history of the town for its tercentenary.[27] In the autumn of 1936 he campaigned for the Republicans, who had nominated that first-rate second-rater Landon.

Despite rheumatism and infected teeth, Bill lectured on propaganda early in 1937 in Maine, Michigan, Ohio, Pennsylvania, and Wisconsin, speaking engagements that brought him, altogether, usually less than one *Liberty* article. With age, it was difficult to keep the ideas, stories, and articles flowing. When his son requested financial aid, he felt that he could not give much assistance. "You may have guessed that things haven't been going so well for me," he wrote to Billy from New York. "They never do for a writer past 60, unless he has been a whale of a best seller and is living on royalties and trimmings. Anything I had ahead went long ago, all except this house, which can't be sold nowadays. And I'm living on somehow from month to month, with only one object in mind; keeping out of debt."[28]

Any sense of accomplishment he might have derived from occasional sales was diminished by doubts that he could continue to produce in the future. Between Christmas and New Year's he noted in his diary, "How long it's been since I wrote anything fluently!"[29] At least Inez had been successful in 1937, with publication of *Good Manners for Girls*.

Early in 1938 his luck began to improve. *Good Housekeeping* bought an appeal for revision of outdated criminal laws and Oursler had several assignments for him, including one for a piece about Hoover.[30] Applause had been greeting the former president's appearances in newsreels, reflecting a recent rise in his popularity, and the editor needed some substantial matter to counterbalance an overload of Roosevelt material. For the first time in forty-four years of friendship, Bill approached Hoover for a formal interview.

They met in Hoover's hotel room on his next visit to New York. In the article, "Herbert Hoover Tells What America Must Do Next," revised by both Hoover and Irwin before publication, Bill depicted his old friend sitting in an easy chair, smoking a pipe, and dispensing advice. "Our first job," he quoted Hoover, "is to get twelve or fourteen million unemployed men and women out of misery and back to work—and at productive jobs in industry, not sad, underpaid, fruitless WPA jobs. They must be jobs that are paid at the rate of private enterprise and not at the rates of relief. Every sensible person should agree to that." When Hoover mentioned that the consumer was jittery, Bill, as a consumer himself, readily agreed. "I've decided against that new summer suit," he quoted himself.[31]

In the autumn he spent most of his time working on an article about the liquor interests for *Scribner's* and the *Reader's Digest*. In a thorough investigation reminiscent of his reporting about the Prohibition issue for *Collier's*, he traveled through the Midwest and East, and found the Anti-Saloon League and the Women's Christian Temperance Union as zealous as they had been in the early twentieth century. They hoped that section by section the country would turn dry again by 1950, with enforcement by local officials. Bill concluded that the drys would find less outside support and more competition than they had found in their previous, temporarily successful battle for Prohibition.[32]

On Christmas Eve, Bill impatiently looked forward to payment from the *Reader's Digest* and wearily looked back on 1938. It had been a busy but difficult year, financially and physically. Despite his deteriorating health, he had continued his usual round of meetings, teas, dinners, parties, plays, movies, golf, visits with Hoover, and of course writing. But he was no longer a tireless walker, and his once-regular Sunday strolls were less frequent and shorter. His blood circulation was poor, arthritis and varicose veins bothered him, and his heavy, bulky hearing aid worked poorly, though he could follow the Munich crisis and the war news on the radio. At home in the evening, he would get up from his easy chair with effort and say sardonically to his harem, "Well, the world's most pathetic invalid will now go up to bed."[33] In public, however, he tried to conceal his ailments.

In the spring of 1939 his earnings were so low that he and Inez considered selling their real estate. For the first time, Bill asked Hoover for financial advice, and when he suggested that they wait until the poor market improved, they decided to hold on to their property, a decision not without cost to Bill's pride. For the first time in twenty-three years of marriage, Inez contributed directly to his bank account, from which he paid the household expenses.

Hoover came to the rescue with a proposal to *Liberty* for a series on Allied and enemy propaganda aimed at Americans before the United States had entered the Great War. At Palo Alto he had endowed the largest collection of war propaganda in the world, and no newspaper or magazine had yet tapped the millions of books, documents, and other items. With another war raging in Europe, *Liberty* editors expected that foreign governments would use similar tactics to drag the United States into the present conflict or to keep it out. Bill went West on the assignment.

San Francisco was "the same romantic don't-give-a-damn city that it always was," he told a reporter.[34] Although the city hadn't changed, its adopted son had. His neck was fleshy and creased, and his bushy auburn hair sprinkled with gray. At a dinner his hosts sang the "Hamadryads" and the "Son of a Gambolier," reviving fond memories, but they were only that. No longer a roistering blade, he was struck by how age, marriage, and experience had changed his life. He saw his son, now divorced, spent a week at a desk in the Hoover War Library, and went to Scituate to write.

Late in August, Bill heard on the radio that the Germans had arranged to sign a nonaggression pact with the Soviets, and on September 1 Hitler's army marched into Poland. Twenty years before, Bill had predicted the development of a system like fascism, but he had assumed that the leaders would emerge from the hereditary aristocracy of Europe and its close ally, the large industrialists. He had not suspected that the leaders would be a chunky Italian journalist and an Austrian paper hanger and that their palace guard would consist of an element similar to American thugs and gangsters. He speculated on the imminent entry into the war of the British and French, and wondered if the isolationist United States would join them again.

While low-flying Navy blimps patrolled off the Scituate cliffs, he kept up with developments in Europe, wishing he was over there covering them. He was burning to write about the war, and he suggested to King Features syndicate a regular summary of the diplomatic, economic, and military aspects of the situation abroad, written from his own point of view. The syndicate did not buy it. At sixty-six, Bill was of a past generation, the Great War generation. He was an old war horse, and the demand was for young lions with energy and contemporary perception, if not seasoning, to cover the new war. An anachronism, he was venerated for his accomplishments rather than for his promise.

In the autumn of 1939 Bill renewed his acquaintance with an Allied spy he had met when he had directed foreign propaganda for the CPI. Between 1914 and 1917, the exploits of Captain Emanuel V. Voska's counterespionage organization of American Czechs and Slovaks had ranged from the capture of a dynamiter to the confirmation of the proposed German-Mexican military alliance against the United States. Voska's exploits in Austria, the Orient, Russia, and America were mentioned in twelve books, but none of the authors knew how he had accomplished his feats. Bill persuaded Voska to reveal the details in memoirs that they would write together.

Wesley Stout, Lorimer's successor at the *Saturday Evening Post*, was skeptical of Voska's credibility. But after Bill assured him that they would carefully check their facts, he agreed to pay $3,000 an installment for the memoirs. Now Bill felt he could afford to turn in his inadequate old carbon hearing aid for a bulky but sensitive new model. After completing the seven-part series, he turned to revising it for a 120,000-word book.[35]

Upon publication of the second installment of "Spy and Counter Spy," Bill was summoned to the chambers of Judge John Knox, who as a federal assistant district attorney had prosecuted a dynamiter whose plot to blow up a bridge had been uncovered by Voska's men. Judge Knox had proof of major inaccuracies in the report of the dynamiter's arrest, discrediting

Voska's principal source of information. The revelations stunned Bill, and he wondered what other inaccuracies had not been discovered. He informed Stout and changed possibly questionable information from the discredited source in subsequent installments.

Soon after Bill had been invited to deliver the commencement address and to receive an honorary degree at Knox College, he received a letter from a former FBI agent, mentioned in the second installment, who objected to statements by the authors. Feeling unworthy of the honors from Knox, Bill offered to cancel his commencement address, but the trustees decided to proceed as scheduled.

On June 12, 1940, Bill delivered his address, "Thoughts in a Crisis," in the Central Congregational Church of Galesburg.[36] Speaking with conviction, he warned of the crisis facing the United States so long as the Nazi menace threatened democracy. As long as the new graduates' freedom was threatened from without, he believed, it was also threatened from within. It was an old theme for Bill, told in the new context of the times, based on lessons of the past.

He cautioned that if the graduates permitted the government to regiment and regulate them by fiat, even for the brief term of a war, their nation might be saved but their national soul lost. Important to the retention of their national soul was freedom of the press and of speech, he said. He believed that insincere propagandists would try to wield that freedom as license.

The great dilemma arose in answering the question:

> Shall we in this time of public danger grant absolutely free speech to men who are agents for governments which, although they are not actually at war with us, are preparing the way and who are professedly inimical to the whole American system? . . . I for one hope that we may solve it without a popular epidemic of witch-hunting and especially without persecution of wholly innocent people who happen to have in their veins the blood of races whose general behavior we dislike. I could even spare a hope for innocent and harmless dissenters, since without some dissent there is no democracy. But as we struggle with those problems, remember that any censorship over press and speech may be the first step toward a regimented people and a totalitarian state.

Building toward his conclusion, Bill acknowledged that his generation had not been alert to challenges to freedom. "We grew careless of the faith; we took our freedoms for granted. . . . We on our part had in 1917 and 1918 a temporary flare-up of the burning faith our forefathers knew; and then we let it die down to embers. It is the time now to dedicate ourselves anew to the ideal which freed men once and will free them again."

Bill was confident that the Axis dictators could not conquer the United States by arms, but could they conquer America in the spiritual sense? It depended wholly on whether or not Americans meant their professions of loyalty to democratic ideals. "If we hold fast to our external principles, we shall be the rock on which a brave new world rebuilds itself," he said, drawing to a conclusion. "That, class of 1940, is the adventure to which life is calling you. . . ."

After his speech, Bill was presented the degree of Doctor of Humane Letters.

In Manhattan, problems regarding the Voska series had been sufficiently resolved for Doubleday, Doran to go ahead with book publication, when another ghost materialized. A figure in the fourth installment strongly objected to accusations that he had almost carried out a plot to blow up the Welland Canal. On Bill's recommendation, the *Saturday Evening Post* issue containing the final installment also carried a statement by Voska correcting errors in his memoirs. Bill revised the page proofs for the book to avoid making the same mistakes twice.

He was at Scituate when the first edition of 2,750 copies of *Spy and Counterspy* came off the press after Labor Day.[37] Sales were considerably slower than what the publisher had expected: by Thanksgiving only 1,185 copies were sold. Readers preferred such books as Osa Johnson's factual *I Married Adventure* and Richard Llewellyn's fictional *How Green Was My Valley*, which headed the best seller lists in 1940.

In 1940 Bill took an intense interest in the presidential campaign, feeling an involvement similar to what he had felt in the elections of 1928 and 1932. He wished Hoover was running again, he said in a letter praising a speech the former president had delivered over radio. "And God knows I wouldn't want to wish the presidency on any man in these days," he told Hoover. "But at this moment I'm thinking as an American citizen, not as a personal admirer."[38]

Hoover was deeply touched. "One comes to realize more and more as time goes on that the only substantial values that one accumulates is such friendship as yours," he replied. "Loyalty and friendship are the greatest gifts a man can have, and I have had a full measure of them from you."[39]

On election day Bill was too excited to work, and "with considerable thrill" he voted a straight Republican ticket for the first time.[40] When Roosevelt won a substantial victory over Wendell L. Willkie, Bill felt that the nation was doomed. The poor market for his kind of copy may have contributed to his feeling that America was on the road to ruin.

After an arduous cross-country lecture tour, Bill had little else to write but his own memoirs, which his agent thought could be sold "with ease."

To gather material about his childhood, he took short trips to upper New York state. When he came to the years when he had written his first books, he took down off a shelf at home *The Picaroons* and *The Reign of Queen Isyl* and read them for the first time in thirty years. "Curiously uneven work," he thought; "and in spots don't even recognize my own writings. Awfully dated. But often vivid reading at that. Picaroons pinches out at end."[41] Looking back on his life gave him a new perspective on opinions and conclusions he had formed on the spot many years before. Reconsidering his criticism of newspapers thirty years before, he thought now that he had been correct. The American newspaper of 1941 was certainly not perfect, no more than its readers were perfect, but, with some exceptions, the contemporary newspaper was no longer a slave to its advertisers, for the enslaved newspaper had nothing to offer them. Commercial common sense had prevailed, much as he had predicted. Remembering, sometimes inaccurately, consulting his own articles and books, and referring to diarylike letters he had written to Inez, he kept on writing, while Bernice Baumgarten of Brandt and Brandt tried to get him an advance from a publisher.

Lacking exercise, Bill let his weight soar to an unhealthy 186 pounds by December 7, 1941. On that date the three-year debate between isolationism and internationalism abruptly ended in the United States with news that the Japanese had attacked Pearl Harbor. Bill's emotions seemed paralyzed. For the first time in his life his own country had been attacked, and without warning—just as he had once suspected it might happen.

Unexpectedly, no publisher could be found for his autobiography. Editors thought that the writing in his early chapters was garrulous and flat and that his story smacked too much of the armchair reminiscences school. Although editors agreed that his career had been colorful and interesting, they thought it was too remote to reach a wide market. In a way, his own life was the point of contention, and the rejections were personal as well as professional affronts.

Emphasizing what he had seen and experienced, and avoiding intimate personal details, he wrote his way through the Great War to the peace negotiations. In retrospect, the Conference of Versailles had resembled a group of "brilliant lunatics trying to solve a new problem in higher mathematics." He thought that Wilson had tried to cover up his declining health by maintaining a hard and fast position when he should have agreed—as Hoover had argued—to changes in the treaty to conciliate the British. Bill thought Wilson had taken too firm a stand against relatively minor changes in the Covenant of the League of Nations to compromise with the Senate and obtain passage of the treaty. He recalled the summer of 1923, when he had been traveling in Europe for *Collier's*, and how inflation had turned German money into wallpaper. Now he could see that the inflation had contributed to the downfall of the infant republic and to the rise of Hitler.

To Bill, the Nazis had been "a lot of brilliant but somewhat delinquent children who had formed a Boys Republic and conducted it without any supervision or advice from experienced elders." He took down from a shelf his favorite book by himself, *The Next War*, and reading it again, he felt "a humiliating sense of its imperfections." But he had prophesied the blitzkrieg, mechanized warfare with tanks of the power, size, and speed unknown in 1922, a longer range and greater payload of airplanes, mobilization of whole populations for war work, incendiary bombing of cities, and unprecedented devastation.[42]

By the end of April 1942 Bill's memoirs had been rejected by eight publishers. On May 19 he heard that the ninth, G. P. Putnam's Sons, would publish it if he would cut it to a reasonable length to meet the exigencies of economics and restrictions on supply of paper. Putnam's offered a meager one thousand dollar advance against a royalty of 10 percent to five thousand copies and 15 percent on additional copies.[43] On Brandt's advice, Bill accepted.

Cutting 270,000 words in almost nine hundred pages to publishable length was a formidable task. With suggestions from Inez, he eliminated all the chapters about his childhood and youth and began his manuscript as a twenty-one-year-old freshman at Stanford. That left 215,000 words. Instead of ending in 1933, where his original manuscript stopped, he ended in 1928 on the Latin American tour with President-elect Hoover. He was cutting and revising in his dreams.

He finally convinced John Timkin of Putnam's to allow him 200,000 words, and in July he sent his manuscript to Timkin in New York and notified Bernice Baumgarten. "Whew!" he wrote. "Traditionally, putting a book to bed is like childbirth. This time it was a Caesarian."[44]

He now had more time for other activities, such as presiding over the Scituate Common Council. The harbor town had changed. Gasoline rationing and the rigors of wartime train travel had reduced the number of visitors, and former regulars such as Franklin P. Adams, Sam Adams, and Burgess were rarely seen at Second Cliff anymore. At night, shore lights and town lights were dimmed. Otherwise, the pattern of Bill's life there remained much the same. He wrote mornings and relaxed the rest of the day and worried about where his next dollar was coming from.

He was collaborating with Thomas M. Johnson on a book about spies and saboteurs for W. W. Norton's successful series about "What Every Citizens Should Know," when his red-bound autobiography, *The Making of a Reporter*, went on sale in November 1942. It was dedicated to his son, who was serving in the Army Engineer Corps. Since reading proofs, Bill had dreaded the reviews, and they did not surprise him.

They ranged from extremely favorable to harshly critical, but even those reviewers who disliked his writing had only admiration for his character and career. Oswald Garrison Villard admired all three. "It goes without saying that this volume is delightfully written," he commented in the *Saturday Review of Literature*. "Indeed it is Will Irwin at his best, and that means a very great deal. It is modest, unassuming, full of humor, and contains that sane judgment of men, women, and affairs which made him for so long one of the most valued and distinguished of our popular journalists." "The making of a reporter in this case included the development of a seeing eye, a discriminating mind and a lucid style," a New York *Times* reviewer commented. Ellery Sedgwick of the *Atlantic* wrote: "Will Irwin is a lovable man believing in his friend Mr. Hoover, through the very thick and the extremely thin, to have a kindly word even for President Harding, to damn the sin and love the sinner. He has lived a good life, a mad life, a successful life, and the record of it is a captivating peep-show of an age that is past." Not all reviewers were so kind. "There are not only gaps and incomplete appraisals," Stanley Walker unsparingly pointed out in the *Herald Tribune*, "but the writing is diffuse, windy and often downright trite." A colorful life colorlessly presented, another reviewer thought, and lamented: "His book makes one regret so much experience was so badly wasted."[45] One of Bill's closest friends had the final word:

"You didn't put enough of yourself into it," Jack Cosgrave told him kindly.

"I couldn't," Bill explained to another friend.

> After it was finished, I realized that no one with even rudimentary instincts of gentility (how old-fashioned that word, and the sentiment it expresses, by the way!) can write a really satisfactory autobiography. Unless one follows Pepys and leaves it, unprinted, for posterity, there are a thousand things about himself and other people that he'd blush to write. The only really good autobiographies—Pepys again excepted—have been done by men with a touch of so-and-so in them. So I had to be merely objective. But of course, my mania for experience plus the trend of my luck at least gave me interesting things to write about objectively.[46]

The Making of a Reporter was an appropriate title for his autobiography not only because he had emphasized his journalistic career, largely omitting his literary aspirations and his personal life, but also because he had written it as a reporter, focusing on the events he had witnessed and especially on the people he had known. His relatives and close friends agreed with Cosgrave that Bill had withheld far too much of his own charm and gaiety from his book. Not the least introspective, he had also withheld the dark, intimate side of his feelings and thoughts, the side that few people realized existed.

For weeks after publication of his autobiography, reviews continued to appear in newspapers and magazines, and he touted it at book luncheons and on radio programs. The day an advertisement for it appeared in the *Times* a newspaper strike curtailed circulation, contributing to what Bill regarded as disappointing sales. After a month, three thousand copies had been sold.

Early in 1943 Bill discovered that working on both a history of the Dutch Treat Club and the spies and saboteurs book under the pressure of deadlines was more than he could handle at sixty-nine. The manuscript of *What You Should Know About Spies and Saboteurs* had to pass through government censors and then parts had to be rewritten, and for the first time in his life he became confused over a manuscript. But he managed to complete his parts of both books in time for publication that year.[47] Then he turned to helping Hoover with his memoirs.

Bill was painstakingly polishing Hoover's prose on Thursday, April 1, 1943, when he began feeling ill. At first he thought it was acidity, which had occasionally bothered him since the advent of his ulcer several years before. During the night he vomited three times. Although he felt wretched the next day, he kept his engagements for a luncheon at the Players Club, a rehearsal for a radio symposium, and the broadcast itself. He was standing at the microphone broadcasting when "something like a sliding door," as he described it, "hit my heart from the right."[48] That night he vomited again and felt pain in his arms, shoulder, and chest, which he recognized as symptoms of heart trouble. In the morning he told Inez, who called in his physician.

Dr. Edmund Devol preliminarily diagnosed Bill's trouble as a coronary occlusion, which was later confirmed by tests. Inez had feared worse. She was also relieved to learn from Hoover that Bill's medical expenses were covered by the insurance fund of the Commission for Relief in Belgium. Bill recovered at a normal rate, and after several weeks in the hospital was taken home in an ambulance.

Convalescing in Manhattan and then Scituate, he caught up on his reading, wrote some, dug dandelions out of the lawn, and followed war news that stirred memories of World War I. His country was enmeshed in the biggest crisis the world had ever known, and he was confined to isolated Second Cliff, feeling "a million miles from the world."[49] The only visible sign of war was an occasional convoy out at sea.

After seven months of convalescence, Bill had a physical examination in Manhattan, and his heart beat was soft and strong and regular. To be safe, he had to live carefully for several more months, but some restrictions were lifted. "Unless you make a damn fool of yourself," one of his physicians told him, "it's a certainty that you won't die of your heart."[50]

Bill was going to bed around nine o'clock on January 7, 1944, when he received a telephone call from the United Press. "Mrs. Hoover dropped dead at seven-thirty tonight," the caller said bluntly. "Will you turn us out a column of appreciation right away and telephone it in?" Wanting to cry, he wrote busily for an hour. Lou Henry had been only six months younger than himself, and they had been in the same class at Stanford. He spent another half hour phoning in his eight-hundred-word story, revising it as he talked. "Seemed quite like old newspaper days," he wrote to his son, "and with all my grief—I'd known Lou Henry for 49 years—I felt bucked up to think that I could still do a rush, emergency newspaper story."[51]

Through 1944 Bill did occasional hack jobs, followed the progress of the war, and attempted to keep up with his son's whereabouts. After camouflaging airfields on the Pacific Coast, Billy, now forty, had been moved to a camp near Spokane, and Bill wrote for more information to his bride, the former Susan Grace Benteen. Much of Bill's income came from writing for the Republican Central Campaign Committee and from sales of miscellaneous earlier works. The army bought the right to publish fifty thousand copies of *The Making of a Reporter* in hip pocket editions, and amateur theater companies occasionally paid small royalties on *Pi-Pa-Ki*. Howard had died in August 1939, and Bill split the money with his collaborator's estate. For eight performances at Carnegie Tech he received $33.75, which prompted him to remark sarcastically, "Playwriting sure is profitable."[52]

Since *Pi-Pa-Ki* had been staged at Stockbridge more than fourteen years before, dozens of prospective Broadway producers had read and rejected the play or, failing to meet the high standards demanded by its authors, been rejected themselves. Then in 1944 Michael Myerberg, producer of the 1943 Pulitzer Prize-winner by Thornton Wilder, *The Skin of Our Teeth*, wanted it. With a musical score, he thought, *Pi-Pa-Ki* would make a great starring vehicle for actress Mary Martin, who had risen to fame singing "My Heart Belongs to Daddy" on Broadway and starring in the comedy *One Touch of Venus*. Shortly before Thanksgiving Day, Bill sold the theatrical rights.[53]

Because the play was too long, he had to eliminate some scenes and condense others, resisting Myerberg's demands here, compromising there. From the beginning of their collaboration, Bill was concerned that the musical production would sacrifice the humanity and tenderness of the story for spectacle. What he wanted was "a golden mean" between spectacle and story, he told his agent.[54]

Revising *Pi-Pa-Ki* and other writing kept him busy through the winter of 1944–1945. At Scituate that spring, he felt so physically fit that he forgot about his heart and his seventy-one years and overexerted. Late on Monday afternoon, May 21, a second heart attack knocked him off his feet. Although this attack, a thrombosis, was lighter than his occlusion of two years before, it was a stern warning to avoid exertion. He wondered if he could stand the pressure of rehearsals.

About four weeks after his heart attack, his "parole board" allowed him to sit in a chair and work on his latest project, a book of letters to Kermit Roosevelt from his father when TR had been president.[55] While Bill was convalescing at Second Cliff, some two thousands miles away in San Francisco the two hundred representatives from forty-six nations, who had been meeting since shortly after FDRs death in April, signed the United Nations covenant, establishing general principles of international decency and human rights. Bill regarded it as a personal victory. "What a triumph for us old boys who went down with the League of Nations!" he noted in his diary.[56]

He felt no sense of triumph, however, when on August 6 he heard that the United States had dropped the first atomic bomb. The news of Hiroshima appalled him. He felt no elation in the certainty of victory. Rather, he feared that "this thing, with man's imperfect nature, means the end of civilization. I saw the tendency begin at second Ypres, April 22, 1915," he recalled. "And it has gone the course I feared. Much disturbed."[57]

In the autumn Bill went to New York for rehearsals of what was now called *Lute Song*. On his first day, Myerberg and Mary Martin asked him to rewrite a couple scenes. The producer wanted the prologue rewritten to take into account the atomic bomb. Miss Martin, who played the wife of the hero, wanted the ending changed so she would not seem to share her husband with the princess, thus changing *Pi-Pa-Ki*'s emphasis on filial devotion and piety to marital fidelity. Although furious, Bill rewrote the scenes.

Directed by John Houseman, *Lute Song* opened in New Haven two weeks before Christmas, and bombed. After improvements, the show received enthusiastic responses in Philadelphia and Boston. On February 6, 1946, the company of eighty opened on Broadway.

Bill sent flowers backstage to the feminine leads, Mary Martin and Helen Craig (the princess), and waited. Thrilled and nervous, he peeked through the curtain of the Plymouth Theatre to watch the first nighters, among them Claudette Colbert, Beatrice Lilly, and Hoover. When the overture ended and the house lights dimmed, Bill took a position standing at the back of the theater, behind the audience.

Through words and music, *Lute Song* told the story of a young husband (Yul Brynner), who responds to the emperor's edict that all the young men of learning go to the capital to take examinations for the exalted imperial service. Young Tsai-Yong goes reluctantly, leaving his blind father and aging mother in the care of his beautiful wife, Tchao-ou-niang (Martin), and taking his lute. Upon winning the examinations, the husband becomes chief magistrate, and the emperor (McKay Morris) forces him to marry his daughter, Princess Nieou-Chi (Craig). The emperor prevents him from sending money back home, and his parents die of age and starvation; Tchao-ou-niang sells her long tresses to give them a decent burial. Instructed by the gods, she goes to the capital as a beggar and holy pilgrim to tell her husband of his parents' death so that he may perform the rites to bring their souls to rest. A Genie gives her the lute, which she gives Tsai-Yong to identify herself. And in a climactic scene, Tsai-Yong, Tchao-ou-niang, and Princess Nieou-Chi confront each other, and the princess finally relinquishes her claim to the young magistrate. Touched by "this unique tale of filial piety," the emperor revokes his imperial decree binding his daughter and Tsai-Yong together. With the husband and wife singing the final bars of "The Lute Song," the play ends.[58]

The applause was thunderous. "Cast rose to the occasion and played in rare form," Bill noted with pleasure.[59]

But the first reviews were disappointing, with only the *Herald Tribune*'s favorable. Reviews could kill a Broadway show, and Bill and the cast felt depressed. As he had feared, spectacle—especially Robert Edmond Jones' masterful designs—had smothered the story.

As *Lute Song* continued its run, the harsh criticism of opening night began to moderate. Lewis Nichols of the influential *Times* hedged on his scathing evaluation of opening night, and conceded that though the ingredients had not been blended, the show "deserves respect." The magazine critics tended to agree. "There should have been less spectacle or less story," *Time* summed up the problem. The production seemed to be too Chinese or not enough Chinese. But George Jean Nathan of the *American Mercury* dissented, charging that *Lute Song* was too delicate for the tastes of New York critics. If the critics had to swallow Chinese drama in any form, he said, they seemed to favor it in Picadilly or Broadway caricatures. He disagreed with the criticism that the elaborate costuming was out of key with the story's simplicity. The theater could, he believed, stand something more elevated, more imaginative, more beautiful than the standard theatrical fare of *Born Yesterday* and *Dream Girl*. Of show biz, Bill thought, "This is the damnedest game!"[60]

For four weeks *Lute Song* did well at the box office. Bill's share of the royalties apparently amounted to several hundred dollars a week when the show was doing well. When Lent affected attendance adversely, he took a 50 percent cut in royalties to help keep the show running.[61] Attendance recovered, and the show ran more than 130 performances on Broadway. Then with a new cast, featuring Dolly Haas as Miss Martin's replacement, the show toured the Midwest, including Chicago. Eventually, the road company worked its way west to San Francisco, where *Lute Song* had begun to take shape in Bill's mind almost fifty years before.

Arriving in San Francisco on Tuesday, November 26, 1946, Bill was immediately caught up in the ballyhoo. Glowing stories appeared in Hearst's *Examiner*, once his arch foe, and in the *Chronicle*, where he had started in daily journalism. The *Chronicle* identified him as the author of "The

City That Was," calling it "one of the great virtuoso performances of American journalism." As usual, the press treated him, in the words of one reporter, as "a long-lost son returning to his native heath after an unconscionable absence."[62] Because of his fragile health, he was accompanied around town by his son.

Despite fog and a dreary drizzle, the first night audience arrived at the Curran Theatre early, almost filling the house. During the performance Bill sat alone in a box near the stage and observed the enthusiastic reception. The reviewers and other members of the audience especially liked the visually exciting costumes and the lavish sets. It looked like the play was off to a good run; but in New York a few days later, he heard that *Lute Song*'s box office had declined. It looked like a "tightwad Christmas."[63]

Bill began 1947 with $3,500 in the bank, much of it earmarked for income taxes. Payments came in for a Union League Club history he was writing and from *Lute Song*. A successful production in Stockholm and prospects for a production in London raised his spirits, but his ears and ulcer bothered him so much it was difficult to write steadily, with self-discipline. When *Lute Song* ended its transcontinental tour in Washington, D.C., he and Inez went down for four performances; Bill thought that Brynner had improved and that the rest of the cast could have performed better. On the way back, the train lurched while he was dining with Inez and he fell into the aisle of the diner, but he was not hurt.

Small disasters seemed to mount. A replacement part for his hearing aid broke, leaving him deaf; an infection spread to his Caporetto ear; his eyes bothered him, making reading difficult; and his weight rose to an uncomfortable 187 pounds. On October 25, 1947, he jotted down in his diary: "life too much for me!"[64]

On Sunday, January 18, 1948, the Irwins entertained Bill's regular physician, Dr. Devol, and two other dinner guests, and they passed a pleasant evening. Dr. Devol left at nine o'clock, and when Inez returned to the living room after seeing him to the door, Bill was standing. "Are you tired, Bill?" she asked.

"A little," he said.

"Then you must go straight to bed." She took him upstairs, helped him undress, and rejoined her guests.

After Emanie Arling and Dr. Michael Heidelberger, the other guests, had left, Inez went back upstairs. Bill's speech had thickened and she could scarcely understand him. It terrified her, but she noticed that he moved his hands and legs easily.

She had no idea where Dr. Devol might be, so she called another local physician, who recommended a Dr. Keating, a local heart specialist. While she tried unsuccessfully to call Dr. Keating, Bill fell asleep peacefully. He had no fever and his color looked normal.

In the morning Dr. Keating came in and, puzzled by the attack, tested Bill for paralysis. "This is not a stroke," he said definitely to Inez.

Bill's voice soon cleared up.[65]

On the following Sunday he suffered another attack, which Dr. Keating diagnosed as a cerebral spasm. Again Bill's condition improved, but Daisy and Inez wisely insisted upon babying him and they developed a routine. Inez would get up earlier than usual and turn on the heat all over the house and pick up the *Herald Tribune* at the front door. While Bill lay in bed reading the newspaper, she might draw his bath. She would permit him to bathe one day and to shave the next, but never do both on the same day. She always helped him dress. Daisy, meanwhile, would arise early and cook his breakfast before the maid arrived. After eating breakfast in bed, he would smoke Sanos and finish reading the newspaper. He avoided going downstairs. After breakfast he went from his bedroom at the front of the house to Inez's room at the back, where he wrote at a large desk in the sunlight. Inez had a trayful of sharpened pencils ready for him on a small table near the desk, just as she saw to it that his cigarettes and matches and a clean ashtray were always on his bedside table. At intervals she would come in and lead him to the easy chair beside another small table supplied with books, magazines, and his smoking things. If he seemed tired, his lunch or dinner was brought to him, but he usually felt like going downstairs to the table. He had a good appetite. Returning to the bedroom floor, he walked like a small child, bringing one foot up from the lower step to the upper step, resting a moment with both feet flat on the step, and then carefully going through the slow process up another step, and then another, until he reached the landing. Inez watchfully rationed his stair climbing.

In the middle of Thursday night, January 29, he suffered another attack. When Inez came into his room, she found him prostrate on the floor. Apparently he had tried to get out of bed. Unable to lift his almost 190 pounds of bulk, she put blankets on him, and he soon rolled over in them. Frantically, she turned aside to call a physician. When she turned back, Bill was scrambling to his knees. She helped him into bed and covered him, and he fell into a natural sleep. Dr. Keating came in the morning.

During the next few days, Bill improved enough to get out of bed and write for half a day. He even felt well enough to venture out two or three times for cigarettes and to his tailor and the Union League Club. One day Inez took him to the physician's office in a taxi. He continued to improve for several days.

Then on Friday, Saturday, and Sunday evenings he suffered successive spasms, all with a frightful thickening of his voice, and the physician came. Everytime Bill stirred or breathed deeply during those nights Inez got up, and all day she took care of him. She and Daisy were often alone in the house when he needed attention, and at times they were frightened.

Daisy thought that he sensed approaching death. He frequently prefaced a comment with "If I should die," but he always smiled. Agnostic, he longed to believe in immortality. "All my days—even my hardest days—I have loved life and this world in which my life has been set," he had written twenty years before. "That I must go out in a final spasm of agony to annihilation seems an intolerable thought."[66]

His spasm on Sunday was protracted, and two days later Inez told the physician that she must have assistance. Her strength was beginning to break.

They decided that they must send Bill to a hospital, and the physician immediately engaged a room at St. Vincent's, just half a block away at the corner of Eleventh Street and Seventh Avenue. That Tuesday morning Bill was carried on a cot downstairs and outside and, amused by the crowd that gathered to watch and comment, put into an ambulance. He had difficulty speaking but otherwise was quite himself all day.

He had an attractive room with a bath and the best of care. A nerve specialist he knew examined him, then told Inez that he had suffered an "occlusion of the artery at the base of his brain."[67] As she understood his condition, the walls of the arteries that fed his brain were breaking down. The specialist, Dr. Mahoney, told her that patients often recovered from this condition, and she refused to despair. She could not believe that he would ever die. With her care, she felt, he would live as long as she would.

Since he could not wear his hearing aid and since the occlusion had paralyzed his swallowing and speaking apparatus, he communicated with her by terse notes in a strange, squiggly hand. "At last I have been caught up with," he wrote, with his usual wry sense of humor. "I've always talked too much." He was fed intravenously and when he saw beside his bed the contraption, as tall as a floor lamp, that held high a container of glucose solution, he scrawled: "What a long meal!"[68] At intervals all day he and Inez communicated by witty, loving notes until his hand could not form letters.

He slept most of Thursday, and when maids Mary Mills and Clara Stevens visited him at the hospital he smiled and shook their hands. When Inez arrived she perceived a marked change; he had sunk into a partial coma. Although he could not speak and his eyes were glazed, he put her hand to his lips.

On Friday his coma deepened, but when she took his hand, he put it to his lips twice, and the second time she realized that he did it intentionally.

She had engaged a male nurse to stay with him from eight o'clock in the evening to eight o'clock in the morning, when the regular nurses came in. Each day she went to the hospital soon after that hour and stayed until the male nurse arrived in the evening. She would have stayed with him twenty-four hours every day if she could have gone without sleep. Over the weekend and into Monday he never spoke nor opened his eyes. He was in a deep coma.

At seven o'clock Tuesday morning, Feburary 24, 1948, the male nurse phoned her to come over immediately. She and Daisy hurriedly dressed and rushed down the block to the hospital and up to his room. Standing at his bedside, they watched over him for about two hours. At nine-thirty o'clock a cerebral occlusion quietly extinguished the life "led more for experience than for achievement."[69]

Inez, Daisy, Ebie, Wallace Jr., and other relatives and many friends, including Hoover, who attended the funeral in St. John's Episcopal Church, a short walk from the Irwin townhouse, remembered him as an amiable, gentle, jovial, kind, often absentminded, and always generous human being. His newspaper friends remembered him as a "genial . . . leader of well-tempered talk, prompt with the ready quip and quick to join a lively time." His Dutch Treat cronies remembered him as "a person of wide-open mind, robust humour, warm and enduring qualities of personality and sturdy faith in the eventual salvation (not necessarily by evangelistic agency) of a sorely bedeviled world"—an appraisal written in 1943 but just as appropriate five years later. To a neighbor he had been "a man of great heart and natural nobility."[70]

Professionally, he was remembered as the author of hundreds of magazine and newspaper pieces and of more than thirty books of fact and fiction, but almost forgotten as a propagandist and, even as *Lute Song* was scheduled to open in London, as a playwright. *Time* aptly called him a "Jack-of-all-letters." "Wide-ranging, versatile," the New York *Times* described him; "he searched and wrote in just about every field available to an extraordinary curiosity." His fellow Bohemians in San Francisco especially remembered him as a poet; Porter Garnett carved in a large panel of Spanish cedar the last seven lines of the prologue to *The Hamadryads* to hang in the club. Other people remembered him as the official biographer of Hoover, a crusading journalist, a press critic, and an ace correspondent. "In the first World War," an obituary writer recalled, "he wrote what were considered some of the best newspaper and magazine dispatches that came from the battle fronts." The authors who completed his Union League history thought he had been "one of the really great journalists of recent times."[71]

Without doubt, he had been a much better journalist than literary artist. His literary gift was narrative and descriptive rather than imaginative. Although his short stories and novels entertained a large, unsophisticated audience in the early twentieth century, their value was ephemeral.

Ironically, his best journalism, such as "The City That Was" and "The American Newspaper," survived his intentionally literary efforts. He was a first-class reporter but, by his own accurate appraisal, a first-class second-class writer.

Of all the people who remembered him, only his second wife really knew him. After twenty years of friendship, author Harvey O'Higgins had realized that he had never known him at all. Who was this man peeping over the Ben-Franklin spectacles like a child playing hide and seek, transparently concealed and mischievous? To O'Higgins, he had been "the Will Irwin whom neither I nor anybody else really knows after we have known him for a lifetime."[72] Only to Inez and Hallie had Bill revealed his subterranean personality, but only Inez had held his complete trust, like the unreserved faith a loving mother receives from her child. She alone understood the sad, despairing melancholy soul who feared life even as he thrived on its variety. She alone understood the temperamental core beneath the genial exterior. She alone had known how to comfort the insecure, tormented child within the man.

She had selected the epitaph for the gravestone that would mark where his ashes would be buried in the family plot at Scituate.[73] The epitaph was from an essay on medieval Italy by John Addington Symonds. "There was a sentence in it, which I have changed a little, that perfectly describes you," she told him. " 'And ever he set his steed, wherever the press was thickest.' How would you like that for an epitaph?"

He smiled brightly. "I'd like it."

And they laughed.

NOTES

ABBREVIATIONS

BB   —Brandt & Brandt, New York City
HH   —Herbert Hoover
IF   —Irwin Family
IHI   —Inez Haynes Irwin
MC   —Margaret Cookman, Westford, Mass.
SEP   —*Saturday Evening Post*
TMOAR   —Will Irwin, *The Making of a Reporter* (New York: G. P. Putnam's Sons, 1942)
WHI   —William Hyde Irwin, Brookdale, Calif.
WI   —Will Irwin
WIJ   —Wallace Irwin, Jr., Larchmont, N.Y.

For further information on sources, see Bibliographical Essay

Preface

1. *Webster's Biographical Dictionary*, s.v. "Irwin, Will, in full William Henry"; *Who Was Who in America*, s.v. "Irwin, William Henry (Will Irwin)"; Stanley J. Kunitz and Howard Haycraft, eds., *Twentieth Century Authors* (New York: Wilson, 1942), p. 706; *Newsweek*, Mar. 8, 1948, p. 58; *Time*, Mar. 8, 1948, p. 100.
2. Feb. 25, 1948.

CHAPTER ONE: *Fledgling*

1. WI, "Biographical Data: Requested by the State Historical Society of Colorado," July 21, 1944, the Historical Society, Denver.
2. "Diploma, Bryant & Stratton's Mercantile College," Apr. 1865, WIJ.
3. WI, "Biographical Data."
4. Ontario County (N.Y.) *Times*, Jan. 1, 1873.
5. WI to Cyril Clemens, July 22, 1935, IF Collection, Bancroft Library, University of California, Berkeley.
6. WI's childhood attempts at poetry did not survive.
7. See WI, "What Is the Western Spirit?" *Sunset*, June 1923, p. 24.
8. WI, "Camps of Yesterday," SEP, Nov. 4, 1922, p. 89.
9. WHI to author, Mar. 4, 1971, gives Herman's birth date as Sept. 5, 1882; WI, "Biographical Data," gives it as Sept. 8, 1881. Wallace Irwin, "I Look at Me" (unpublished autobiography), n.d., p. 14B, IF Collection.
10. WI, *Propaganda and the News: Or, What Makes You Think So?* (New York: Whittlesey House, McGraw-Hill, 1936), p. 77.
11. Denver *Post*, Oct. 10, 1920.
12. June 18, 1892 (typescript), WHI; the published poem was unavailable.

13. June 10, 1892 (typescript), WHI; Denver *Times*, June 11, 1892. It is my conclusion that "Hanging Up the Sword" was his prize-winning essay.
14. Denver *Post*, Oct. 10, 1920.
15. TMOAR, p. 5.
16. Ibid., pp. 14, 15.
17. WI, *Herbert Hoover: A Reminiscent Biography* (New York: Century, 1928), pp. 59, 60.
18. TMOAR, p. 17.
19. *Daily Palo Alto*, Jan. 7, 1896.
20. *Sequoia*, Sept. 6, 1895, p. 51; *Sequoia*, Jan. 10, 1896, p. 226.
21. TMOAR, pp. 22, 32.
22. WHI to author, Apr. 17, 1971.
23. TMOAR, p. 28.
24. R. G. O'Neil and J. F. Van Der Kamp, *The Stanford Axe: 1899–1930* (n.p., 1930), p. 8.
25. Dec. 16, 1896.
26. *Sequoia*, May 14, 1897, p. 372.
27. *Sequoia*, Oct. 1, 1897, p. 54.
28. May 5, 1898, WHI.
29. TMOAR, p. 32.
30. Ibid., p. 34.
31. Marriage License and Certificate of Marriage, San Francisco, July 7, 1898, WHI.
32. Feb. 23, 1899, Coolidge Collection, Bancroft Library, University of California, Berkeley.
33. Nov. 1, 1898, WHI.
34. Feb. 23, 1899.
35. Charles K. Field and Will H. Irwin, *Stanford Stories: Tales of a Young University* (New York: Doubleday, Page, 1900). During Irwin's college years books of short stories about eastern universities, such as *Princeton Stories* by Jesse Lynch Williams and *Harvard Episodes* by Charles Macomb Flandrau, were in vogue. In 1896 Field, the campus wit at Stanford, published a volume of light verse, *Four Leaved Clover*, perhaps the first book about the new university.
36. WI to Coolidge, Feb. 23, 1899.
37. O'Neil and Van Der Kamp, *The Stanford Axe*, pp. 24–25.
38. William Henry Irwin, Diploma, The Leland Stanford Junior University, Bachelor of Arts in English degree, May 24, 1899, WHI.
39. TMOAR, pp. 39, 40.
40. Ibid., p. 40.

CHAPTER TWO: *Newspaperman*

1. TMOAR, p. 39.
2. *Wave*, Jan. 13, 1900.
3. This is Wallace Irwin's phrase for those expelled from Stanford, according to WI, *Herbert Hoover: A Reminiscent Biography* (New York: Century, 1928), p. 43.
4. *Wave*, May 26, 1900.
5. TMOAR, p. 32.
6. Ibid., p. 50.
7. Ibid.
8. Ibid., p. 51.
9. Dec. 26, 1900, WIJ.
10. Quotations in this and the next four paragraphs are from TMOAR, p. 52.
11. Ibid.
12. This episode is based on the *Chronicle*, Feb. 11, 1902, and TMOAR, pp. 57–64.
13. TMOAR, p. 72.
14. *Chronicle*, Feb. 22, 1902.
15. This episode is based on TMOAR, p. 73.
16. John Philip Young, *Journalism in California* (San Francisco: Chronicle Publishing, 1915), p. 159.

17. TMOAR, p. 79.
18. "Richly Endowed Stanford University," *World's Work*, May 1902.
19. Gelett Burgess and Will Irwin, *The Picaroons* (New York: McClure, Phillips, 1904).
20. The serial began in vol. 9, Feb. 1903, and concluded in vol. 11, Feb. 1904.
21. Gelett Burgess and Will Irwin, *The Reign of Queen Isyl* (New York: McClure, Phillips, 1903).
22. The serial ran in vol. 9, July through Nov. 1903. Also see nn. 19, 20.
23. Interview with WHI, Aug. 18, 1969.
24. TMOAR, p. 87.
25. WHI to author, Apr. 17, 1971.
26. Diary of Harriet Hyde Irwin, Jan. 7, 1904, cited in WHI to author, Apr. 17/20, 1971.
27. TMOAR, p. 92.
28. Irwin would finish his script of the Bohemian Club play, *The Hamadryads*, in New York; it was produced on Aug. 20, 1904, at the club's encampment, "surrounded by giant trees at the foot of a wooded hillside," on the Russian River north of San Francisco. See WI and W. J. McCoy, *The Hamadryads: A Masque of Apollo* ([San Francisco: Bohemian Club,] 1910). McCoy composed the music.
29. Diary of Harriet Hyde Irwin, May 29, June 2, 1904, cited in WHI to author, Apr. 17/20, 1971.
30. WI, *The City That Was: A Requiem of Old San Francisco* (New York: B. W. Huebsch, 1906), p. 47.

CHAPTER THREE: *Reporter*

1. In TMOAR, pp. 95-98 WI recalled his first day in the *Sun* local room and his first assignment.
2. WI, *Highlights of Manhattan* (New York: Century, 1927), p. 146.
3. WI, "The Spending Jag in New York," SEP, Dec. 14, 1912, p. 41.
4. TMOAR, p. 99.
5. This episode is based on ibid., pp. 102-5.
6. Ibid., p. 102.
7. This episode is based on ibid., pp. 108-9.
8. IHI, "Adventures of Yesterday" (unpublished autobiography), n.d., pp. 550, 551, IHI Collection, Schlesinger Library, Radcliffe College, Cambridge, Mass.
9. WI to IHI, May 30, 1905, WI Collection, Beinecke Rare Book and Manuscript Library, Yale University, New Haven, Conn.
10. WI to IHI, Apr. 12, 1905, WI Collection.
11. WI to IHI, Apr. 17, 1905, WI Collection.
12. WI to IHI, June 15, 1905, WI Collection.
13. WI to IHI, June 24, 1905, WI Collection.
14. WI, "The American Newspaper," *Collier's*, Feb. 4, 1911, pp. 16, 17.
15. WI, "The Job of Reporting," *Scribner's*, Nov. 1931, p. 493.
16. WI to IHI, Aug. 10, 1905, WI Collection.
17. TMOAR, pp. 124, 125.
18. WI to IHI, Aug. 22, 16–24, 28, 1905, WI Collection.
19. New York *Sun*, Aug. 31, 1905.
20. TMOAR, p. 107; WI to IHI, n.d. [1905]; WI Collection.
21. WI to IHI, Oct. 3, 1905, WI Collection.
22. WI to IHI, Dec. 13, 1905, WI Collection.
23. WI to IHI, Oct. 3, 1905, WI Collection.
24. WI to IHI, Jan. 21, 1905 [1906], WI Collection.
25. WI to IHI, Feb. 7, 1906, WI Collection.
26. TMOAR, p. 130.
27. This episode is based upon ibid., pp. 130-36; WI, "Job of Reporting," pp. 494-96; WI to IHI, Apr. 19, 21, 22, 1906, YU; New York *Sun*, Apr. 19-26, 1906.
28. Louis L. Snyder and Richard B. Morris, *A Treasury of Great Reporting* (New York: Simon and Schuster, 1949), p. 274. The rival newspaper is unnamed.

29. See WI, *The City That Was: A Requiem of Old San Francisco* (New York: B. W. Huebsch, 1906).

30. This episode is based on TMOAR, p. 136, and WI to IHI, Apr. 24, 1906, WI Collection.

31. WI to IHI, Apr. 29, May 3, 1906, WI Collection.

CHAPTER FOUR: *Muckraker*

1. Peter Lyon, in his *Success Story: The Life and Times of S. S. McClure* (New York: Charles Scribner's Sons, 1963), p. 297, stated that WI had reported for work on May 15 "and a few days later S. S. told him he was managing editor." But in WI to IHI, May 6, 1906, WI Collection, Beinecke Rare Book and Manuscript Library, Yale University, New Haven, Conn., Irwin said he had already been offered the managing editor's job; and in WI to IHI, May 10, 1906, WI Collection, Irwin stated that McClure had officially hired him as managing editor of *McClure's*.

2. WI to IHI, June 8, 22, n.d. [23], n.d. [July 6], 1906, WI Collection; Lyon, *Success Story*, p. 299. Irwin eventually rewrote the Christian Science series, according to WI to IHI, Nov. 8, 1906, Jan. 5, 1907, WI Collection.

3. WI to IHI, Nov. 16, 1906, WI Collection.

4. TMOAR, p. 129.

5. WI to IHI, Dec. 10, 1906, WI Collection.

6. WI to IHI, Feb. 22, [1907], WI Collection.

7. WI to IHI, July 16, 1906, Feb. 2, 5, 1907, WI Collection.

8. TMOAR, p. 137.

9. Ibid.

10. This episode is based on ibid., 129–141.

11. WI, "The Medium Game: Behind the Scenes with Spiritualism," *Collier's*, Sept. 14, 1907, p. 13. This is the first of the installments, which ran in consecutive issues.

12. TMOAR, p. 159.

13. WI to IHI, Aug. [1907], WI Collection.

14. San Francisco *Call*, Mar. 12, 1910; WI to IHI, Aug. 11, 1907, WI Collection.

15. WI to IHI, Aug. 20, 1907, WI Collection.

16. WI to IHI, Sept. 5, 1907, WI Collection.

17. WI, "The Japanese and the Pacific Coast," *Collier's*, Oct. 12, 1907, p. 15, and Oct. 19, 1907, pp. 16, 17. The other installments ran Sept. 28 and Oct. 26.

18. WI to IHI, Sept. 16, 1907, WI Collection.

19. WI to IHI, n.d., WI Collection.

20. This episode is based on TMOAR, pp. 159–64; WI, "The American Saloon," *Collier's*, Mar. 21, 1908, pp. 11, 12; WI, "More About 'Nigger Gin'," *Collier's*, Aug. 15, 1908, p. 28; WI, "Arthur Gleason's Job," *Collier's*, Jan. 26, 1924, p. 37.

21. WI, "The American Saloon," *Collier's*, May 16, 1908, p. 10.

22. TMOAR, p. 161.

23. March 8, 1910.

24. IHI to WI, Feb. 1, 1908, WI Collection.

25. IHI to WI, Apr. 3, 1908, WI Collection.

26. Arnold Genthe, *Pictures of Old Chinatown: With Text by Will Irwin* (New York: Moffat, Yard, 1908); New York *Times*, Jan. 9, 1909.

27. *The Confessions of a Con Man* (New York: B. W. Huebsch, 1909).

28. "The McGregor Rose," SEP, May 1, 8, 1909.

29. WI to IHI, June 11, 1909, WI Collection.

30. *Warrior, the Untamed: The Story of an Imaginative Press Agent* (New York: Doubleday, Page, 1909); WI to IHI, Mar. 14, 1910, WI Collection.

31. *The House of Mystery: An Episode in the Career of Rosalie Le Grange, Clairvoyant* (New York: Century, 1910).

32. WI to IHI, Apr. 25, 1910, WI Collection.

33. *The Readjustment* (New York: B. W. Huebsch, 1910).

34. TMOAR, p. 164; WI to IHI, Sept. 23, 1909, WI Collection.

35. Mar. 10, 1910, WI Collection.
36. June 4, 1910, WI Collection.
37. Unidentified newspaper clipping, n.d., WI Collection.
38. This episode is based on TMOAR, p. 167. Neither the newspaperman nor his newspaper is identified.
39. WI to IHI, Oct. 12, 1910, WI Collection. Also see WI, "O. Henry, Man and Writer," *Cosmopolitan*, Sept. 1910, and WI, "Children and Edged Tools," *Everybody's*, Nov. 1910.
40. "The American Newspaper," *Collier's*, Feb. 18, 1911, p. 15, and June 3, 1911, pp. 17–19, 28.
41. "The American Newspaper," *Collier's*, July 22, 1911, pp. 13, 25, 26. Quotations in this Pittsburgh episode are from George Seldes, *Freedom of the Press* (Garden City, N.Y.: Garden City Publishing, 1935), pp. 25–27.
42. WI to IHI, Sept. 7, 1911, WI Collection.
43. *Call*, Jan. 27, 1911; *Daily Times*, May 25, 1911.
44. Publication in book form was planned, but Hearst's pending libel suit and Irwin's other work delayed production indefinitely. The series was finally reprinted as *The American Newspaper: A Series First Appearing in Collier's, January-July, 1911* (Ames: Iowa State University Press, 1969), with comments by Clifford F. Weigle and David G. Clark. Also see my "Will Irwin's Pioneering Criticism of the Press," *Journalism Quarterly* 47 (1970): 263–71.
45. TMOAR, pp. 180, 182.
46. Arthur M. Schlesinger, Jr., *The Age of Roosevelt: The Crisis of the Old Order, 1919–1933* (Boston: Houghton Mifflin, 1957), 1:79.
47. WI, *Herbert Hoover: A Reminiscent Biography* (New York: Century, 1928), p. 123.
48. (Indianapolis: Bobbs-Merrill, 1912).
49. This title was used for both the magazine article, Dec. 1911, and the book (New York: D. Appleton, 1912).
50. *The Thirteenth Chair* by Bayard Veiller was a three-act play based on Irwin's Rosalie Le Grange stories; it ran 328 performances on Broadway in 1916–1917, according to Burns Mantle and Garrison P. Sherwood (eds.), *The Best Plays of 1909–1919: And The Year Book of the Drama in America* (New York: Dodd, Mead, 1933), pp. 587, 588.
51. "Golden Water" ran Jan. 25, Feb. 8, Feb. 22, 1913.
52. Al Jennings and WI, "Beating Back," SEP, ran Sept. 6–Nov. 29, 1913. Also see *Beating Back* (New York: D. Appleton, 1914).
53. WI, "Dr. Arnold Genthe," *American*, May 1913; Arnold Genthe and WI, *Old Chinatown: A Book of Pictures by Arnold Genthe with Text by Will Irwin* (New York: Mitchell Kennerley, 1912).
54. TMOAR, p. 195.
55. WI to IHI, Apr. 17, 19, 1914, WI Collection.
56. "What's Wrong with the Associated Press," Mar. 28, 1914, and "The United Press," Apr. 14, 1914; "The Floating Laborer," SEP, May 9, June 6, July 4, 1914.
57. TMOAR, p. 204.
58. Ibid.
59. Grace A. Luce, daughter of a San Diego judge and a Stanford alumna, had married Wallace in 1901.
60. TMOAR, p. 204.

CHAPTER FIVE: *War Correspondent*

1. "England Faces the Music," *Collier's*, Sept. 19, 1914, p. 9.
2. Quotations in this Louvain episode are from WI, *Men, Women and War* (London: Constable, 1915), pp. 22–26, 31, 36, 37, 41.
3. Ibid., pp. 58, 59.
4. WI, *A Reporter at Armageddon: Letters from the Front and Behind the Lines of the Great War* (New York: D. Appleton, 1918), p. 190.

5. Ibid., p. 192; WI, *The Next War: An Appeal to Common Sense* (New York: E. P. Dutton, 1921), p. 113.
6. WI, "England: The Puzzle," *American*, Feb. 1915, p. 81.
7. Quotations in this episode are from TMOAR, pp. 252, 253.
8. Ibid., p. 249.
9. WI, "The 'Glory' of War," *American*, Dec. 1914, p. 53.
10. WI, *Men, Women and War*, p. 127.
11. WI, "War Madness," SEP, Feb. 26, 1916, p. 7.
12. Publicity included WI, *The Babes of Belgium* (New York: Commission for Relief in Belgium, n.d.), which emphasized the desperate need for milk for Belgian babies.
13. TMOAR, p. 257.
14. Ibid., p. 258.
15. Ibid., p. 291.
16. Ibid., p. 261.
17. WI, *Men, Women and War*, pp. 190–92.
18. Quoted in "An American War Correspondent," *Literary Digest*, Apr. 24, 1915, pp. 954, 955.
19. TMOAR, p. 262.
20. Ibid., p. 263.
21. WI to IHI, Apr. 11, [1915], WI Collection, Beinecke Rare Book and Manuscript Library, Yale University, New Haven, Conn.
22. TMOAR, p. 276; "Skeletons in the Newspaper Closet," *Literary Digest*, Sept. 18, 1915, pp. 592, 593.
23. New York *Tribune*, Apr. 25, 27, 1915.
24. WI, "War Madness," p. 7.
25. TMOAR, pp. 289, 290.
26. This episode, including quotations, is based on ibid., pp. 293–95.
27. Ibid., p. 295.
28. Aug. 1915.
29. In New York by D. Appleton, and in London by Constable.
30. "Literature," *Nation*, Oct. 21, 1915, p. 501; "The New Books," *Independent*, Oct. 11, 1915, p. 72.
31. IHI to WI, Dec. 21, 1915, WI Collection.
32. IHI to WI, Dec. 25, 1915, WI Collection.
33. TMOAR, p. 299.
34. Ibid., p. 301.
35. WI, *The Latin at War* (New York: D. Appleton, 1917), p. 90.
36. WI, "The Roof of Armageddon," SEP, June 24, 1916, p. 6.
37. TMOAR, p. 317.
38. WI, *Christ or Mars?* (New York: D. Appleton, 1923), p. 7.
39. Quotations in this episode are from TMOAR, p. 297.
40. Ibid., p. 323.
41. Ibid., p. 324.
42. WI's interview with Wilson is based on ibid., pp. 325, 326.
43. Ibid., p. 221.
44. SEP, Jan. 27, 1917.
45. WI, *Reporter at Armageddon*, p. 32.
46. "The Autocrat of the Dinner Table," SEP, June 23, 1917.
47. WI, "Letters from the Front," SEP, July 21, 1917, p. 41.
48. TMOAR, p. 340.
49. Quotations in this episode are from WI, *Reporter at Armageddon*, pp. 311, 312.

CHAPTER SIX: *Propagandist*

1. WI, "Report on Foreign Propaganda" (unpublished draft), [1918], p. 1, CPI Records, National Archives and Records Service, Washington, D.C.; "Statement of Federal Employ-

ment," Sept. 16, 1970, National Personnel Records Center, St. Louis, Mo.; James R. Mock and Cedric Larson, *Words that Won the War: The Story of the Committee on Public Information, 1917–1919* (Princeton, N.J.: Princeton University Press, 1939), p. 270.

2. WI to Thomas A. Storey, Mar. 19, 1918, CPI Records.
3. Mar. 18, 1918, CPI Records.
4. WI to W. O. Reed, Mar. 29, 1918, CPI Records.
5. WI, "An Age of Lies," *Sunset,* Dec. 1919, p. 54.
6. WI to George Horace Lorimer, June 14, 1918, CPI Records.
7. George Creel, *How We Advertised America* (New York: Harper & Brothers, 1920), p. 200.
8. Lorimer to WI, July 10, 1918, Legislative, Judicial, and Diplomatic Records, National Archives and Records Service, Washington, D.C.; TMOAR, p. 362.
9. July 15, 1918, Legislative, Judicial, and Diplomatic Records.
10. "Statement of Federal Employment," Sept. 16, 1970; this source identifies Irwin's position as Director of Foreign Educational Work. Jackson A. Giddens indicated in letters to me of Aug. 28, 1967, and Mar. 22, 1972, that his extensive research on American foreign propaganda in World War I left him with the impression that Irwin was fired, but I found no evidence that Irwin had left the CPI involuntarily.
11. WI, "Age of Lies," p. 54.
12. "The New Books: The War and Allied Topics," *American Review of Reviews,* Oct. 1918, p. 438; Springfield *Republican*, Sept. 19, 1918.
13. Quotations in this episode are from WI, *Christ or Mars?* (New York: D. Appleton, 1923), pp. 185, 186.
14. TMOAR, p. 365.
15. Ibid., p. 367.
16. Ibid., p. 368.
17. WI to Carl Brandt, Sept. 26, 1939, WI magazine file, BB.
18. Lincoln Steffens, *The Letters of Lincoln Steffens* (New York: Harcourt, Brace, 1938), 1:444. Steffens thought that Walter Lippmann understood the whole situation better, however.
19. See WI, "Into Alsace with the Tricolor," SEP, Feb. 22, Mar. 1, 1919.
20. Dec. 15, 1918, MC.
21. WI to Edith Haynes Thompson, Jan. 16, 1919; WI to IHI, Jan. 18, 21, 29, 1919; all MC.
22. WI to IHI, Feb. 1, 1918 [1919], MC.
23. WI to IHI, Feb. 5, [1919], MC.
24. Albert M. Bender to WI, Feb. 3, 4, 1919, MC.
25. WI to IHI, Feb. 8, 1919, MC.
26. Feb. 10, [1919], MC.
27. WI to Edith Haynes Thompson, Feb. 13, [1919], MC.
28. WI to IHI, Feb. 12, 13, [1919], MC.
29. Feb. 14, [1919], MC.
30. Feb. 16, [1919], MC.
31. WI to IHI, Feb. 17, 1919, MC.
32. Feb. 20, 1919, MC.
33. WI to IHI, Feb. 26, [1919], and Feb. 23, 1919 (WI's italics), MC.
34. Feb. 26, [1919], MC.
35. Ibid.
36. Mar. 3, [1919], MC.
37. WI to IHI, first letter of Mar. 4, 1919, MC.
38. See WI's "England and the New Age," SEP, May 24, 1919, and "France and Us," SEP, May 17, 1919.
39. Quotations from this episode are from TMOAR, p. 385.
40. IHI, "Adventures of Yesterday" (unpublished autobiography), n.d., p. 412, IHI Collection, Schlesinger Library, Radcliffe College, Cambridge, Mass.
41. May 8, 1919, Wallace Irwin Collection, Bancroft Library, University of California, Berkeley.
42. San Francisco *Call* and *Post*, May 10, 1919.

43. Unidentified newspaper clipping, n.d., in IHI, California Scrapbook, n.d., MC.
44. San Francisco *Bulletin*, May 12, 1919.
45. Invitation from Albert M. Bender to Mr. and Mrs. Will Irwin, May 13, [1919], MC.
46. "Copper Dan Imbibes," SEP, Dec. 20, 1919, and "The Moral Weapon," SEP, Sept. 13, 1919.
47. WI, "Our Big Chance," *Independent*, Nov. 15, 1919, p. 100, and Nov. 29, 1919, p. 117.
48. "France Worries Through," SEP, Mar. 13, 1920, p. 22.
49. [About Feb. 7, 1920], Pre-1921 Hoover Papers, HH Presidential Library, West Branch, Iowa; "Hoover as an Executive," SEP, Mar. 27, 1920, p. 70.
50. The article may have been "Common Sense About Germany," SEP, May 8, 1920.
51. WI, "The Ruhr Aflame," SEP, June 5, 1920, p. 85.
52. Quotations in this episode are from ibid., p. 89.
53. WI, "The Ruhr Aflame," SEP, June 19, 1920, p. 148.
54. Ibid., p. 154.
55. Ibid.
56. "Common Sense in Belgium," SEP, July 17, 1920, p. 10.

CHAPTER SEVEN: *Crusader*

1. WI, "Private Bullard," *Independent*, Mar. 15, 1924, p. 150.
2. Mar. 19, 26, Apr. 2, 1921.
3. TMOAR, p. 396.
4. Quotations in this summary of *The Next War* are from that source, in the following order: pp. 127, 49, 5, 140, 146, 149.
5. "The Suicidity of Suicide," *Nation*, May 11, 1921, p. 691.
6. WI to Fremont Older, June 7, 1921, Older Collection, Bancroft Library, University of California, Berkeley.
7. WI, *Columbine Time* (Boston: Stratford, 1921), p. 1.
8. Nov. n.d., 1921, WI Collection, Beinecke Rare Book and Manuscript Library, Yale University, New Haven, Conn.
9. Interview with Constance Smith Whitman, Dec. 17, 1968, New York, N.Y.
10. Quotations in this anecdote are from WI, "The Irwin Boys Decide To Tell All," *Collier's*, Aug. 30, 1924, p. 29.
11. WI to George Horace Lorimer, Feb. 13, 1923, Lorimer Collection, Historical Society of Pennsylvania, Philadelphia.
12. Lorimer to WI, Feb. 14, 1923, Lorimer Collection.
13. "To An Unknown Soldier," *Collier's*, May 26, 1923, pp. 10, 11.
14. "If You See It in the Paper, It's—?" *Collier's*, Aug. 18, 1923, p. 28; "You Have a Sixth Sense for the Truth," *Collier's*, Aug. 25, 1923, p. 28.
15. See articles by WI, "Mr. Porter Visits Geneva," *Collier's*, Sept. 8, 1923, p. 29; "Did the League of Nations Fail?" *Collier's*, Nov. 3, 1923, p. 13. See also by WI in *Collier's*, "League Adopts a Nation," Sept. 22, 1923; "Firing 100,000 Officeholders," Sept. 29, 1923; "Getting at the Truth About Folks," Oct. 20, 1923.
16. "Half a League, Onward," *Collier's*, Nov. 24, 1923, p. 18.
17. WI, "My Religion," in *They Believe*, as told to Otis Skinner et al. (New York: Century, 1928), pp. 82–83.
18. Quotations in this three-paragraph summary of WI, *Christ or Mars?* are from that source, pp. 37, 63, 85, 9, 40, 187, 188.
19. "Youth Rides West," *Collier's*, Feb. 16–April 26, 1924; "Arthur Gleason's Job," *Collier's*, Jan. 26, 1924; "Flis," *Collier's*, Feb. 14, 1925; "The Irwin Boys Decide To Tell All," with a companion essay by Wallace, *Collier's*, Aug. 30, 1924; "Does a Moment of Revolt Come to Every Married Man?" *McCall's*, Mar. 1924; "Going to School for Peace," *Ladies Home Journal*, Nov. 1924; Denver *Post*, Apr. 6, 1924.
20. WI, "Patriotism that Pays," *Nation*, Nov. 12, 1924, p. 515; Denver *Post*, Oct. 10, 1920.
21. WI, "Patriotism that Pays," p. 516.
22. WI to Carl Brandt, Jan. 16, 1925, Sidney Howard *Lute Song* file, BB.

23. Denver *Post*, Mar. 22, Apr. 3, 1925.
24. June 4, [1925], Wallace Irwin Collection, Bancroft Library, University of California, Berkeley.
25. *Youth Rides West: A Story of the Seventies* (New York: A. A. Knopf, 1925), p. 26.
26. Ibid., pp. 62, 63.
27. *Tribune*, Feb. 15, 1925; *Times*, Feb. 8, 1925.
28. "The Cloudburst," *Collier's*, Mar. 14, 1925; "Richest People on Earth," *Collier's*, Aug. 22, 1925.
29. "When a Swelled Head Bursts," *Liberty*, July 25, 1925.
30. IHI, "Adventures of Yesterday" (unpublished autobiography), n.d., p. 583, IHI Collection, Schlesinger Library, Radcliffe College, Cambridge, Mass.
31. WI to Herbert J. Hagerman, July 7, 1925, Hagerman Papers, National Archives and Records Service, Washington, D.C.
32. IHI, "Adventures of Yesterday," p. 583, IHI Collection; *Carbonate Chronicle*, July 20, 1925.
33. "The Contender," SEP, Mar. 27, 1926; WI to Herbert J. Hagerman, Nov. 16, 1925, Hagerman Papers.
34. WI, *Christ or Mars?* pp. 107, 108.
35. WI, Diary, 1925, p. 362, WI Collection.
36. Hallie's reason for termination of alimony is unclear. According to WHI to author, Mar. 4, 1971, Hallie and Herman Irwin were married July 7, 1948.
37. New York *Times*, Apr. 16, 1926.
38. WI to Wallace Irwin, June 4, [1926], Wallace Irwin Collection.
39. WI, *Highlights of Manhattan*, p. 113; "Through a Loophole in the Law," *Liberty*, Feb. 12, 1927.
40. WI, Diary, 1926, p. 356; WI, Diary, 1927, p. 58, WI Collection.
41. (New York: J. H. Sears, 1927), p. 7.
42. "Books in Brief," *Nation*, Oct. 5, 1927, p. 343.
43. "Havoc Beyond the Levees," *World's Work*, July 1927; "Can We Tame the Mississippi?" *World's Work*, Aug. 1927. See also WI, "The Aftermath: Mud and Money," *Survey*, July 1, 1927.
44. TMOAR, p. 409.
45. Ibid., p. 410.
46. Nov. 13, 1927.
47. 1927, p. 357, WI Collection.
48. WI to Corinne (Roosevelt) Robinson, June 29, 1928, Robinson Collection, Harvard College Library, Harvard University, Cambridge, Mass.
49. WI, Diary, 1927, p. 357, WI Collection.
50. (Garden City, N.Y.: Doubleday, Doran, 1928).
51. "Campaign Panegyrics," *Bookman*, Nov. 1928, p. 347; New York *Herald Tribune*, Apr. 8, 1928.
52. WI, *Herbert Hoover*, pp. 3, 23.
53. "Mr. Irwin on Mr. Hoover," *Nation*, May 9, 1928, p. 541.
54. Edwin Emerson, *Hoover and His Times: Looking Back Through the Years* (Garden City, N.Y.: Garden City Publishing, 1932), p. 563.
55. TMOAR, p. 416.
56. The others: two from Belgium and one from France (Legion of Honor).
57. WI, Diary, 1929, p. 46, WI Collection.
58. TMOAR, p. 399.
59. Authur M. Schlesinger, Jr., *The Age of Roosevelt, The Crisis of the Old Order, 1919–1933* (Boston: Houghton Mifflin, 1957), 1:155.
60. IHI, "Adventures of Yesterday," p. 581.
61. 1929, p. 323, WI Collection.
62. Ibid., pp. 365, 367; WI, Diary, 1930, back of title page, WI Collection.

CHAPTER EIGHT: *Man of Letters*

1. See "Give 'Em the Ax!" New York *Herald Tribune*, May 18, 1930; "Herbert Hoover, an Intimate Portrait by His Friend," *American*, May 1930; "Andrew Mellon Stripped of His Mystery," *American*, July 1930; and "Faithful Fido," *Liberty*, Apr. 11, 1931.
2. New York *Times*, June 21, 1930.
3. "Putting Copyright to Rights," *World's Work*, Dec. 1930; "Red Ballyhoo," SEP, Nov. 22, 1930; "Portrait of a President," SEP, Jan. 17, 1931; "The President's Job," SEP, Mar. 7, 1931.
4. P. 365, WI Collection, Beinecke Rare Book and Manuscript Library, Yale University, New Haven, Conn.
5. "Beware of the Shadow," *Pictorial Review*, Oct., Nov. 1931, Jan. 1932.
6. "These Whispers About Mr. Hoover," *Liberty*, May 21, 1932; New York *Times*, Apr. 24, 1932.
7. WI, Diary, 1933, p. 1, WI Collection.
8. Ibid., p. 18.
9. Ibid., p. 61.
10. WI to HH, Apr. 28, 1933, Post-Presidential Papers, HH Presidential Library, West Branch, Iowa.
11. See *Liberty* articles: "After Repeal—Watch Out!" Aug. 26, 1933; "The New Racketeer— America's Greatest Danger," June 4, 1932; "The Blackjack of Extortion," June 11, 1932; "The Toll of the New Racketeer," June 18, 1932; "What America Pays the Racketeer," July 2, 1932.
12. WI to HH, n.d. [summer 1933], Post-Presidential Papers.
13. Marchette Chute, *PEN American Center: A History of the First Fifty Years* (New York: PEN American Center, 1972), p. 18.
14. HH to WI, Dec. 16, 1933, Post-Presidential Papers; *Liberty*, Feb. 24, 1934, p. 21.
15. HH to WI, Dec. 16, 1933, Post-Presidential Papers.
16. WI to HH, Dec. 23, 1933, Post-Presidential Papers.
17. WI to HH, n.d. [spring 1934], Post-Presidential Papers.
18. WI to HH, June 9, 1934, Post-Presidential Papers.
19. WI, Diary, Sept. 16, 1935, WI Collection. Diary dates, instead of page numbers, are given when the pages are unnumbered.
20. WI, Diary, 1935, Jan. ledger page; WI, Diary, Jan. 29, Feb. 5, 1936; IHI, Diary, 1936, p. 30, WI Collection.
21. *Times*, Jan. 26, 1936; WI, Diary, Jan. 22, 1936, WI Collection.
22. Jan. 28, 1936, Post-Presidential Papers.
23. WI, *Propaganda and the News*, p. 297.
24. E. D. Kennedy, "Chronicle Without Criticism," *Saturday Review of Literature*, Feb. 8, 1936, p. 7; "Book Reviews," *Social Education* 1 (1937):74, 75.
25. See "Saving the American Child," *Forum and Century*, April 1936, condensed as "They Brought Our Children Health," *Reader's Digest*, May 1936; "The Pleasures of Hate," *Survey Graphic*, June 1936. Also see, for example, the Denver *Post*, Mar. 8, 15, 22, 29, 1936, for the Universal Service series.
26. *Liberty*, March 21, 1936; see "Should Congressmen Be Held Responsible for Slander?" Aug. 15, "Sweepstakes Riches," Mar. 28, "Gambling Mad America," July 11, "Are They Putting J. Edgar Hoover on the Spot?" Oct. 17, "Does John L. Lewis Want to Be President?" Dec. 5, "Are the Republican Candidates Physically Fit To Be President?" May 16, "Will the Veterans Demand More Millions?" Nov. 14; Diary, April 21, 1936.
27. *Highlights of Manhattan*, rev. ed. (New York: D. Appleton-Century, 1937); WI, *Scituate, 1636–1936: An Illustrated Historical Account of an Old New England Town Wherein History and Literature Have Gone Hand in Hand and Where an Old Oaken Bucket Has Played a Famous Part* (Scituate, Mass.: Scituate Tercentenary Committee, 1936).
28. WI to WHI, Apr. 1, [1937], WHI.
29. Dec. 27, 1937.
30. "It Is the Law," *Good Housekeeping*, May 1938.

31. *Liberty*, July 16, 1938, pp. 12, 13.
32. "The Resurrection of Mr. Volstead," *Scribner's*, Feb. 1939.
33. Interview with Inez Elizabeth Sturges, June 21, 1971, Syosset, N.Y.
34. San Francisco *Chronicle*, June 8, 1939.
35. See Emanuel V. Voska with Will Irwin, "Spy and Counter Spy," SEP, May 4, 11, 18, 25, June 8, 15, 29, 1940.
36. Ninety-fifth Commencement Speech, Knox College, June 12, 1940, college archives, Galesburg, Ill. Irwin's remarks are summarized in this and the following four paragraphs.
37. Emanual Victor Voska and WI, *Spy and Counterspy* (New York: Doubleday, Doran, 1940).
38. June 27, 1940, Post-Presidential Papers.
39. July 7, 1940, Post-Presidential Papers.
40. WI, Diary, Nov. 5, 1940, WI Collection.
41. Handwritten note on WI to Carl Brandt, July 13, 1941, WI book file, BB; WI, Diary, June 1, 1941, WI Collection.
42. TMOAR, pp. 370, 395–97.
43. Bernice Baumgarten to WI, May 18, 1942, WI book file, BB.
44. WI to Bernice Baumgarten, July 14, 1942, WI book file, BB.
45. "Personal History of Three Decades," *Saturday Review of Literature*, Nov. 14, 1942, p. 11; *Times*, Nov. 22, 1942; "Atlantic Bookshelf," *Atlantic*, Jan. 1943, p. 136; *Herald Tribune*, Nov. 15, 1942; unidentified newspaper clipping, Western History Dept., Denver Public Library.
46. WI to Belle Kant, June 14, 1946, IF Collection, Bancroft Library, University of California, Berkeley.
47. See WI and Thomas M. Johnson, *What You Should Know About Spies and Saboteurs* (New York: W. W. Norton, 1943), and WI et al., *Thirty-Eighth Anniversary of the Dutch Treat Club: With a Documentary History of the Club by Will Irwin; A Play, with a Moral, by Westbrook Pegler; Contributions by a Score, or so, of Members; Portraits of Nine Club Functionaries; Twelve Illustrations in Colour* (New York: Privately Printed, 1943).
48. WI, Diary, Apr. 2, 1943, WI Collection.
49. WI to HH, Aug. 25, 1943, Post-Presidential Papers.
50. WI to HH, Nov. 18, 1943, Post-Presidential Papers.
51. Jan. 3, 1944, WHI.
52. WI, Diary, Apr. 27, 1944, WI Collection.
53. Irwin received a $500 advance from Myerberg, 10 percent of which went to Brandt & Brandt and 1 percent to the Dramatists Guild. He declined an invitation to invest in the show.
54. WI to Harold Freedman, Nov. 22, 1944, Sidney Howard *Lute Song* file, BB.
55. In WI, Diary, June 19, 1945, WI Collection, Irwin jocularly referred to those who watched over his health, probably including his physician and Inez, as his "parole board." WI, ed., *Letters to Kermit from Theodore Roosevelt, 1902–1908* (New York: Charles Scribner's Sons, 1946), which includes a brief biography of father and son as well as summaries of matters of state for each section, was the first presentation of the complete collection.
56. Diary, June 26, 1945, WI Collection.
57. Ibid., Aug. 6, 1945.
58. Burns Mantle, ed., *The Best Plays of 1945–46: And the Year Book of the Drama in America* (New York: Dodd, Mead, 1946), pp. 346–71.
59. WI, Diary, Feb. 6, 1946, WI Collection.
60. *Times*, Feb. 17, 1946; "The Theater," *Time*, Feb. 18, 1946, p. 49; "The Theatre," *American Mercury*, May 1946, pp. 587, 588, 590; WI, Diary, May 4, 1946, WI Collection.
61. The authors normally split an 8 percent royalty with the composer and lyric writer, taking 4 percent. Irwin split that with the Howard estate, which reduced his normal share to 2 percent of the gross or $500 on a $25,000 week. Out of that was deducted 10 percent for his agent and an assessment for the Dramatists Guild.
62. *Chronicle*, Nov. 29, 1946; Oakland *Tribune*, Dec. 8, 1946.
63. WI, Diary, Dec. 25, 1946, WI Collection. Irwin occasionally took reductions in royalties during the Broadway and road runs to help keep *Lute Song* going.

64. WI Collection.
65. Quotations in the above episode are from IHI to Wallace and Laetitia Irwin, Feb. 29, 1948, WIJ.
66. Edith Haynes Thompson to William Hyde and Susan Irwin, Feb. 24, 1948, WHI; WI, "My Religion," p. 86.
67. IHI to Wallace and Laetitia Irwin, Feb. 29, 1948.
68. Edith Haynes Thompson to William Hyde and Susan Irwin, Feb. 24, 1948.
69. TMOAR, p. 3.
70. New York *Times*, Feb. 26, 1948; WI et al., *Thirty-Eighth Anniversary of the Dutch Treat Club*, p. 82; William Rose Benét, "The Phoenix Nest," *Saturday Review of Literature*, June 12, 1948, p. 36.
71. "Milestones," *Time*, March 8, 1948, p. 100; *Times*, Feb. 25, 1948; Denver *Post*, Feb. 25, 1948; WI, Earl Chapin May and Joseph Hotchkiss, *A History of the Union League Club of New York City* (New York: Dodd, Mead, 1952), p. v.
72. Denver *Post*, Nov. 2, 1926. O'Higgins died in 1929.
73. This incident is from IHI, "Adventures of Yesterday," p. 589.

BIBLIOGRAPHIC ESSAY

BIOGRAPHERS whose subject has written an autobiography have a running start on their biography; not that their work has been done, but at least it has been cut out for them. So it was with this biography of Will Irwin. His autobiography, *The Making of a Reporter* (New York: G. P. Putnam's Sons, 1942), provided little more than a skeleton—and that limited to his twenty-first to fifty-fifth years, since he omitted his formative and waning years. In reminiscing about his most productive years, even, he was occasionally inaccurate and rarely introspective or candid about his aspirations, feelings, and personal life. He described the events he had covered and the people he had known more than he analyzed himself. To verify and correct and to fill in and expand, I consulted many other sources, particularly those closer in time and proximity to significant events.

Also, Irwin seldom expressed his private feelings explicitly—except on politics and war—in the hundreds of books, articles, short stories, poems, newspaper pieces, pamphlets, and other published works he wrote before and after his autobiography. So to plumb his character it was necessary to study his unpublished papers, in which he wrote more subjectively, as well as his published works. Published and unpublished comments by others— from documents and interviews—added further dimensions to a portrayal of his character and career.

The most significant single depository of papers concerning Will Irwin is in the Collection of American Literature, Beinecke Rare Book and Manuscript Library, Yale University, New Haven. His 22 diaries and his 1,145 letters to Inez Haynes Irwin often reveal the peaks and valleys of his psychological state. His diaries also contain abundant financial data. His letters depict many of his wartime experiences abroad that are highlighted in *The Making of a Reporter* and in his war correspondence, and at times I have cautiously used his autobiography and his reportage, rather than his letters, for the sake of convenience. The Will Irwin collection also contains 59 letters from Inez to him before their marriage. In letters to and from her, and in 43 volumes of her diaries, he is frequently mentioned.

The other major source of Mrs. Irwin's papers, the Inez Haynes Irwin Collection in the Schlesinger Library at Radcliffe College, Cambridge, Massachusetts, includes more than ten diaries containing detailed accounts of trips with Will and her unpublished autobiography, "Adventures of Yesterday" (n.d.), in which he is a key figure. As a successful writer and an early liberated woman, Mrs. Irwin herself is a ripe topic for a biography.

Although the Will Irwin holdings of the Bancroft Library, University of California, Berkeley, are not so comprehensive as those at the Beinecke Library, they do contain important unpublished documents. Among the papers are letters by Irwin after his expulsion from Stanford University and the unpublished autobiography of his close, writing brother. Wallace Irwin's "I Look at Me" (n.d.) is the best single source for a description of the childhood and youth the two Irwin brothers shared.

For the background on the Colorado of Irwin's youth, the best sources are Don L. and Jean Harvey Griswold's *The Carbonate Camp Called Leadville* (Denver: University of Denver Press, 1951) and Charlyle Channing Davis's *Olden Times in Colorado* (Los Angeles: Phillips Publishing, 1916). I was unable to find several thousand words about Irwin's childhood and youth cut from the manuscript of his autobiography, but visits to Denver and Leadville (as well as to Canandaigua, Clayville, and Oneida) helped me understand the profound effect of that rugged terrain on Irwin.

I also visited his alma mater. The Stanford registrar's file, the libraries, and especially the archives contain primary and second sources that reveal Irwin's personal and professional interests during the period in which his ambitions crystalized. His poetry and fiction in *The Stanford Quad*, the yearbook, and *The Sequoia*, the literary magazine, are signed and thus readily identifiable; but his journalism in the *Daily Palo Alto*, the student newspaper, is anonymous and therefore almost impossible to identify conclusively. Secondary sources describe the academic requirements of his day and his roles in the founding of campus traditions.

Two government depositories hold many valuable unpublished documents concerning Irwin. The Herbert Hoover Presidential Library, West Branch, Iowa, holds correspondence and other papers that reflect the long, unwavering friendship of the writer and the engineer-politician. The George E. Akerson Papers there indicate how Irwin and Hoover worked together on the latter's campaign biography. The National Archives and Records Service, Washington, D.C., is the principal depository for papers illuminating Irwin's role in the Committee on Public Information. These papers are supplemented by published sources; the most important are cited in the notes to the text of this biography.

Several private files contain unpublished documents that shed light on Irwin's personal and professional life. Those at Brandt and Brandt, his literary agency, present additional perspectives on his successes and failures as a free-lance writer, particularly during those later years not covered in his autobiography. Documents in the possession of Wallace Irwin, Jr., provide perspectives on family background and on his uncle's health. William Hyde Irwin's collection of correspondence among members of the Hyde and Irwin sides of the family and excerpts from his mother's diary help to explain the sometimes turbulent relationship between Will and his first wife, Hallie Hyde. Also, Mr. Irwin's *Augusta Bixler Farms: A California Delta from Reclamation to the Fourth Generation of Owners* ([Brookdale, Calif.: William Hyde Irwin], 1973) yields useful geneological background. Two visits to Mr. Irwin's home, near Brookdale in the Santa Cruz mountains, helped me understand his parents' feelings about that locale.

I also visited, interviewed, and corresponded with other relatives of Will Irwin, on both his and the Haynes sides. A trunk of Inez's memorabilia in the possession of Margaret W. Cookman, Westford, Massachusetts, revealed, among other things, the conflict between Will's professional ambition and his devotion to Inez immediately after the Great War. Mrs. Cookman arranged my second interview with Inez's surviving sister, Edith Haynes Thompson, with whom I had extensive correspondence.

Two uniquely useful sources for leads and information about Irwin's life and work in the West were the morgues of the San Francisco *Chronicle* and the Denver *Post*. The Denver Public Library western history collection and the Colorado State Historical Society, Denver, yielded valuable material, too.

Many books, aside from those already mentioned, provided context and background for this biography. The second and third editions of Edwin Emery's interpretative *The Press and America* (Englewood Cliffs, N.J.: Prentice-Hall, 1962, 1972) provided a definitive overview of journalism during Irwin's lifetime. Three books by the late Frank Luther Mott, whom Emery succeeded as the leading historian of the mass media, were frequently consulted. Mott's *A History of American Magazines*, particularly the fourth and fifth volumes (Cambridge, Mass.: Belknap Press of Harvard University Press, 1957, 1968), describes magazines Irwin wrote for, supplementing old copies of the magazines themselves. To put Irwin's published books in context, I relied mostly on Mott's *Golden Multitudes: The Story of Best Sellers in the United States* (New York: R. R. Bowker, 1947). I used two periodicals, the *Book Review Digest* and *Publishers Weekly*, to verify or track down publication dates of Irwin's books. I found colorful background on San Francisco journalism at the turn of the century in John Bruce's *Gaudy Century: The Story of San Francisco's Hundred Years of Robust Journalism* (New York: Random House, 1948) and John Philip Young's *Journalism in California* (San Francisco: Chronicle Publishing, 1915). The New York *Sun* of Irwin's day is aptly described in several books, but no author does it better than Irwin himself. Of the several books concerning muckraking, three were most useful, although I do not completely agree with their authors' interpretations. Those three are *The Muckrakers:*

Crusaders for American Liberalism (Chicago: Henry Regnery, 1968) by Louis Filler, *The Social and Political Ideas of the Muckrakers* (New York: Citadel Press, 1964) by David Mark Chalmers, and *The Age of Reform: From Bryan to F.D.R.* (New York: Vintage Books, 1955) by Richard Hofstadter. Directly or indirectly, William Randolph Hearst was a force in Irwin's career, and two biographies were useful especially for their author's views of the press tycoon: Ferdinand Lundberg's anti-Hearst *Imperial Hearst: A Social Biography* (New York: Equinox Cooperative Press, 1936) and John Tebbel's mildly favorable *The Life and Good Times of William Randolph Hearst* (New York: E. P. Dutton, 1952). For background to Irwin's campaign for copyright reform I consulted volume two of Stephen P. Ladas's *The International Protection of Literary and Artistic Property: Copyright in the United States of America and Summary of Copyright Law in Various Countries* (New York: Macmillan, 1938) and volume two of Arthur Fisher's *Studies on Copyright*, memorial edition (South Hackensack, N.J.: Fred B. Rothman, and Indianapolis: Bobbs-Merrill, 1963). To better understand Irwin's attitude against war, I read *War and the Breed: The Relation of War to the Downfall of Nations* (Boston: Beacon Press, 1915), by his mentor David Starr Jordan. I also read many other works that had influenced Irwin.

For general cultural, economic, political, and social backgrounds to his changing times, three books were of exceptional interest. They were Frederick Lewis Allen's *Only Yesterday: An Informal History of the Nineteen-Twenties* (New York: Harper & Row, 1931); Allen's *Since Yesterday: The Nineteen-Thirties in America, Sept. 3, 1929–Sept. 3, 1939* (New York: Bantam Books, 1940); and Lloyd Morris's *Postscript to Yesterday: American Life and Thought, 1896–1946* (New York: Harper & Row, 1947). Other major background sources are cited in the notes.

I also used a wide variety of other kinds of sources. They include standard biographical and historical reference works and hundreds of newspapers, as well as census lists, city directories, diplomas, invitations, maps, marriage certificates, medals, pamphlets, passports, photographs, postal guides, programs, scrapbooks, and wills. Some are cited in the notes.

Since the notes in effect provide a highly selective bibliography of Irwin's published works and since comments in the texts substitute for annotations to those citations, a discussion of his works is omitted here. A chronology of Irwin's major works has been provided.

INDEX